2 Quickstart

2.1
Start your engines

2.2
Load a scene

2.3
A first render

2.4
Adding an object

2.5
Position the sphere

2.6
Add a material

2.7
Texture

2.8
Simple animation

2.9
Rendering

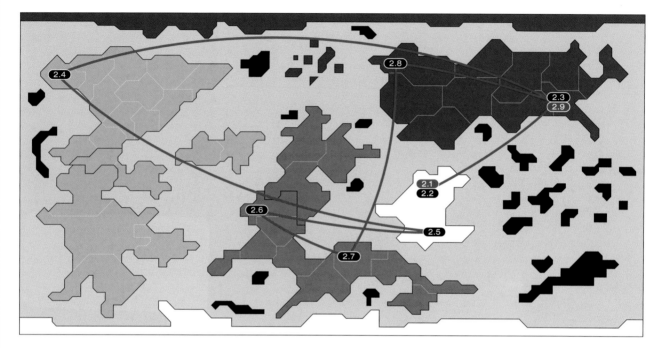

Part A
Using Blender

Part B
Model

Part C
Render

Part D
Animation

Part E
Reference

LEGEND

10 Particle effects

10.1
A first particle system

10.2
Rendering a particle system

10.3
Making fire with particles

10.4
A simple explosion

10.5
Fireworks

10.6
A shoal of fish

10.7
Static particles

12 The interface

12.1
Blender windows

12.2
InfoWindow

12.3
FileWindow

12.4
3DWindow

12.5
IpoWindow

12.6
SequenceWindow

12.7
OopsWindow

12.8
TextWindow

12.9
SoundWindow

12.10
ImageWindow

12.11
ImageSelectWindow

12.12
AnimPlaybackWindow

13 The buttons

13.1
ButtonsWindow

13.2
ViewButtons

13.3
LampButtons

13.4
MaterialButtons

13.5
TextureButtons

13.6
AnimButtons

13.7
RealTimeButtons

13.8
EditButtons

13.9
WorldButtons

13.10
Paint/Face Buttons

13.11
RadiosityButtons

13.12
ScriptButtons

13.13
DisplayButtons

PLANET BLENDER

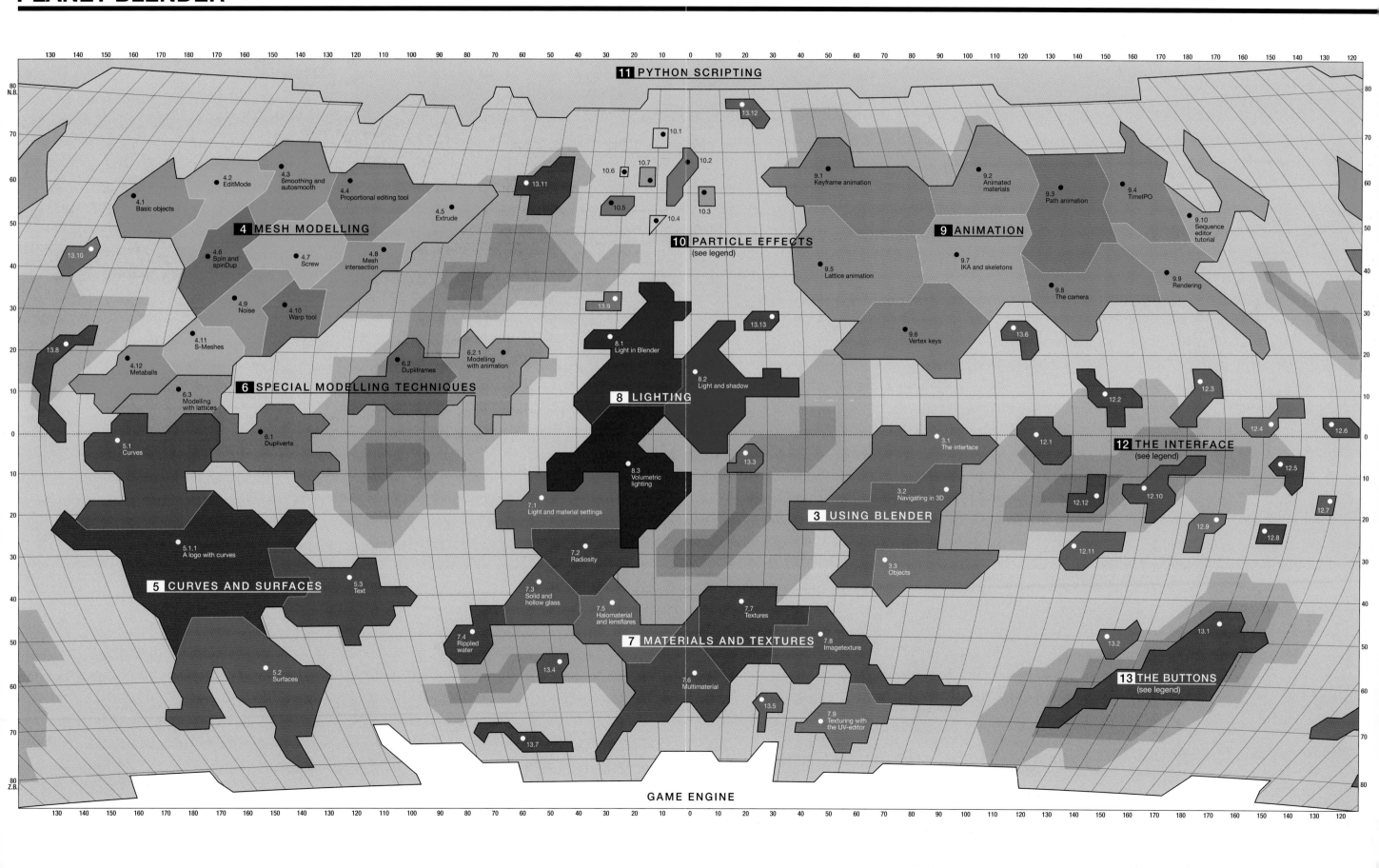

11 PYTHON SCRIPTING

10.1

10.6 10.7 10.2

10.5 10.3

10.4

10 PARTICLE EFFECTS
(see legend)

13.11

13.12

4.2 EditMode
4.3 Smoothing and autosmooth
4.1 Basic objects
4.4 Proportional editing tool
4.5 Extrude

4 MESH MODELLING

13.10

4.6 Spin and spinDup
4.7 Screw
4.8 Mesh intersection

4.9 Noise
4.10 Warp tool

4.11 S-Meshes

13.8

4.12 Metaballs

6.2 Dupliframes
6.2.1 Modelling with animation

6.3 Modelling with lattices

6 SPECIAL MODELLING TECHNIQUES

6.1 Dupliverts

5.1 Curves

13.9

8.1 Light in Blender

13.13

8.2 Light and shadow

8 LIGHTING

5.1.1 A logo with curves

8.3 Volumetric lighting

13.3

5 CURVES AND SURFACES

5.3 Text

7.1 Light and material settings

7.2 Radiosity

3.3 Objects

5.2 Surfaces

7.3 Solid and hollow glass

7.5 Halomaterial and lensflares

7.7 Textures

7.4 Rippled water

7 MATERIALS AND TEXTURES

7.8 Imagetexture

13.4

7.6 Multimaterial

13.5

7.9 Texturing with the UV-editor

13.7

9.1 Keyframe animation
9.2 Animated materials
9.3 Path animation
9.4 TimeIPO

9 ANIMATION

9.10 Sequence editor tutorial

9.5 Lattice animation

9.7 IKA and skeletons

9.9 Rendering

9.6 Vertex keys

9.8 The camera

13.6

12.2

12.3

12.4

12.6

3.1 The interface

12.1

12 THE INTERFACE
(see legend)

12.5

3.2 Navigating in 3D

12.12

12.10

12.7

3 USING BLENDER

12.9

12.8

12.11

13.2

13.1

13 THE BUTTONS
(see legend)

GAME ENGINE

The official **Blender 2.0** guide

- Ton Roosendaal
- Carsten Wartmann

3D Development

Not a Number

The official **Blender 2.0** guide

- Ton Roosendaal
- Carsten Wartmann

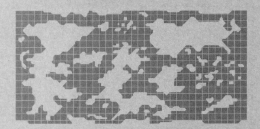

Not a Number bv
Van Eeghenstraat 84
1071 GK Amsterdam
the Netherlands

www.blender.nl
info@blender.nl

Design
·Riff Raff, Amsterdam, the Netherlands

DTP
·Rob Debrichy
·Janno Heck

Authors
·Ton Roosendaal
·Carsten Wartmann

Tutorial Authors
·Randall Rickert
·Reevan McKay
·Willem Zwarthoed
·Bart Velhuizen
·Geno Ruffalo

CD Design and Layout
·Joeri Kassenaar

Production
·Sven Wouter
·Sian Lloyd
·Jacco Marks
·Tricia Hughes
·Jan Wilmink
·Ian Ginn
·Chris Knight
·Loran Kuijpers

The Official Blender Book
ISBN 0-7615-3513-6
Library of Congress Catalog Card Number: 00-11772

Printed in the United States of America
02 03 04 GG 10 9 8 7 6 5 4 3 2

When I wrote the preface for the first book about Blender, over two years ago now, it was with a true feeling of mixed emotions. On the one hand, I had just finished a period with many of my old friends at the animation studio NeoGeo in Eindhoven, while on the other hand, I was beginning to realise what an amazing impact Blender was having in opening up the world of 3D animation to thousands of people around the world.

So much has happened in the intervening time that I could fill an entire book without giving you all of the wealth of knowledge that has been built up around Blender over the years to help you to realise your own creative ambitions.

Since the founding of Not a Number in 1998 the company has grown from a single person to over forty people. Crucial for this fast development were two major decisions I chose to make. First was the introduction of the much praised/despised Ckey, a commercial addition to Blender costing about 100 USD. This enabled me to invest further, both in people and marketing. Second was the decision to join partnership with Ian Ginn, who was able to develop and establish an ambitious and exciting business model for NaN. Since then we have worked to create a dedicated team of people that enabled us to provide tools and support for the ever-expanding community of Blender users, and that enabled new and unexpected possibilities for the company to establish business with.

As many of you will know, Blender was initially published as a freeware gift to the worldwide computer graphics community, giving design and animation professionals and enthusiasts alike access to the same tools as the expensive programs available on the market. We intend to maintain this free access for Blender users - NaN is not in the business of selling tools! Instead, Blender's unique and future-proofed technology creates a wealth of opportunities for licensing and partnership deals with major industry players. We intend to use these deals to create a standard for distributing and enjoying real-time interactive content, which will allow us to maintain Blender's freeware status on the PC market.

We could never have done it without you, so it is to all of the Blender community that my thanks go first and foremost. On top of that, I must also mention my many colleagues at NaN for their invaluable efforts and commitment to Blender over the past year. A special thanks goes to Carsten Wartmann, who wrote and edited a large part of this book. Special thanks also are for the contributions by Bart Veldhuizen, Geno Ruffalo, Randall Rickert and Reevan McKay. I was very pleased to work with Riff Raff again for an exciting graphical design; they developed the concept for this "Blender world atlas".

I wish you all a pleasant journey and lots of amazing discoveries! :-)

Amsterdam, January 2001
Ton Roosendaal

TABLE OF CONTENTS

Part A / Introduction

Chapter 1

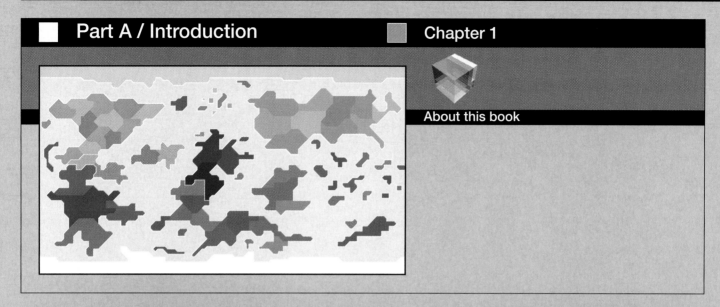

About this book

Chapter 2

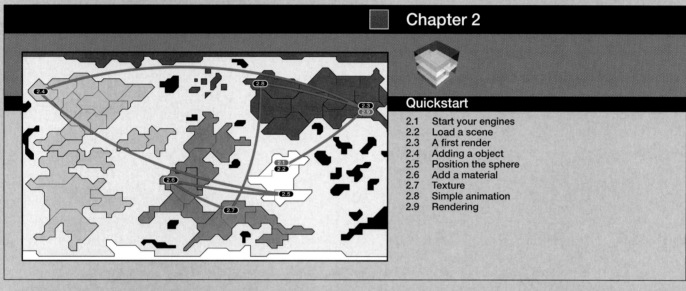

Quickstart

Chapter 3

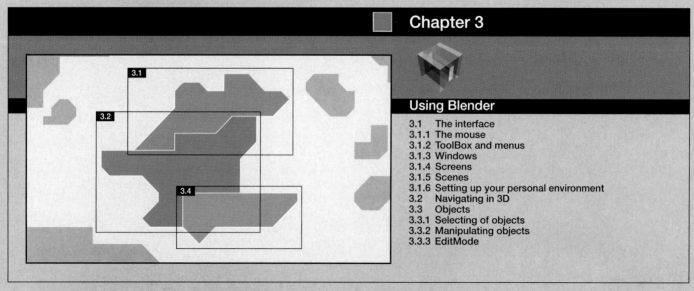

Using Blender

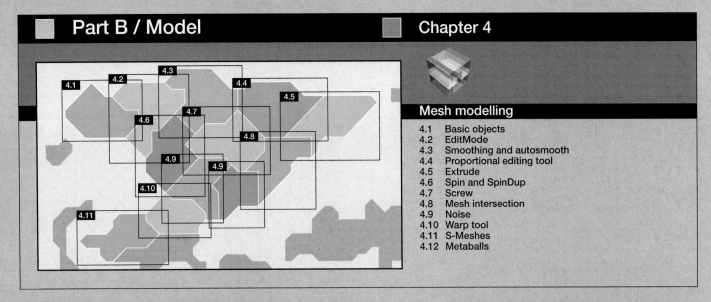

Part B / Model

Chapter 4

Mesh modelling

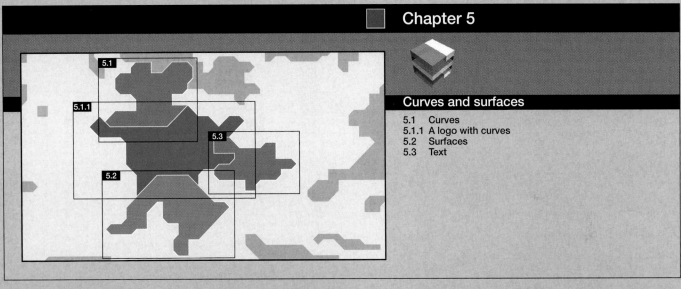

Chapter 5

Curves and surfaces

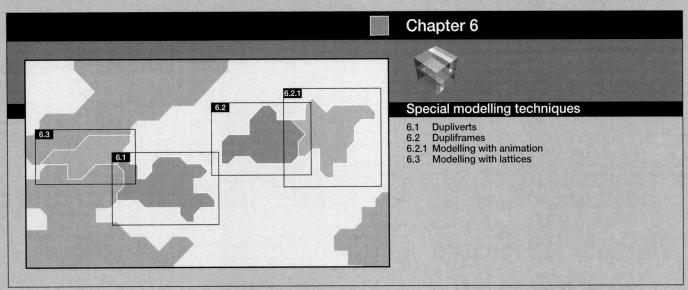

Chapter 6

Special modelling techniques

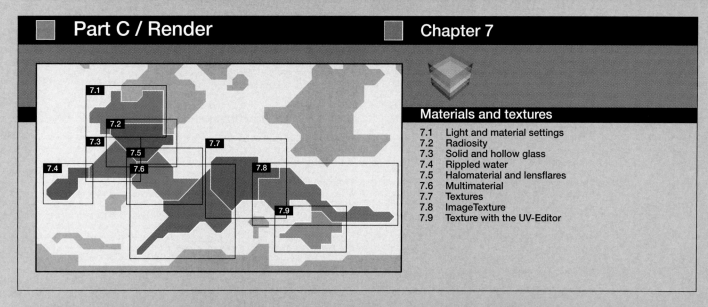

Part C / Render

Chapter 7

Materials and textures

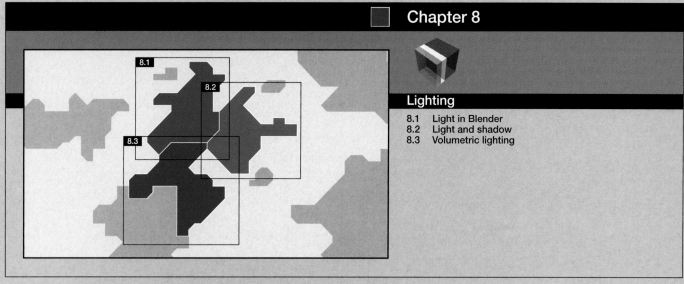

Chapter 8

Lighting

Part D / Animation

Chapter 9

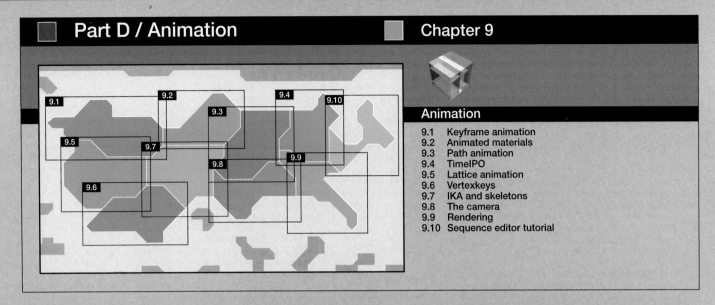

Animation

Chapter 10

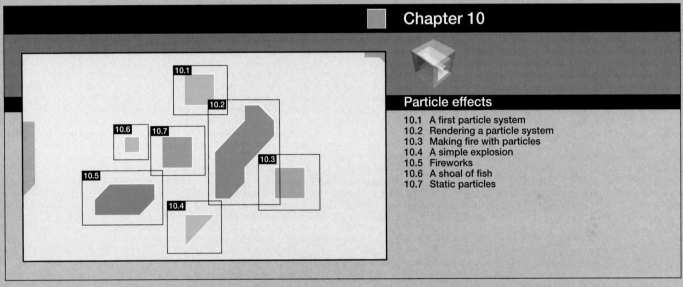

Particle effects

Chapter 11

Python scripting

Part E / Reference

Chapter 12

The interface

Chapter 13

The buttons

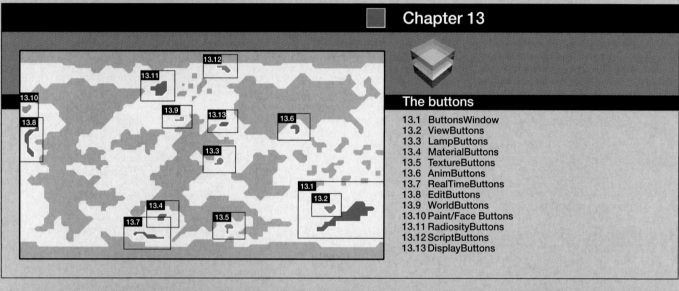

Chapter 14

Appendix

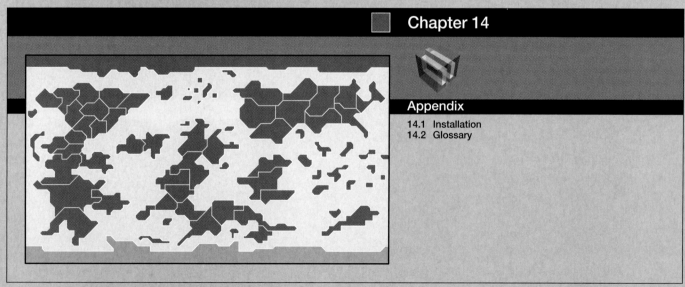

CONTINENT OVERVIEW

Part A / Introduction

1 About this book	2 Quickstart	3 Using Blender

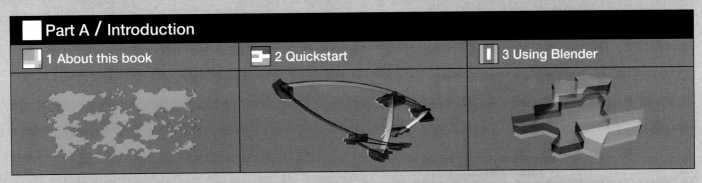

Part B / Model

4 Mesh modelling	5 Curves and surfaces	6 Special modelling techniques

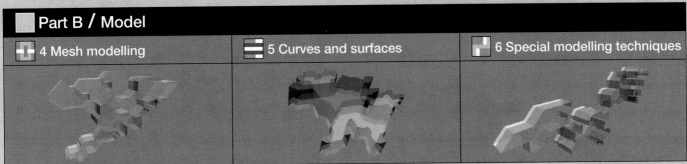

Part C / Render

7 Materials and textures	8 Lighting	

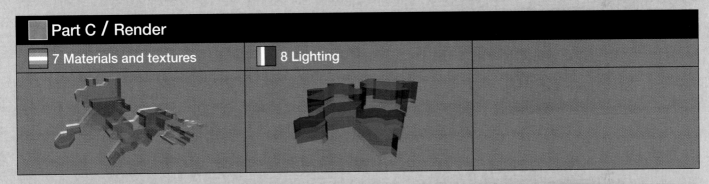

Part D / Animation

9 Animation	10 Particle effects	11 Python scripting

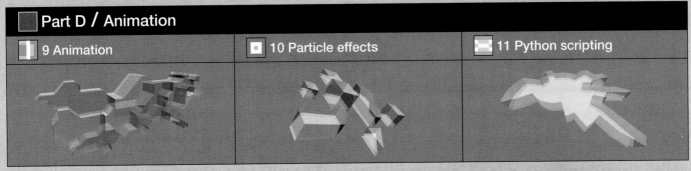

Part E / Reference

12 The interface	13 The buttons	14 Appendix

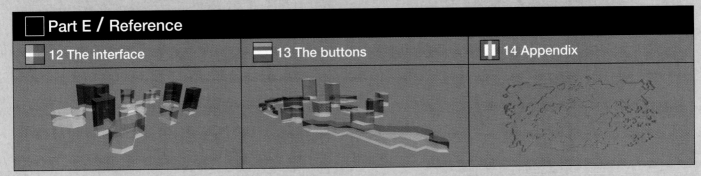

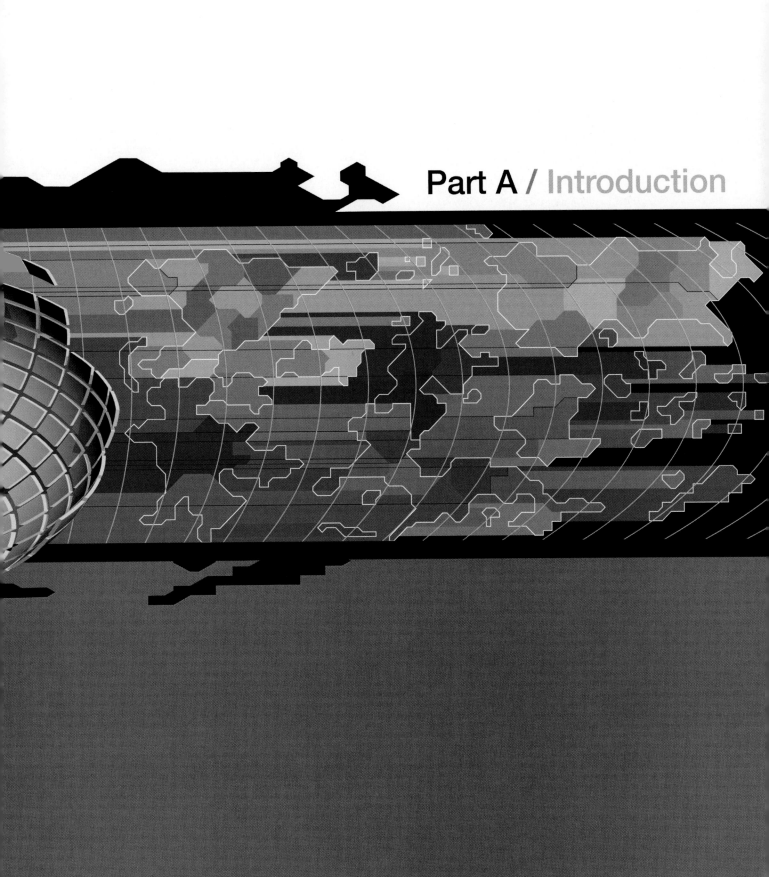

Part A / Introduction

Chapter 1
About this book

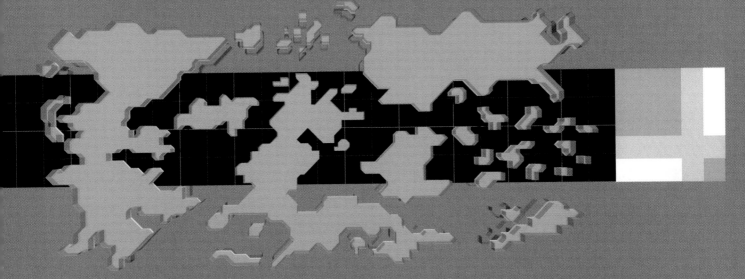

Blender has grown into a mature 3D design suite, a fully integrated package that allows artists to do the modelling, animation, rendering and post production. To complete the 3D suite, Blender has recently evolved into a realtime 3D creation and playback tool. Just as the original freeware Blender allowed individuals to make their first steps in the world of 3D design, the new software can now also be used by budding game designers to show the world what they are capable of.

Since Blender is a product that evolves continuously, with new releases coming available every 2 to 4 weeks, it is impossible to 'freeze' development to enable a manual to be valid for a longer period. That's why we had to decide to base this manual on Blender V2.03, one of the first 'gameBlender' releases, with interactive 3D features still under beta. This manual covers all of the 2.0 functionality to build, render and to animate, but is not intended as a guide how to create games with Blender. That will be in another book which will be published later this year.

This Blender 2.0 Guide covers all changes that have been made in Blender in the past 2 years. We have tried to collect as many tutorials and micro-guides as possible to update our last manual (1.5-1.8) and to help newcomers to Blender to get started with the software. Inside, users should easily be able to find help and references covering all aspects of Blender 2.0x to let them bring their creative ideas to completion.

This book is intended as your travel guide, an atlas to the Blender World. The first part contains a general introduction to Blender and a quick tour with some short visits to essential Blender countries. The second part thoroughly explores each Blender continent, with fun travels and practical examples. The third part is a complete reference for the experienced traveler, e.g. a full description of the hotkeys and buttons in Blender.

Other interesting resources for Blender users:

Our website, "http://www.blender.nl". The discussion forums here provide an excellent support and feedback, here is where you can meet with other Blender users and discuss or view the artworks they make.

Direct NaN support for users: "support@blender.nl". You can also use this email address to ask questions about this book or to point us to the inevitable mistakes that might have sneaked in!

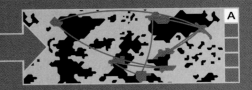

Chapter 2
Quickstart

Welcome to the wonderful world of Blender! The Quickstart will take you on a tour of the basic functions of this remarkable suite of 3D creation tools.

I am sure you have already installed Blender and know how to launch it. If not, then please refer to the "Installation" section in the appendix of this book. Basically the installation procedure consists of unpacking the archive onto your hard disk, and then starting it from there. The start procedure will depend on your operating system.

Once you have started Blender, it presents you with a screen with a big 3D view and many buttons. This is the default scene in Blender. Later in this book, you will see how to customise that default scene to suit your needs.

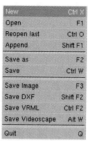

New	Ctrl X
Open	F1
Reopen last	Ctrl O
Append	Shift F1
Save as	F2
Save	Ctrl W
Save Image	F3
Save DXF	Shift F2
Save VRML	Ctrl F2
Save Videoscape	Alt W
Quit	Q

Usually, after experimenting with a few mouse clicks in a new program, one wants to load up some scenes to test what can be done with the program. The easiest way to do this in Blender is to use the "File" menu at the top of the screen. Click on "File" and choose "Open". The keyboard shortcut for opening a new file is F1.
Blender makes extensive use of shortcuts for speedier functionality.

and, on Windows operating systems, a list of your drives.

The directory you are currently in is shown in the top text-field. The ParentDir button allows you to go up one directory.

Using these possibilities, go to your CD-rom drive and browse for the folder containing the file "Stage.blend". Now click with the middle mouse button (MMB) on the filename "Stage.blend". The file will be loaded immediately. Alternatively, you can click with the LMB and then confirm your selection with ENTER.

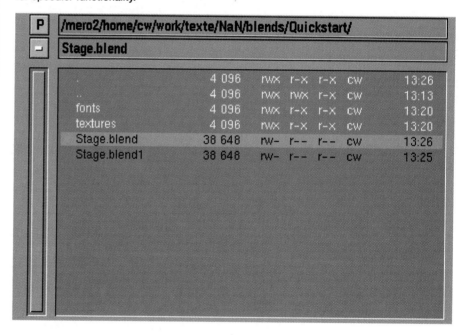

P	/mero2/home/cw/work/texte/NaN/blends/Quickstart/					
-	Stage.blend					
.		4 096	rwx r-x r-x	cw		13:26
..		4 096	rwx rwx r-x	cw		13:13
fonts		4 096	rwx r-x r-x	cw		13:20
textures		4 096	rwx r-x r-x	cw		13:20
Stage.blend		38 648	rw- r-- r--	cw		13:26
Stage.blend1		38 648	rw- r-- r--	cw		13:25

You will see that you have a FileWindow from which you can browse through all of the files on your computer.

Pressing and holding the MenuButton with the left mouse button (LMB) will give you a choice of recently browsed paths

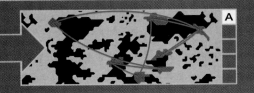

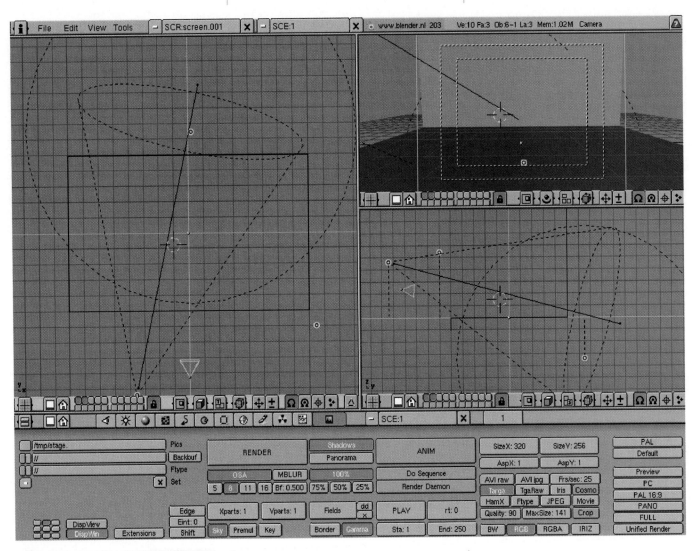

→ *Blender works best with a 3-button mouse. To compensate for the lack of a middle mouse button, hold ALT and press the LMB instead.*

The screen will now show four windows: a top view on the top-left, a camera-view on the top right, a side-view on the right middle. All three 3DWindows visualize the 3D space. The wide window at the bottom is the ButtonsWindow. In this instance it contains the DisplayButtons that control the rendering.

Just click on the big "RENDER" button in the ButtonsWindow and Blender will render the actual camera view and display it. You can see a brick wall at the back, and a wooden stage lit by a spotlight. This will be our stage for the next steps in this quick tour of Blender. Close the render-window with ESC, or F11.

Move your mouse cursor over the big 3DWindow and press SPACE, but without moving the mouse. The Toolbox, which is Blender's main-menu, will appear. Move your mouse over "MESH" and click with the LMB, the "MESH" submenu will appear.

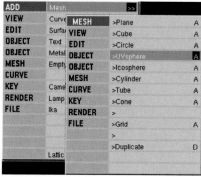

Move your mouse down to ">UVSphere" (it will be highlighted in blue) and click the LMB again. A PopupMenu will prompt you, asking how many segments the sphere should have. Just click on "OK" for now. Leaving the PopupMenu with the mouse will cancel the creation. A second Popup will now appear and ask for the number of rings for the sphere. Just click on "OK" as you did before.

The sphere is now in the so-called "EditMode", a mode where we can edit every single point of the sphere in order to shape it the way we like. For now we want to manipulate the object as a whole and so we'll need to leave the EditMode. Press TAB and you will see the sphere drawn in pink in the 3DWindows and shaded in the CameraView.

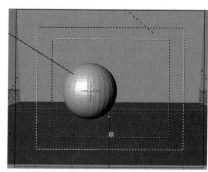

You can now do another rendering (F12, then close with ESC or F11) and watch how the sphere casts shadows onto the scene.

So far the sphere looks a little blocky. You can see the single polygons that make up the appearance of the sphere. We will change this now. Press F9, and the ButtonsWindow will change to EditButtons.

Here we have several buttons with which we can change the mesh object, but for now we only need one. Locate the "Set Smooth" button in the third row of buttons in the EditButtons, and click it with the LMB. The sphere is now drawn smooth in the shaded camera view, and in a rendering.

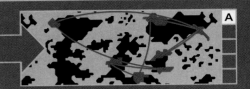

Newly created objects will always appear at the position of the 3D cursor.

 You can use the 3DCursor to place an object in 3D space without using multiple views. Position the 3DCursor with a LMB click. What is very helpful here is that you can snap the cursor to the grid, other objects, or vertices (SHIFT-S).

Most of the time you will create an object at a random position (without caring where the 3DCursor happens to be) and then move the object visually into position.

Now select the Sphere in one of the 3DWindows with the right mouse button (RMB). The colour of the wireframe views of the sphere will change to purple, indicating the selected objects in Blender.

Once you have selected an object, you can manipulate it. Move your mouse cursor to the big 3DWindow (the top view) and press GKEY to start the grab mode. The sphere turns white and follows the movements of your mouse in the window. In the other windows, you can see that it only moves in the two directions that you can control with the mouse. In this instance it moves around on the stage without either moving up or down.

When you are satisfied with the position of the sphere, click with the LMB to confirm the new position. If you don't want to change anything, or if you should accidently move an object, click with the RMB to cancel.

 ESC and the RMB both cancel Blender operations.

Now try to move the sphere a little bit above the stage. This can be achieved by moving the sphere in the side view (the 3DWindow below the camera view). Change the position until you are satisfied that you have a feeling for moving objects in the Blender windows. Do some test renderings to see how the position changes the scene and influences the shadow.

Select the sphere and switch the ButtonsWindow to the MaterialButtons by pressing F5. You will get a near empty window. Locate the so-called "MenuButton" in the header of the MaterialButtons.

Now, press and hold it with the LMB. A menu will appear in which you can select "ADD NEW" with the mouse.

Stage
Wall
ADD NEW

A clutch of Buttons will appear in the ButtonWindow, but don't worry -- we do not need to touch them all just now. The most prominent property of a surface is the colour. Locate the colour sliders to the right of the material preview.

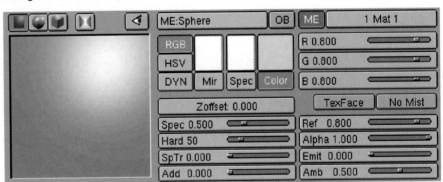

The colour sliders are labeled with "R, G, and B" which stand for the base colours Red, Green and Blue. You can adjust each of them, in a range from 0.0 to 1.0, to get every colour you could possibly want. Also, you can use a different way of setting up colours if you click on the "HSV" button. The colour slider will change to "H, S and V", with the "H" slider you choose a hue, and then adjust its saturation with "S", and its brightness (Value) with "V". Experiment with both of these methods for choosing a colour and see which suits you best. I have chosen a gold tone, which is a setting of R=0.80, G=0.74 and B=0.00 on the RGB sliders.

Textures are patterns or structures on the surface of an object. Blender has several types of textures to simulate different materials.

With the sphere selected, press F6 to switch to the TextureButtons. Locate the MenuButton again and add a new texture in the way we did for the material. Now Bender presents you with the built-in texture types.

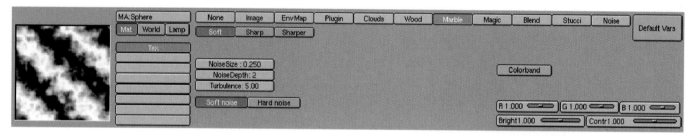

Choose a marble texture by clicking on the button "Marble". Blender shows you a preview of the texture in the TexturePreview on the left of the window.

For the purpose of this quickstart, we won't care too much about the settings we'll just go with the defaults. You can now do a render by pressing F12 to see a purple and gold marbled sphere. To change the colour of the marble texture go back to the MaterialButtons with F5 and locate the colour settings for textures to the right side of the window.

You can now change the colour of the texture, just as we did for the material. If you choose to use the HSV colour setting you will also see the HSV sliders here.

➡ *You should name objects, materials, textures, etc., in Blender to help you keep track on them in bigger scenes. Just click on the appropriate TextButton in the header of a window and edit the name with the QWERTY keys. A special function here is the little button with the car on it, if clicked upon, Blender names the object itself.*

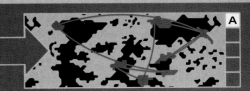

One of the great strengths of Blender is its animation functionality. We will now make a simple animation in just a few steps.

Select the sphere, move your mouse cursor to the big 3DWindow (the top view), and press GKEY to move it. Move it to the left and watch the camera view while so doing. The sphere should be outside the outer dotted line in the camera view. This dotted line denotes the area that will be rendered by Blender.

Now we'll instruct Blender that this will be the initial position of the Sphere. Press IKEY and choose "LOC" from the appearing menu.

Blender will now remember this position, but we still have to tell it where the sphere should go. For that we need two pieces of information: the new position, and the time when the sphere should reach that position.

We already know how to do this for the location. The time we set with the 'FrameSlider' that is located in the header of the ButtonsWindow. It now is at frame one. Press UPARROW six times and look at the FrameSlider. It has advanced 60 frames. You can now move the Sphere to the final position that you want it to be, and insert a new keyframe with IKEY (again choose "LOC").

> Blender counts time in frames. The 60 frames we have used here are roughly equal to two seconds of animation.

Now move your mouse cursor over the camera view and press SHIFT-LEFTARROW to set the FrameSlider to the first frame, and then ALT-A, which will play the animation in the 3DWindow as a preview. Depending on the speed of your computer, and the graphics card installed, you will get a real time preview of your animation.

In this latter stage of the production, Blender will calculate every picture and save it to your harddisk. You can then play the animation or edit it for use on the internet or on video.

The ButtonsWindow, which we will need for this step, is accessed by pressing F10. The DisplayButtons will appear.

The first thing we need to tell Blender is precisely where the calculated pictures, or the animation, should be stored. This is done using the buttons on the left in the DisplayButtons. In the input field labeled "Pics", you can enter a directory and filename in which Blender should store the pictures (or animation). Click on the square button to the left of the textfield to get a FileWindow in order to browse for a directory and enter a filename.

> Make sure the directory you enter exists, otherwise Blender will not save any of your pictures.

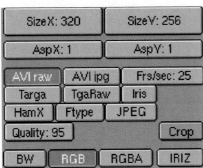

Now enter a size for your animation using the size buttons in the DisplayButtons. Bigger sizes will, of course, increase the rendering time, so if you don't have a fast computer, or your patience is limited, don't choose too big a size. Under the size buttons you can tell Blender in which file format you want to save the animation. For now, I suggest we use "AVI raw".

Below the "ANIM" button, you can adjust the length of the animation. For the purpose of this quickstart, it should be "Sta: 1" and "End: 61" because your animation lasts for that amount of time measured in frames.

Now click "ANIM" with the LMB, and Blender will render every single picture of the animation. When Blender has finished, press "PLAY" and Blender will play back the rendered animation.

> You can always cancel the rendering with ESC if you don't like the result, or if it takes too long.

And that's it! You have just completed your first 3D animation. By now you should have a good general idea of the steps required in order to make animations in Blender.

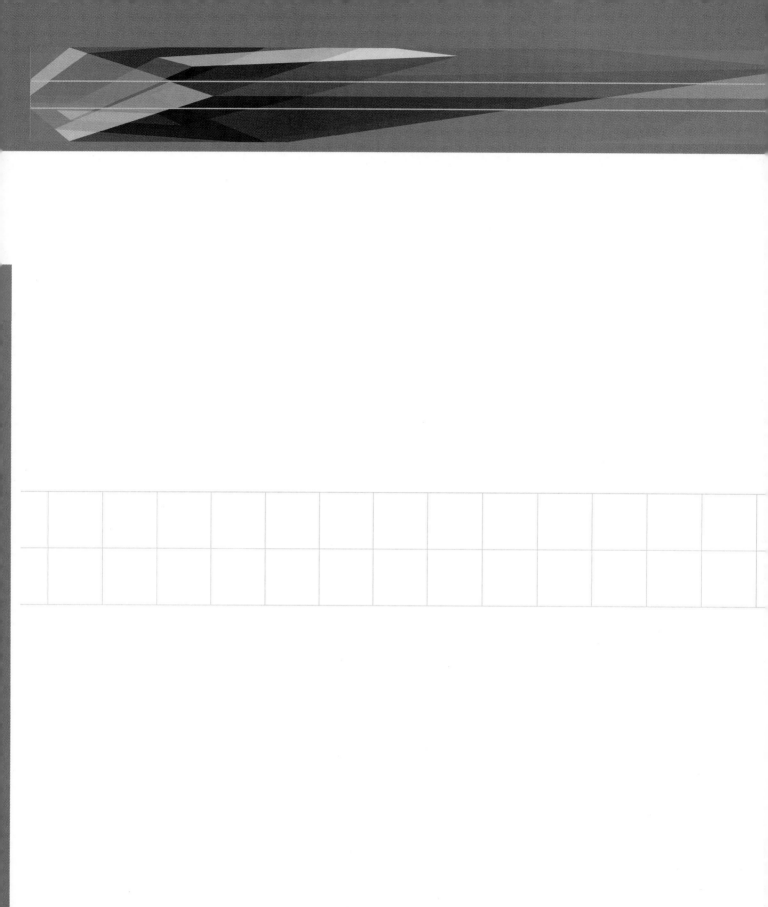

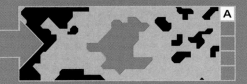

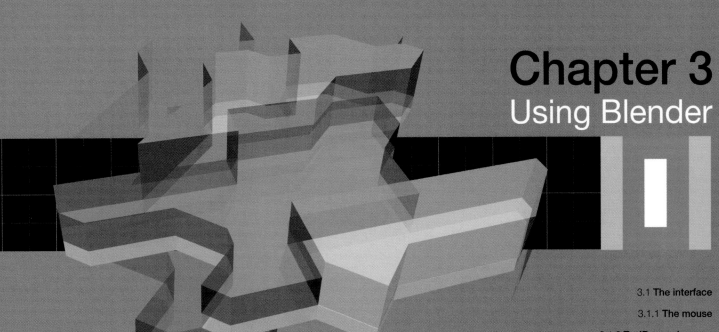

Chapter 3
Using Blender

For beginners the Blender user interface can be a little confusing as it is different than other 3D software packages. But persevere! After familiarising yourself with the basic principles behind the user interface, you'll start to realise just how fast you can work in your scenes and models. Blender has optimized the day-to-day work of an animation studio, where every minute costs money.

Figure 1: The first start

→ *The installation of Blender is simple, just unpack and put it in a directory of your chosing. Installation is described in detail in the section "Installation".*

After starting Blender a screen will appear as shown in figure 1. The big Window is a 3DWindow where your scene and objects are displayed and manipulated.

The smaller window, located below the 3DWindow, is the ButtonsWindow where you can edit the various settings of selected objects, and the scene.

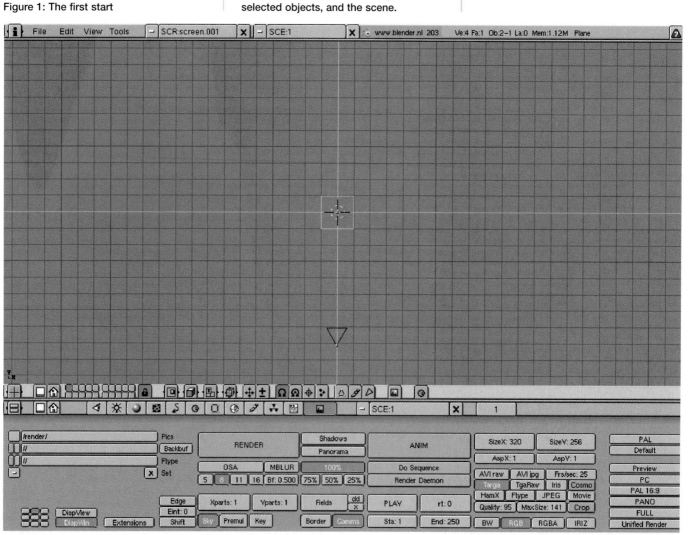

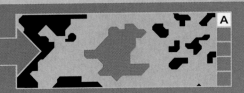

Each window has a Header. Here you can control aspects of the window that contains this header. The Headers are described in detail in the "Reference" section of this manual. Here, I will only explain the basic funtions that will allow us to get started on the first tutorial.

3.1.1 The mouse

Blender is designed to be used with two hands: one hand using the keyboard, the other hand the mouse. This prompts me to mention here the 'Golden Rule of Blender':

➜ *Keep one hand on your keyboard and one hand on your mouse!*

The mouse is particularly important because by using it you can control more than one axis at the same time. As far as possible, in every section and window of Blender, the mouse has the same functionality.

(LMB)
With the left mouse button you can activate buttons and set the 3DCursor. Often 'click and drag the left button' is used to change values in sliders.

(MMB)
The middle mouse button is used predominantly to navigate in the windows. In the 3DWindow it rotates the view. Together with SHIFT it drags the view, and with CTRL it zooms. While manipulating an object, the middle mouse is also used to constrain a movement to a single axis.

➜ *On systems with only two mouse buttons, you can substitute the middle mouse button with the ALT key and the left mouse button.*

(RMB)
The right mouse button selects or activates objects for further manipulation.

Objects change colour when they are selected. Holding SHIFT while selecting with the right mouse button adds the clicked object to the selection. The last selected object is the active object that is used for the next action. If you SHIFT-RMB an already selected object, it gets the active object. One more click and you can deselect it.

3.1.2 ToolBox and menus

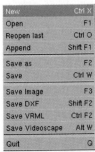

New	Ctrl X
Open	F1
Reopen last	Ctrl O
Append	Shift F1
Save as	F2
Save	Ctrl W
Save Image	F3
Save DXF	Shift F2
Save VRML	Ctrl F2
Save Videoscape	Alt W
Quit	Q

In the header of the InfoWindow, normally located on the top of the screen, you will find a menu. It offers you standard operations like File Operations and Changing of Views.

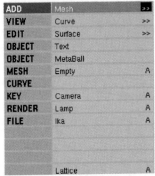

ADD	Mesh	>>
VIEW	Curve	>>
EDIT	Surface	>>
OBJECT	Text	
OBJECT	MetaBall	
MESH	Empty	A
CURVE		
KEY	Camera	A
RENDER	Lamp	A
FILE	Ika	A
	Lattice	A

The SPACE -key brings up the Toolbox, a large PopupMenu offers you the most commonly used operations in Blender. The "FILE" entry allows you also to action file operations. Behind every command you will find the associated hotkey.

➜ *Use the toolbox to learn the hotkeys in Blender!*

The most common file operations in Blender are the loading and saving of scenes. The quickest way to action these common functions is via the hotkeys. F1 offers you a FileWindow to load a scene, F2 a FileWindow to save a scene. To save a rendered picture, use the F3 -key.

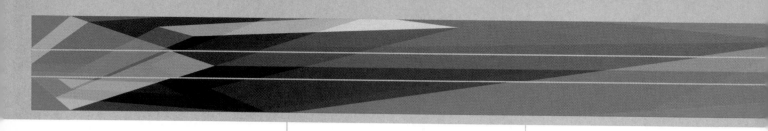

FileWindow

By the same token, however you initiate a file operation, you will always get its appropriate FileWindow.

The MenuButton below it offers you the last directories you have visited, as well as your drives in Windows.

The button labeled "A/Z" uses an alphabetical sorting, the clock button sorts by filedate, and the next button by the file size. Right of these Buttons there is a piece of text that shows what kind of operation the FileWindow will do, e.g. "LOAD FILE". The next button selects between long (size, permissions, date) and short filenames. The little ghost hides all files beginning with a dot. After that button, you have information about the free space which remains on the disk, and how many megabytes the selected files are.

3.1.3 Windows

All Blender screens consist of Windows. The Windows represent data, contain buttons, or request information from the user. You can arrange the Windows in Blender in many ways to customise your working environment.

Header

Every Window has a Header containing Buttons specific for that window or presenting information to the user. As an example, the header of the 3DWindow is shown here.

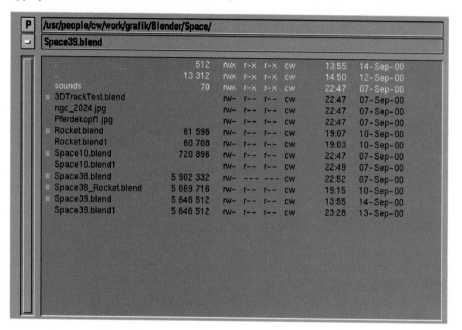

The main part of a FileWindow is the listing of directories and files. Filetypes known by Blender are allocated a yellow square. A click with the LMB selects a file and puts the name into the filename-input. A RETURN will then load the file. A LMB -click on a directory enters it. A shortcut to load files is the MMB, which quickly loads the file. You can also enter the path and filename by hand in the two inputs at the top of the FileWindow.

With the RMB, you can select more than one file. The selected files are highlighted blue.

> The PAD+ and PAD- keys increase and decrease the last number in a filename. This is handy for saving versions while you work.

The button labeled with a "P" at the upper left corner of the FileWindow puts you one directory up in your path.

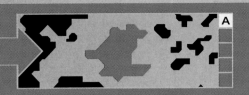

The left-most Button shows the type of the Window, clicking it, produces a PopupMenu in which you can change the Window type.

The next button switches between a full screen and a tiled screen window. The Button featuring a house graphic fills the window to the maximum extent with the information it is displaying.

A RMB -click on the Header pops up a menu asking you to place the Header at the "Top", the "Bottom", or to have "No Header" for that Window.

Click and hold with the MMB on the header, and then drag the mouse to scroll the header in case it doesn't fit the width of the window.

Edges

Every time you place the mouse cursor over the edge of a Blender window, the mouse cursor changes shape. When this happens, the following mouse keys are activated:

Drag the window edge horizontally or vertically while holding down the LMB. The window edge always moves in increments of 4 pixels, making it relatively easy to move two window edges so that they are precisely adjacent to each other, thus joining them is easy.

Clicking an edge with MMB or RMB pops up a menu prompting you to "Split Area" or "Join Areas".

"Split Area" lets you choose the exact position for the border. Split always works on the window from which you

entered the edge. You can cancel the operation with ESC.

"Join Areas" joins Windows with a shared edge, if possible, which means that joining works only if you don't have to close more than one Window for joining.

The Buttons

Buttons offer the quickest access to DataBlocks. In fact, the buttons visualise a single DataBlock and are grouped as such. Always use a LMB click to call up Buttons. The Buttons are described below:

Button
This button, which is usually displayed in salmon colour, activates a process such as "New" or "Delete".

TogButton
This button, which displays a given option or setting, can be set to either OFF or ON.

Tog3Button
This button can be set to off, positive or negative. Negative mode is indicated by yellow text.

RowButton
This button is part of a line of buttons. Only one button in the line can be active at once.

NumButton
This button, which displays a numerical value, can be used in three ways:
Hold the button while moving the mouse. Move to the right and upwards to assign a higher value to a variable, to the left and downwards to assign a lower value. Hold CTRL while doing this to change values in steps, or hold SHIFT to achieve finer control.

Hold the SHIFT + LMB to change the button to a "TextBut". A cursor appears, indicating that you can now enter a new value. Enter the desired value and press ENTER to assign it to the button. Press ESC to cancel without changing the value.
Click the left-hand side of the button to decrease the value assigned to the button slightly, or click the right-hand side of the button to increase it.

NumSlider
Use the slider to change values. The left-hand side of the button functions as a "TextBut".

TextButton
This button remains active (and blocks the rest of the interface) until you again press LMB, ENTER or ESC . While this button is active, the following hotkeys are available:
ESC: restores the previous text.
SHIFT+BACKSPACE: deletes the entire text.
SHIFT+ARROWLEFT: moves the cursor back to the beginning of the text.
SHIFT+ARROWRIGHT: moves the cursor to the end of the text.

MenuButton
This button calls up a PopMenu. Hold LMB while moving the cursor to select an option. If you move the mouse outside of the PopupMenu, the old value is restored.

IconButton
Button type "But", it activates processes.

IconToggle
Button type "TogBut", it toggles between two modes.

IconRow
As button type "RowBut", only one button in the row of buttons can be active at once.

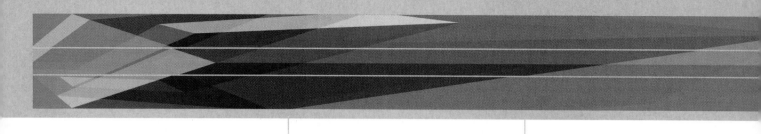

IconMenu
This button is actually a "RowBut", but only the active button is displayed. Hold the button while moving the mouse horizontally to view the available options.

Windowtypes

DataSelect,
For browsing the data structure of the scene, and selecting objects from it.

3DWindow, SHIFT - F5
Main window while working in the 3D-space. Visualizes the scene from orthogonal, perspective, and camera views.

IpoWindow, SHIFT - F6
Creating and manipulating of so called IpoCurves, the animation curve system of Blender.

ButtonWindow, SHIFT - F7
The ButtonWindow contains all the Buttons needed to manipulate every aspect of Blender. A brief overview follows after this section; for a more detailed explanation see the Reference section of this manual.

SequenceEditor, SHIFT - F8
Post-processing and combining animations and scenes.

OopsWindow, SHIFT - F9
The OopsWindow (Object Oriented Programming System) gives a schematic overview of the current scene structure.

ImageWindow, SHIFT - F10
With the ImageWindow you can show and assign images to objects. Especially important with UV-texturing.

InfoWindow
The header of the InfoWindow shows useful information, it contains the menus and the scene and screen MenuButtons. The InfoWindow itself contains the options by which you can set your personal preferences.

TextWindow, SHIFT - F11
A simple texteditor, mostly used for writing Python-scripts, but also a useful means by which you can insert comments about your scenes.

ImageSelectWindow
Lets you browse and select images on your disk. Includes thumbnails for preview.

SoundWindow, SHIFT - F12
For the visualisation and loading of sounds.

©2000 Marius Cienski

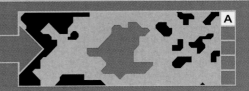

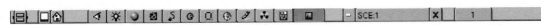

ButtonWindow

The ButtonsWindow contains the Buttons needed for manipulating objects and changing general aspects of the scene.

The ButtonsHeader contains the icons to switch between the different types of ButtonsWindows.

ViewButtons
The 3DWindow settings for a Window. It only features buttons if selected from a 3DWindow.

LampButtons, F4
The LampButtons will only display when a lamp is selected. Here you can change all of the parameters of a lamp, like its colour, energy, type (i.e. Lamp, Spot, Sun, Hemi), the quality of shadows, etc.

MaterialButtons, F5
The MaterialButtons appears when you select an object with a material assigned. With this group of Buttons you can control every aspect of the look of the surface.

TextureButtons, F6
These Buttons let you assign Textures to Materials. These Textures include mathematically generated Textures, as well as the more commonly used Image textures.

AnimationButtons, F7
The AnimationButtons are used to control various animation parameters. The right section of the Buttons are used for assigning special animation effects to objects, e.g. particle systems, and wave effects.

RealTimeButtons, F8
These Buttons are part of the real time section of Blender. This manual covers only linear animation.

EditButtons, F9
The EditButtons offer all kinds of possibilities for you to manipulate the objects themselves. The Buttons shown in this window depend on the type of object that is selected.

WorldButtons
Set up global world parameters, like the colour of the sky and the horizon, mist settings, and ambient light settings.

Face/PaintButtons
These Buttons are used for colouring objects at vertex level, and for setting texture parameters for the UV-Editor.

RadiosityButtons
The radiosity renderer of Blender.

ScriptButtons
Assigning of Python scripts to world, material, and objects.

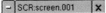

DisplayButtons, F10
With the DisplayButtons you can control the quality and output-format of rendered pictures and animations.

3.1.4 Screens

Screens are the major frame work of Blender. You can have as many Screens as you like, each one with a different arrangement of Windows. That way you can create a special personal workspace for every task you do. The Screen layout is saved with the Scene so that you can have scene-dependant work spaces. An example of this is to have a Screen for 3D work, another for working with Ipos and, a complete file manager to arrange your files and textures.

3.1.5 Scenes

Scenes are a way to organise your work. Scenes can share objects, but they can, for example, differ from each other in their rendered resolution or their camera view.

Together with the SequenceEditor, you can then compose videos in much the same way as in a TV-production.

While you are adding a new scene, you have these options:

"Empty": create a completely empty scene.
"Link Objects": all Objects are linked to the new scene. The layer and selection flags of the Objects can be configured differently for each Scene.
"Link ObData": duplicates Objects only. ObData linked to the Objects, e.g. Mesh and Curve, are not duplicated.
"Full Copy": everything is duplicated.

3.1.6 Setting up your personal environment

With the possibilities listed above, you can create your own personal environment. To make this environment a default when Blender starts, or you reset Blender with CTRL-X, use CTRL-U to save it to your home directory.

Blender is a 3D program, so we need to be able to navigate in 3D space. This is a problem because our screens are only 2D. The 3DWindows are in fact "windows" to the 3D world created inside Blender.

3.2.1 Using the keyboard to change your view

Place your mouse pointer over the big window on the standard Blender screen. This is a 3DWindow used for showing and manipulating your 3Dworlds.

→ *Remember that the window with the mouse pointer located over it (no click needed) is the active window! This means that only this window will respond to your key presses.*

Pressing PAD1 gives you a view from the front of the scene. In the default Blender scene, installed when you first start Blender, you will now be looking at the edge of a plane with the camera positioned in front of it.

PAD7 returns you to the view from the top. Now use the PAD+ and PAD- to zoom in and out. PAD3 gives you a side view of the scene.

PAD0 switches to a cameraview of the scene. In the standard scene you only see the edge of the plane because it is at the same hight as the camera.

PAD/ only shows selected objects; all other objects are hidden. PAD. zooms to the extent of the selected objects.

Switch with PAD7 back to a top view, or load the standard scene with CTRL-X. Now, press PAD4 four times, and then PAD2 four times. You are now looking from the left above and down onto the scene. The 'cross' of keys PAD8, PAD6, PAD2 and PAD4 are used to rotate the actual view.
Pressing PAD5 switches between a perspective view and an orthogonal view.

→ *Use CTRL-X followed by RETURN to get a fresh Blender scene. But remember, this action will discard all changes you have made!*

You should now try experiementing a little bit with these keys to get a feel for their operation and function. If you get lost, use CTRL-X followed by RETURN to get yourself back to the default scene.

3.2.2 Using the mouse to change your view

The main button for navigating with the mouse in the 3DWindow is the MMB. Press and hold the MMB in a 3DWindow, and then drag the mouse. The view is rotated with the movement of your mouse. Try using a perspective view (PAD5) while experimenting – it gives a very realistic impression of 3D.

With the SHIFT key, the above procedure translates the view. With CTRL, it zooms the view.

With the left-most icon, you can switch the window to different window types (e.g. 3DWindow, FileWindow, etc.). The next icon in the line toggles between a full screen representation of the window and its default representation. The icon displaying a house on it zooms the window in such a way that all objects become visible.

Next in the line, including the icon with the lock on it, are the LayerButtons, which we will cover later.

The next icon switches the modes for the local view, and is the mouse alternative for the PAD/ key.

With the following icon you can switch between orthogonal, perspective, and camera views (keys PAD5 and PAD0).

The next button along toggles between the top, front, and side views. SHIFT selects the opposite view, just as it does when you use the keypad.

This Button switches between different methods of drawing objects. You can choose from a bounding box, a wireframe, a faced, a gouraud-shaded, and a textured view.

With these icons you can translate and zoom the view with a LMB click on the icon and a drag of the mouse.

This overview should provide you with an idea of how to look around in 3D-scenes.

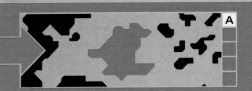

3.3.1 Selecting of objects

Selecting an object is achieved by clicking the object using the RMB. This operation also deselects all other objects. To extend the selection to more than one object, hold down SHIFT while clicking. Selected objects will change the colour to purple in the wireframe view. The last selected object is coloured a lighter purple and it is the active object. Operations that are only useful for one object, or need one object as reference, always work with the active object.

Objects can also be selected with a 'border'. Press BKEY to action this, and then draw a rectangle around the objects. Drawing the rectangle with the LMB selects objects; drawing with RMB deselects them.

Selecting and activating

Blender makes a distinction between selected and active.
Only one Object can be active at any time, e.g. to allow visualisation of data in buttons. The active and selected Object is displayed in a lighter colour than other selected Objects. The name of the active Object is displayed in the InfoHeader. A number of Objects can be selected at once. Almost all key commands have an effect on selected Objects.

A single RMB click is sufficient to select and activate an Object. All other Objects (in the visible layers) are then deselected in order to eliminate the risk of key commands causing unintentional changes to those objects. All of the relevant buttons are also drawn anew. Selections can be extended or shrunk using SHIFT+RMB. The last Object selected (or deselected) then becomes the active Object. Use Border Select (BKEY) to more rapidly select a number of Objects at one time. None of the Objects selected using this option will become active.

3.3.2 Manipulating objects

Most actions in Blender involve moving, rotating, or changing the size of certain items. Blender offers a wide range of options for doing this. See the 3DWindow section for a fully comprehensive list. The options are summarised here.

Grab

GKEY, Grab mode. Move the mouse to translate the selected items, then press LMB or ENTER or SPACE to assign the new location. Press ESC to cancel. Translation is always corrected for the view in the 3DWindow.

Use the middle mouse toggle to limit translation to the X, Y or Z axis. Blender determines which axis to use, based on the already initiated movement.

RMB and hold-move. This option allows you to select an Object and immediately start Grab mode.

Rot

RKEY, Rotation mode. Move the mouse around the rotation center, then press LMB or ENTER or SPACE to assign the rotation. Press ESC to cancel. Rotation is always perpendicular to the view of the 3DWindow.

The center of rotation is determined by use of these buttons in the 3DWindow-header. The left-most button rotates around the center of the bounding box of all selected objects. The next button uses the median points (shown as yellow/purple dots) of the selected objects to find the rotation center. The button with the 3DCursor depicted on it rotates around the 3DCursor. The last Button rotates around the individual centers of the objects.

Size

SKEY, Scaling mode. Move the mouse from the rotation center outwards,

then press LMB or ENTER or SPACE to assign the scaling. Use the MiddleMouse toggle to limit scaling to the X, Y or Z axis. Blender determines the appropriate axis based on the direction of the movement.

The center of scaling is determined by the center buttons in the 3DHeader (see the explanation for the rotation).

While in scaling mode, you can mirror the object by pressing XKEY or YKEY to mirror at the x- or y-axis.

NumberMenu

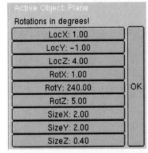

To input exact values, you can call up the NumberMenu with NKEY. SHIFT-LMB - click to change the Buttons to an input field and then enter the number.

3.3.3 Editmode

When you add a new object with the Toolbox, you are in the so-called Edit-Mode. In EditMode, you can change the shape of an Object (e.g. a Mesh, a Curve, or Text) itself by manipulating the individual points (the vertices) which are forming the object. Selecting works with the RMB and the BorderSelect also works to select vertices.

While entering EditMode, Blender makes a copy of the indicated data. The hotkey UKEY here serves as an undo function (more accurately it restores the copied data).

As a reminder that you are in EditMode, the cursor shape changes to that of a cross.

Part B / Model

Chapter 4
Mesh modelling

Chapter 5
Curves and surfaces

Chapter 6
Special modelling techniques

Chapter 4
Mesh modelling

Blender offers a set of basic objects, that you can use as the starting point for any model you may care to create.

You can access these basic objects via the Toolbox, which you can call up by using SPACE or SHIFT-A. The difference between the two is that SHIFT-A places the highlighted menu-entry in the add menu, while SPACE displays the last selected option.

With the mouse you can call up the Toolbox by left clicking on the Toolbox icon located at the upper right corner of the Blender screen.

Set Blender to the default scene by pressing CTRL-X, remembering that this action will delete your current scene, so you should be sure to save if you want to keep it.

Bring the mouse cursor over a 3DWindow and press SHIFT-A. The Toolbox with the activated ADD menu will pop up.

ADD	Mesh	>>
VIEW	Curve	>>
EDIT	Surface	>>
OBJECT	Text	
OBJECT	MetaBall	
MESH	Empty	A
CURVE		
KEY	Camera	A
RENDER	Lamp	A
FILE	Ika	A
	Lattice	A

Next, click with the LMB (left mouse button) on the menu-entry "MESH". The menu changes and will show the different possibilities for adding mesh-objects.

MESH	>Plane	A
VIEW	>Cube	A
EDIT	>Circle	A
OBJECT	>UVsphere	A
OBJECT	>Icosphere	A
MESH	>Cylinder	A
CURVE	>Tube	A
KEY	>Cone	A
RENDER	>	
FILE	>Grid	A
	>	
	>Duplicate	D

Select "Plane", the Toolbox disappears and a Plane appears at the 3DCursor. We are currently in the EditMode where we can edit the shape of the mesh itself. Now press TAB to leave EditMode, and the Plane changes to purple in the 3DWindow.

It is very likely that this Plane is positioned exactly above the default Plane, so press GKEY to enter the grab mode, then move the plane with the mouse a little way off and confirm the new position with a LMB click.

We are now going to add a more interesting object. Press SHIFT-A again, and then choose "UVSphere" from the "MESH" section.

In this instance, the Sphere does not appear at once, but Blender instead asks you for more information. The "Segment" and "Rings" input fields are prompting for the resolution of the Sphere we are going to create. For this, just click "OK" or press RETURN. Again, leave EditMode and move the Sphere to a position of your choosing.

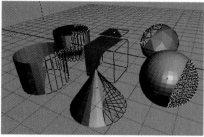

You can add a few more objects from the Toolbox with the procedures described above. Then use the middle mouse button (MMB) to rotate the view and explore the objects you have just created. Use the MMB together with SHIFT and CTRL to translate and zoom the view. Use a perspective view (PAD5) to get more of a 3D look.

Notice how the objects are composed from lots of single edges. Use the Edit-Mode (TAB) to explore the vertices of a selected object.

Press ZKEY to toggle on and off the filled view for objects in the 3DWindow.

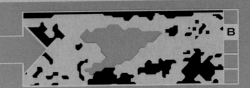
When working in 3D space, basically you can perform two types of operations: operations that affect the whole object, and operations that affect only the geometry of the object itself but not its global properties, such as the location or the rotation.

In Blender, you switch between these two modes using the TAB-key. A selected object outside EditMode is drawn in purple in the 3DWindows (in wireframe mode). To indicate the EditMode, the Objects vertices are drawn. Selected vertices are shown in yellow; non-selected vertices are shown in purple.

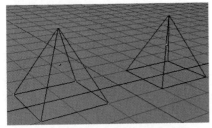

Like objects, vertices can be selected with the RMB (right mouse button). Holding SHIFT allows you to select more than one vertex. With some vertices selected you can use GKEY, RKEY or SKEY for manipulating the vertices, just as you can do for whole objects.

Now add a Cube to the default scene. Use the 3DCursor to place the cube away from the default plane, or use GKEY to move it away after leaving EditMode.

Switch the 3DWindow to a side view (PAD3), select the cube (if it is deselected) and press TAB to enter the EditMode again. Now, press BKEY for the BorderSelect and draw a rectangle with the LMB around the top four vertices of the cube. You will only see two vertices, because the other two are hidden directly behind the first two.

The top vertices have changed to yellow to indicate that they have been selected. You can rotate the view to make sure you really have selected all four vertices.

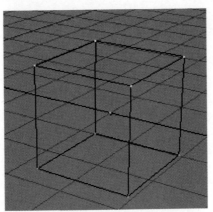

Now, press SKEY and move the mouse up and down. You can see how the four vertices are scaled. Depending on your movements, you can make a pyramid or a chopped off pyramid. You can also try to grab and rotate some vertices of the other objects to get a better feel for EditMode.

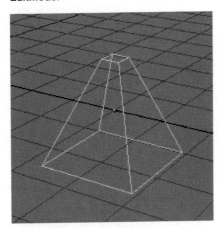

With WKEY, you can call up the "Specials" menu in EditMode. With this menu you can quickly access functions which are frequently required for polygon-modelling. You will find the same functionality in the EditButtons F9.

➡ *You can access the entries in a PopupMenu by using the corresponding numberkey. For example, the key presses WKEY, 1KEY, will subdivide the selected vertices without you having to touch the mouse.*

Smoothing and autosmooth by Reevan McKay

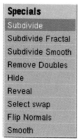

Specials
Subdivide
Subdivide Fractal
Subdivide Smooth
Remove Doubles
Hide
Reveal
Select swap
Flip Normals
Smooth

Most objects in Blender are represented by polygons. In Blender, truly curved objects are often approximated by polygon meshes. When rendering images, you may notice that these objects appear as a series of small flat facets. (Fig. 1). Sometimes this is a desirable effect, but usually we want our objects to look nice and smooth. This tutorial guides you through the steps of smoothing an object and applying the AutoSmooth filter to quickly and easily combine smooth and faceted polygons in the same object.

The object used in this demo can be found on the CDROM.

Figure 1

There are two ways of activating the face smoothing features of Blender. The easiest way is to set an entire object as smooth or faceted. This can be accomplished by selecting a mesh object, switching to the EditButtons window (F9), and clicking the Set Smooth button shown in Fig. 2. You will notice that the button does not stay pressed, but Blender has assigned the "smoothing" attribute to each face in the mesh. Rendering an image with F12 will produce the image shown in Fig. 3.

Notice that the outline of the object is still strongly faceted. Activating the smoothing features doesn't actually modify the object's geometry. Instead, it changes the way the shading is calculated across the surfaces, giving an illusion of a smooth surface.

Clicking the Set Solid button reverts the shading to what is shown in Fig. 1.

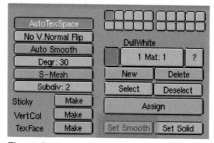

Figure 2

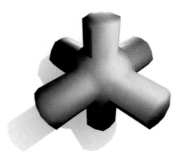

Figure 3

An alternative method of selecting which faces to smooth can be done by entering EditMode for the object with TAB, selecting faces and clicking the Set Smooth button (Fig. 4). When the mesh is in EditMode, only the faces that are selected will receive the "smoothing" attribute. You can set solid faces (removing the "smoothing" attribute) in the same way: by selecting faces and clicking the Set Solid button.

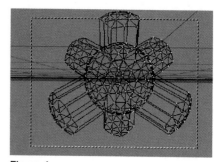

Figure 4

It can be difficult to create certain combinations of smooth and solid faces using the above techniques alone. Though there are workarounds (such as splitting off sets of faces by selecting them and pressing YKEY), there is an easier way to combine smooth and solid faces.

Pressing the AutoSmooth button in the EditButtons (Fig. 5) makes Blender decide which faces should and should not be smoothed based on the angle between faces (Fig. 6). Angles on the model that are sharper than the angle specified in the "Degr" NumBut will not be smoothed. You can change this value to adjust the amount of smoothing that occurs in your model. Higher values will produce more smoothed faces, while the lowest setting will look identical to a mesh that has been set completely solid.

Only faces that have been set as smooth will be affected by the AutoSmooth feature. A mesh, or any faces that have been set as solid will not change their shading when Auto-Smooth is activated. This allows you extra control over which faces will be smoothed and which ones won't by overriding the decisions made by the AutoSmooth algorithm.

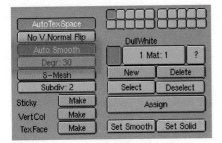

Figure 5

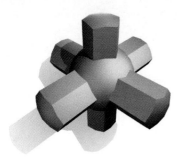

Figure 6

When working with dense meshes, it can become difficult to make subtle adjustments to the vertices without causing nasty lumps and creases in the model's surface. The proportional editing tool works like a magnet to smoothly deform the surface of the model.

Step By Step

In a top-down view, add a plane mesh to the scene with SHIFT+A >>MESH>>PLANE. Subdivide it a few times with WKEY >>SUBDIVIDE (or by clicking on the SUBDIVIDE button in the EditButtons) to get a relatively dense mesh (Fig. 1). When you are done, deselect all vertices with AKEY.

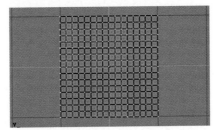

Figure 1

Select a single vertex in the mesh by clicking it with the RMB (Fig. 2).

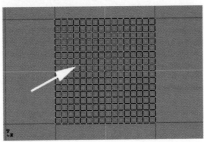

Figure 2

Still in EditMode, activate the proportional editing tool by pressing OKEY or by clicking on the grid icon in the header bar of the 3DWindow.

> → *If the icon isn't visible in the header bar because your window is too narrow, you can scroll the header bar by clicking with the MMB on it and and dragging it left or right.*

You should see the icon change to a distorted grid with two curve-shape buttons positioned next to it (Fig. 3).

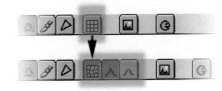

Figure 3

Switch to a front view (KEYPAD_1) and activate the move tool with GKEY. As you drag the point upwards, notice how other nearby vertices are dragged along with it in a curve similar to the one selected in the header bar.

You can change which curve profile is used by either clicking on the corresponding icon in the header bar, or by pressing SHIFT+O. Note that you cannot do this while you are in the middle of a proportional editing operation; you will have to press ESC to cancel the editing operation before you can change the curve.

When you are satisfied with the place-ment of the vertex, confirm its position with LMB. Pressing ESC will cancel the operation and reverts your mesh to the way it looked before you started dragging the point.

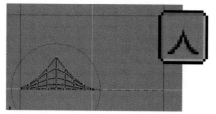

Figure 4

You can increase or decrease the radius of influence (shown by the dotted circle in Fig. 4) while you are editing by pressing KEYPAD_PLUS and KEYPAD_MINUS respectively. As you change the radius, you will see the points surrounding your selection adjust their positions accordingly.

You can get great effects using the proportional editing tool with scaling (SKEY) and rotation (RKEY) tools.

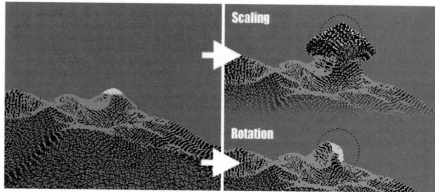

Figure 5

Combine these techniques with vertex painting to create fantastic landscapes.

Fig. 6 shows the results of proportional editing after the application of textures and lighting.

Figure 6

Extrude

by Willem Zwarthoed

The most important tool for working with Meshes is the "Extrude" command (EKEY). This command allows you to create cubes from rectangles, and cylinders from circles. The Extrude command allows you to create objects such as tree limbs very easily.

Although the process is quite intuitive, the principle behind Extrude is outlined below:

- First, the application determines the outside 'edge' of the Extrude, i.e. which selected edges are allowed to be changed into faces. By default, the application ignores edges with two or more selected faces.
- The edges in question are then changed into faces.
- If the edges in question had only one face, all of the selected faces are duplicated and linked to the newly created faces, e.g. rectangles result in cubes during this stage.
- In other cases, the selected faces themselves are linked to the newly created faces. This prevents undesired faces from being retained 'inside' if Extrude is invoked again later. This distinction is extremely important, e.g. during smoothing. The distinction ensures the construction of consistently coherent, closed volumes at all times when using Extrude.
- Edges without selected faces are simply Extruded.
- Vertices without selected edges are turned into edges.

Grab mode is automatically started when Extrude is invoked.

Using Extrude

Extrude is one of the most frequently used modelling tools in Blender. It's simple, straightforward, and easy to use, yet it is also very powerful. In this tutorial you'll learn how to use Extrude to model a sword in a very short time.

The Blade

Start Blender and delete the default plane. In top view, add a mesh circle with 8 vertices. Move the vertices so they represent the figure below.

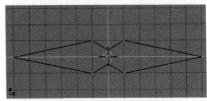

Select all the vertices and scale them down with the SKEY so the shape fits in 2 grid units. Switch to front view with Keypad_1.

The shape we've created is the base of the blade. Using extrude we'll create the blade in a few simple steps. With all vertices selected press EKEY, or click the button labeled 'extrude' in the EditButtons (F9). A box will pop up asking 'Ok? Extrude'.

Click it or press RETURN to confirm. If you move the mouse now, you'll see the following has happened: Blender has duplicated the vertices, connected them to the original ones with edges and faces, and has entered grab mode. Move the new vertices up 30 units, constraining the movement with CTRL. Click the LMB to confirm their new position, and scale them down a little bit with the SKEY.

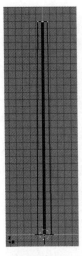

Press EKEY again to extrude the tip of the blade. Move the vertices five units up. To make the blade end in one vertex, scale the top vertices down to 0.000 (hold CTRL for this) and press WKEY>'Remove Doubles' or click the "Rem Doubles" button in the EditButtons (F9). Blender will inform you it has removed seven of the eight vertices and only one vertex remains: the blade is done!

The Handle

Leave edit mode and move the blade to the side. Add a UVsphere with 16 segments and rings and deselect all the vertices with the AKEY. Borderselect the top three rings of vertices with BKEY and delete them with XKEY>'Vertices'.

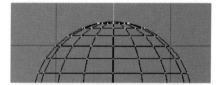

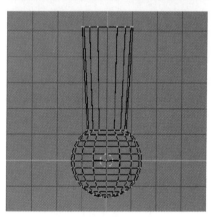

Select the top ring of vertices and extrude them. Move the ring up four units and scale them up a bit, extrude and move 4 units again twice and scale the last ring down a bit. Leave EditMode and scale the entire handle down so it's in proportion with the blade. Place it under the blade.

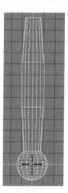

The Hilt

By now you should be used to the 'extrude>move>scale' sequence, so try to model a nice hilt with extrude. Start out with a cube and extrude different sides a few times, scaling them where needed. You should be able to get something like this:

After texturing, the sword looks like this:

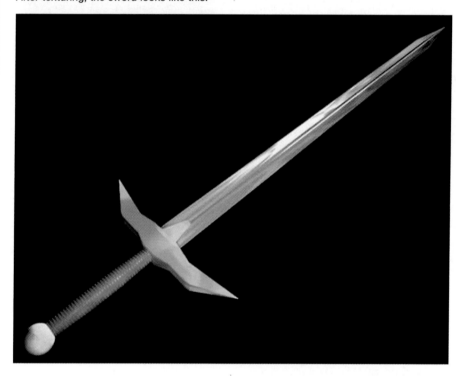

As you can see, extrude is a very powerful tool allowing you to model relatively complex objects very quickly (the entire sword was created in less than a half hour!). Getting the hang of the extrude>move>scale will make your life as a Blender modeller so much easier.

Spin

The Spin tool in Blender is designed for creating the sort of objects that you can produce on a lathe. This tool is often referred to as "lathe"-tool or "sweep"-tool in the literature.

First you must create a mesh representing the profile of your object. If you are modelling a hollow object, it is a good idea to give a thickness to the outline. Fig. 1 shows the profile for a wine glass. This file can be found on the CDROM.

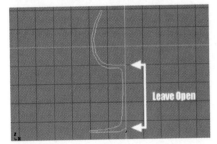

Figure 1

With all the vertices selected and in Edit-Mode, access the EditButtons window (F9). The "Degr" button indicates the number of degrees to spin the object (in this case we want a full 360 degrees sweep). The "Steps" button specifies how many profiles there will be in the sweep (Fig.2).

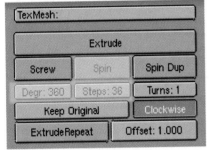

Figure 2

As with Spin Duplicate (covered by the next section), the effects of Spin depend on the placement of the cursor and which window (view) is active. We will be rotating the object around the cursor

in the top view. Switch to the top view with KEYPAD_7. The cursor should be placed along the center of the profile. This is easily accomplished by selecting one of the vertices along the center, and snapping the cursor to that location with SHIFT+S >>CURS->SEL.

Fig. 3 shows the wine glass profile from top view, with the cursor correctly positioned.

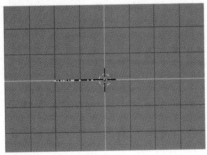

Figure 3

Before continuing, make a note of the number of vertices in the profile. This information can be found in the Info bar at the top of the Blender interface (Fig. 4)

Figure 4

Click the "Spin" button. If you have more than one window open, the cursor will change to an arrow with a question mark and you will have to click in the window containing the top view before continuing. If you have only one window open, the spin will happen immediately.

Fig. 5 shows the result of a successful spin.

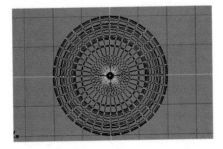

Now for the tricky part! The spin operation leaves duplicate vertices along the profile. Unfortunately, these duplicates do not always exactly match the original profile. In order to remove them, and thereby close the object, we need to take a few steps.

Use the boundary select tool (BKEY) to select all of the vertices that lie along the "seam". The white rectangle in Fig. 6 shows the vertices that must be selected.

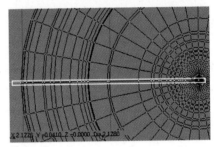

Figure 6

Press PERIOD to scale around the location of the cursor. We'll do this to scale the selected points into a line that passes through the center of the object.

Press SKEY to start scaling. Drag the mouse cursor vertically and press the middle mousebutton. If done correctly, this will constrain scaling operations to the Y axis. If not, you can click MMB again to turn off the constraint and try again (Fig.7).

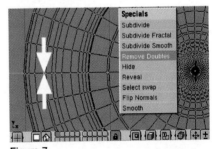

Figure 7

While scaling, hold down the CONTROL key to scale in 0.1 unit increments. Scale the line of points down to 0 in the Y axis, and clicking the LMB to complete

the scaling operation. If you like, you can revert to the default rotation/scaling pivot by pressing COMMA when you have finished.

Remove doubles in the current selection set by pressing WKEY >>REMOVE DOUBLES. A small box will appear saying how many points were removed. Dismiss this box by moving the mouse, pressing ESC or by clicking the LMB or clicking the RMB.

Notice the selected vertex count before and after the "Remove Doubles" operation (Fig. 8). If all goes well, the final vertex count (38 in this example) should match the number from Fig. 4. If not, some vertices were missed and you will have to go and weld them manually.

> **→** To weld two vertices together, select both of them by holding SHIFT and click RMB on them. Press SKEY to start scaling and hold down CONTROL while scaling to scale the points down to 0 units in the X,Y and Z axis. LMB to complete the scaling operation and click the "Remove Doubles" button in the EditButtons window.

Figure 8

All that remains now is to recalculate the normals by selecting all vertices and pressing CONTROL+N >>RECALC NORMALS OUTSIDE. At this point you can leave EditMode and apply materials or smoothing, set up some lights, a camera and make a rendering. Fig. 9 shows our wine glass in a finished state.

Figure 9

SpinDup

The SpinDup tool is a great way to quickly make a series of copies of an object laid out in a circular pattern. The "clock.blend" file on the CDROM contains a clock that is missing the hour marks.

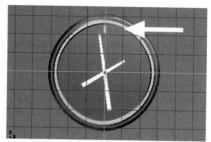

Figure 1

Select the object you wish to rotate (in this example, it is the small rectangle at the 12:00 position on the clock, indicated by the arrow in Fig. 1) and switch to the EditButtons window with F9. Set the number of degrees in the "Degr"

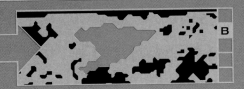

NumBut to 360. We want to make 12 copies of our object, so set the "Steps" to 12 (Fig. 2).

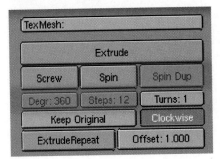

Figure 2

Switch the view to the one in which you wish to rotate the object by using the keypad. Note that the result of the "Spin-Dup" command depends on the view you are using when you press the button. Position the cursor at the center of rotation. The objects will be rotated around this point.
Select the object you wish to duplicate and enter EditMode with TAB.
In EditMode, select the vertices you want to duplicate (note that you can select all vertices with AKEY or all of the vertices linked to the point under the cursor with LKEY). See Fig. 3.

→ If you want to place the cursor at the precise location of an existing object or vertex, select the object or vertex, and press SHIFT+S >>CURS->SEL.

Figure 3

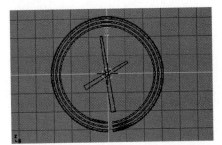

Press the "SpinDup" button. If you have more than one 3DWindow open, you will notice the mouse cursor change to an arrow with a question mark. Click in the window in which you want to do your rotation. In this case, we want to use the front window (Fig. 4).

If the view you want is not visible, you can dismiss the arrow/question mark with ESC until you can switch a window to the appropriate view with the keypad

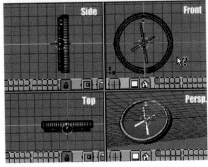

Figure 4

When spin-duplicating an object through 360 degrees, a duplicate object is placed at the same location of the first object, producing duplicate geometry. You will notice that after clicking the "SpinDup" button, the original geometry remains selected. To delete it, simply press XKEY >>VERTICES. The source object is deleted, but the duplicated version beneath it remains (Fig. 5).

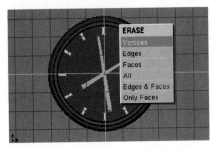

Figure 5

The "clock.blend" file on the CDROM contains the rest of the clock details and lighting on layers two and three (Fig. 6). Fig. 7 shows the final rendering of the clock.

Figure 6

Figure 7

This tool starts a repetitive "Spin" with a screw-shaped revolution on the selected vertices. You can use this to create screws, springs or shell-shaped structures.

This Image shows how to make a spring (Fig. 1).

Figure 1

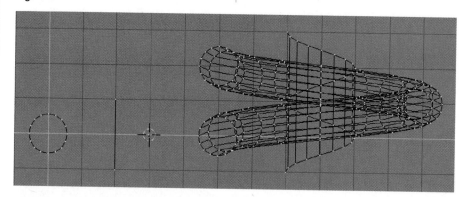

The method for using the "Screw" function is strict: (Fig. 2)

• Set the 3DWindow in front view, NUMPAD_1.
• Place the 3DCursor at the position through which the rotation axis must pass, vertically on the screen.
• Ensure that an open poly line is always available. This can be a single edge or half a circle, or ensure that there are two 'free' ends; two edges with only one vertex linked to another edge. The "Screw" function localises these two points and uses them to calculate the vector that is added to the "Spin" per full rotation. If these two vertices are at the same location, this creates a normal "Spin". Otherwise, interesting things happen!
• Select all vertices that must participate in the "Screw".
• Give the buttons "Steps" and "Turns" the desired value.
• Press "Screw"!

If there are multiple 3DWindows, the mouse cursor changes to a question mark. Click at the 3DWindow in which "Extrude" must be executed.

Figure 2

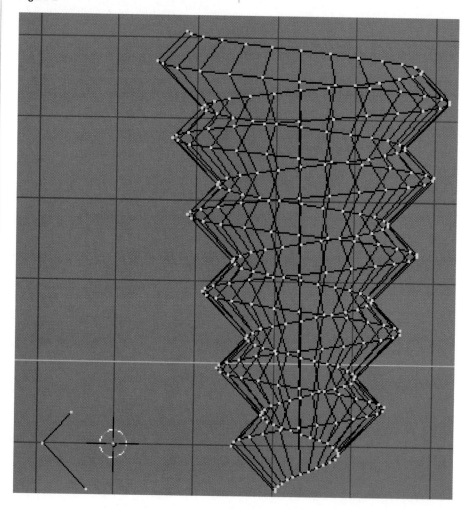

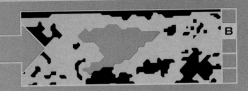

Mesh Intersection, often called "boolean functions", is a different way to model. The Blender way is to model around holes, but with Mesh Intersection first you do your models and then you cut holes in them.

Mesh Intersect is available in the Editbuttons, F9. Select the faces (this means, select the vertices in EditMode which form the desired face) that need an intersection, and press this button. Blender now intersects all selected faces with each other.

For the best example to test this out, use an IcoSphere and a Cube. After intersection, you can select the individual parts LKEY. By removing certain parts, a user can easily obtain a boolean operation like OR, AND or XOR.

To ensure a proper intersection, it is important to follow these guidelines carefully:

• Make sure no co-planar faces intersect.
• Always make sure faces have as few intersections as possible, for example,

intersecting a single plane with a tube works better when the plane is subdivided a few times.
• The 'trick': rotate each part slightly, just a fraction of a degree.
• Before intersecting, save the file or press TAB -TAB to create an UNDO possibility. It is possible to make Blender crash with this routine.

by Randall Rickert

The noise function allows you to displace vertices in meshes based on the gray-values of a texture. That way you can generate great landscape or carve text into meshes.

Specials

Subdivide
Subdivide Fractal
Subdivide Smooth
Remove Doubles
Hide
Reveal
Select swap
Flip Normals
Smooth

Add a plane and subdivide it at least five times with the special menu WKEY >Subdivide. Now add a material and assign a clouds texture to it. Adjust the "NoiseSize" to 0.500. Choose white as the color for the material and black as the texture color. This, will give us good contrast for the noise operation.

Ensure that you are in EditMode and all vertices are selected, then switch to the EditButtons F9. Press the "Noise" button several times until the landscape looks attractive. You should now remove the texture from the landscape because it will disturb the look. Now you can add some lights and do a render. Press "SetSmooth" in the EditButtons to get a smooth landscape.

The Warp Tool is a little-known tool in Blender, partly because it is not found in the edit buttons window, and partly because it is only useful in very specific cases. It is not something the average Blender-user will need every day.

A piece of text wrapped into a ring shape is useful in flying logos, but it would be difficult to model without the Warp Tool.

Add the text in top view, set "Extrude" to 0.1 and set "Bevel" to 0.01. Lower the resolution so that the vertex count will not be too high when you subdivide the object later on. Convert the object to curves, then to a mesh, because the Warp Tool does not work on text or on curves. Subdivide the mesh twice, so that the geometry will change shape cleanly, without artifacts.

Switch to front view and move the mesh away from the 3DCursor. This distance defines the radius of the warp. See Figure 1.

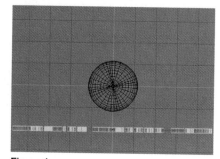

Figure 1

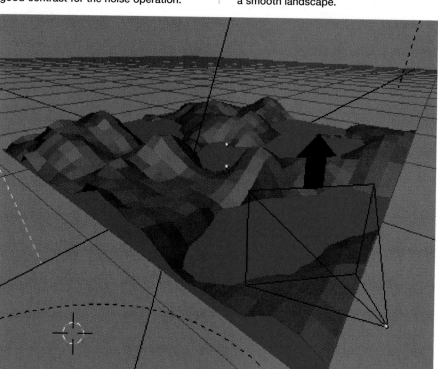

Place the mesh in edit mode and press SHIFT+W to activate the warp tool. Move the mouse upward to interactively define the amount of warp. See Figure 2.

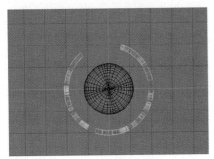

Figure 2

Now you can switch to side view and rotate the ring of text to face the camera. The result is warp.blend. See Figure 3.

Figure 3

S-Mesh is short for Subdivision-Meshes. With any regular Mesh as a starting point, Blender can calculate a smooth sub-division on the fly, that is while modelling or while rendering. This allows high resolution Mesh modelling without the need to save and maintain vast amounts of data.

In fact, you can now work with Meshes as if it were Nurbs Surfaces, but with a more precise control and a more flexible modelling freedom.

"S-mesh" is a Mesh option. The button to activate this is in the EditButons F9. The second button Subdiv allows you to indicate the resolution for the smooth subdivision.

Blender's subdivision system is based at the vertex normals in a Mesh. For regular Mesh modelling, it doesn't really matter how the normals point. For S-Meshes however, it is necessary to have them all pointing inside or outside consistently.

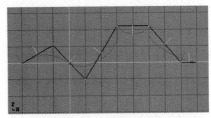

Use the CTRL+N command to make Blender recalculate the normals.

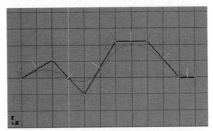

In the above image, the face normals are drawn in cyan, the vertex normals are drawn in blue. You can enable drawing normals in the F9 menu as well.

Blender's S-Meshes are still under development. The current system best allows for the modelling of smooth and organic shapes. Also bear in mind that a regular Mesh with square faces will give the best result.

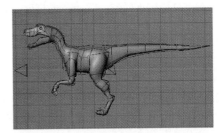

This cool raptor is modelled by Hiroshi Saito and is a good example of modelling organic objects with s-meshes. The file is included on the CDROM ("raptor.blend").

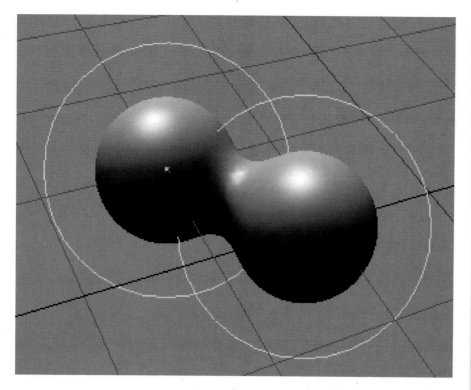

Modelling with MetaBalls

In EditMode, you can move and scale the balls or rounded tubes as you wish. This is the best way to construct static (not animated) forms. MetaBalls can also influence each other outside EditMode. Now you have much more freedom in which to work. The balls can rotate or move and they benefit from every transformation of the Parents' Objects. This method does, however, require more calculation time and is thus a little slower to execute.

The following rules describe the relation between MetaBall Objects:

All MetaBall Objects with the same 'family' name (the name without the number) influence each other. For example "Ball", "Ball.001", "Ball.002", "Ball.135". Note here that we are not talking about the name of the MetaBall ObData block.
The Object with the family name, without a number determines the basis, the resolution and the transformation of the polygonise. It also has the Material and texture area.

To be able to display animated MetaBalls 'stably', it is important to first determine what Object forms the basis. If the basis moves, and the rest remains still, you will see the polygonised faces move 'through' the balls.

The "Threshold" in EditButtons is an important setting for MetaBalls. You can make the entire system more fluid, less detailed, or harder by using this option. The resolution of polygonise is also specified in EditButtons. This is the big memory consumer, however, it is released immediately after polygonise. It works more efficiently and faster with multiples, more compact 'families' of balls. Because it is slow, the polygonise is not immediately recalculated for each change. It is always recalculated after a Grab, Rotate, or Size command.

MetaBalls consist of spherical or tubular elements that can operate on each other's shape. You can only create round and fluid, 'mercurial' or 'clay-like' forms that exist procedurally.
Use MetaBalls for special effects, or as a basis for modelling.

MetaBalls are little more than mathematical formulas that perform logical operations on one another (AND, OR), and that can be added and subtracted. This method is also called CSG, Constructive Solid Geometry. Because of its mathematical nature, CSG can be displayed well, and relatively quickly, with Ray Tracing. Because this is much too slow for interactive displays, polygonise routines were developed. The complete CSG area is then divided into a 3D grid, and for each edge in the grid a calculation is made if, and more importantly where, the formula has a turning point, a 'vertex' for the polygonise is created there.

The available quantity of CSG primitives and tools in Blender is limited. This will be developed further in future versions of Blender. The basis is already here and it is outstandingly implemented. Blender has little need for modelling systems that are optimized for Ray Tracing, even though they are great fun to play with!

A MetaBall is displayed with the transformations of an Object and an exterior determined by the Material. Only one Material can be used here. In addition, MetaBall saves a separate texture area which normalises the coordinates of the vertices. Normally the texture area is identical to the bound box of all vertices. The user can force a texture area with the TKEY command (outside EditMode).

MetaBalls are very compact in memory and in the file. The requisite faces are only generated upon rendering. Be aware that this can take up a great deal of calculation time and memory.

©2000 Aaron Hilton

©2000 Willem Zwarthoed

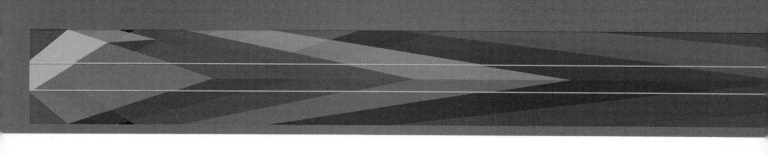

Curves and surfaces

Chapter 5
Curves and surfaces

Beziers

Bezier curves are the most commonly used type for designing letters or logos.

A curvepoint consists of three handles. The middle handle is used to move the entire vertex, selecting it will also select the other two handles, and allow you to move the complete vertex. Selecting one or two of the other handles will allow you to change the shape of the curve by dragging.

There are four types of handles:
Free Handle (black). This can be used in anyway you wish. Hotkey: HKEY (toggles between Free and Aligned).
Aligned Handle (pink). These handles always lie in a straight line. Hotkey: HKEY (toggles between Free and Aligned).
Vector Handle (green). Both parts of a handle always point to the previous handle or the next handle. Hotkey: VKEY.
Auto Handle (yellow). This handle has a completely automatic length and direction. Hotkey: SHIFT+H.

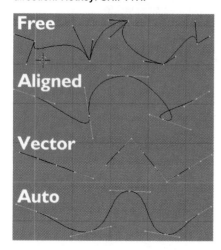

Handles can be rotated by selecting the end of one of the vertices. Again, use the grabber with RMB -hold-move.

As soon as the handles are rotated, the type is modified automatically:
Auto Handle becomes Aligned.
Vector Handle becomes Free.

A separate resolution can be set for each Bezier curve (the number of points generated between two points in the curve).

Nurbs

Nurbs curves have a large set of variables, which allow you to create mathematically pure forms. However, working with them requires a little more intuition:

Knots. Nurbs curves have knots, a row of numbers that specify the precise curve. Two pre-sets are important for this. "Uniform" produces a uniform division, for closed curves. "Endpoint" sets the knots in such a way that the first and last vertexes are always included.
Order. The order is the 'depth' of the curve calculation. Order '1' is a point, order '2' is linear, order '3' is quadratic, etc. Always use order '5' for Curve paths; this behaves fluidly under all circumstances, without irritating discontinuities in the movement.
Weight. Nurbs curves have a 'weight' per vertex - the extent to which a vertex participates in the interpolation.

Just as with Beziers, the resolution can be set per curve.

Poly

If no interpolation is needed, you can use the "Poly" type. This has all the facilities, such as extrude and beveling.

5.1.1 A Logo with Curves
by Reevan McKay

Blender's curve tools provide a quick and easy way to build great looking extruded text and logos. We will use these tools to turn a rough sketch of a logo into a finished 3D object. Fig. 1 shows the design of the logo we will be building.

Figure 1: The sketched logo

Preparing the Template

First, we will import our original sketch so that we can use it as a template. Blender supports both TGA and JPG format images. To load the image, move the cursor over a 3DWindow and press SHIFT+F7 to get to the view settings for that window. Activate the Back-GroundPic button and use the LOAD button to locate the image you want to use as a template (Fig. 2). If you do not have one, you can load the LOGO-SM.JPG image from the CDROM.

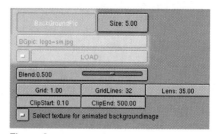

Figure 2

Return to the 3DView by pressing SHIFT+F5 (Fig. 3). You can hide the background image when you are finished using it by returning to the SHIFT+F7 window and deselecting the BackGroundPic button.

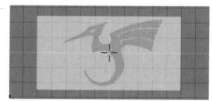

Figure 3

Trace the curves

Add a new curve by pressing SHIFT+A >>CURVE>>BEZIER CURVE. A curved segment will appear and Blender will enter Editmode. We will move and add points to make a closed shape that describes the logo you are trying to trace.

You can add points to the curve by selecting one of the two endpoints, then holding CONTROL and LMB. Note that the new point will be connected to the previously selected point. Once a point has been added, it can be moved by selecting the control vertex and pressing GKEY. You can change the angle of the curve by grabbing and moving the handles associated with each vertex (Fig 4).

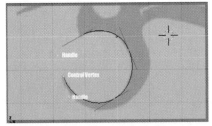

Figure 4

You can add a new point between two existing points by selecting the two points and pressing WKEY >>SUBDIVIDE (Fig. 5).

Figure 5

Points can be removed by selecting them and pressing XKEY >>SELECTED. You cut a curve into two curves by selecting two adjacent control vertices and pressing XKEY >>SEGMENT.

To make sharp corners, you can select a control vertex and press VKEY. You will notice the colour of the handles change from purple to green (Fig. 6). At this point, you can adjust the handles to adjust the way the curve enters and leaves the control vertex (Fig. 7).

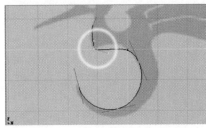

Figure 6

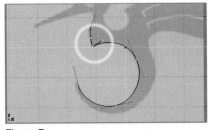

Figure 7

To close the curve and make it into a single continuous loop, select at least one of the of the control vertices on the curve and press CKEY. This will connect the last point in the curve with the first one (Fig. 8).
You may need to manipulate some more handles to get the shape you want.

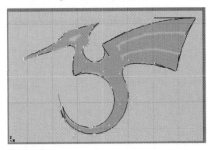

Figure 8

Cut Holes

Leaving editmode with TAB and entering shaded mode with ZKEY should reveal that the curve renders as a solid shape (Fig. 9). We want to cut some holes into this shape to represent the eyes and wing details of the dragon. When working with curves, Blender automatically detects holes in the surface and handles them accordingly. Return to wireframe mode with ZKEY and enter editmode again with TAB.

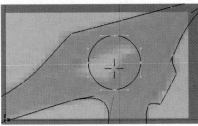

Figure 9

While still in editmode, add a circle curve with SHIFT+A >>CURVE>>BEZIER CIRCLE (Fig. 10). Scale the circle down to an appropriate size with SKEY and move it with GKEY.

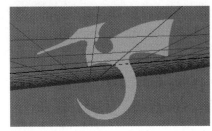

Figure 10

Shape the circle using the techniques we have learned (Fig. 11). Remember that you can add vertices to the circle with WKEY >>SUBDIVIDE.

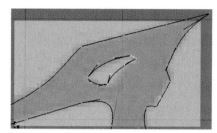

Figure 11

Create a wing cutout by adding a Bezier circle, converting all of the points to sharp corners, and then adjusting as necessary. You can duplicate this outline to save time when creating the second wing cutout. To do this, make sure no points are selected, then move the cursor over one of the vertices in the first wing cutout and select all linked points with LKEY (Fig. 12). Duplicate the selection with SHIFT+D and move the new points into position.

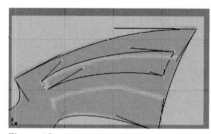

Figure 12

If you want to add more geometry that is not connected to the main body (placing an orb in the dragon's curved tail for example), you can do this by using the SHIFT+A menu to add more curves as shown in Fig. 13.

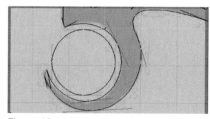

Figure 13

Extruding the Curve

Now that we have the curve, we need to set its thickness and beveling options. With the curve selected, go to the Edit-Buttons (F9). The Ext1 parameter sets the thickness of the extrusion while Ext2 sets the size of the bevel. BevResol sets how sharp or curved the bevel will be.

Fig. 14 shows the settings used to extrude this curve.

Figure 14

If you want to perform more complex modelling operations, you can convert the curve to a mesh with ALT+C >>MESH. Note that this is a one-way operation: you cannot convert a mesh back into a curve.

When your logo model is complete, you can add materials and lights and make a nice rendering (Fig. 15).

Figure 15

Surfaces are actually an extension of Nurbs Curves. In Blender they are a separate ObData type. Whereas a curve only produces one-dimensional inter-polation, Surfaces have a second extra dimension, called the U and V directions. These allow you to create curved sur-faces; a two-dimensional network of vertices defines the form for this.

Use Surfaces to create and revise fluid curved surfaces. They can be cyclical in both directions, allowing you to easily create a 'donut' shape. Surfaces can also be drawn as 'solids' in EditMode (zbuffered, with OpenGL lighting). This makes working with surfaces quite easy.

Currently Blender has a basic tool set for Surfaces. It has limited functionality regarding the creation of holes and for melting surfaces. Future versions will contain increased functionality in these areas.

Modelling with Surfaces

You can take a 'primitive' from the ADD menu as a starting point, or duplicate a single point from an existing surface with SHIFT+D. Nurbs curves are also a normal part of a Surface; they can be processed and drawn as described above.

SURF	>Curve	A
VIEW	>Circle	A
EDIT	>Surface	A
OBJECT	>Tube	A
OBJECT	>Sphere	A
MESH	>Donut	A
CURVE		
KEY		
RENDER		
FILE		
	>Duplicate	D

Create a surface by extruding an entire curve (EKEY). Each edge of a surface can then be extruded any way you wish to form the model. Use CKEY to make the U or V direction cyclic. It is important to set the 'knots' to "Uniform" or "End-point" with one of the pre-sets from the EditButtons

A surface becomes active if 1 of its vertices is selected with the RMB. This causes the EditButtons to be re-drawn.

When working with surfaces, it is handy to always work on a complete column or row of vertices. Blender provides a selection tool for this: SHIFT+R , "Select Row". Starting from the last selected vertex, a complete row of vertices is extend selected in the 'U' or 'V' direction. Choose Select Row again with the same vertex and you toggle between the 'U' or 'V' selection.

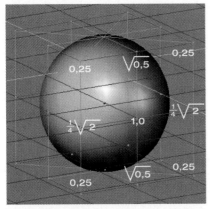

To create pure circles, globes or cylinders, you must set the weights of the vertices. The example shows this for a globe. Three standard numbers are included as pre-sets in the EditButtons. Read the weight of a vertex with the NKEY.

A complete overview of all the tools and options is contained in the Reference section for "3DWindow" and "EditButtons".

Text is a special curve type for Blender. Only Postscript Type 1 fonts are supported by Blender.

Start with a fresh scene by pressing CTRL-X and add a TextObject with the Toolbox (ADD->Text). In EditMode you can edit the text with the keyboard, a text cursor shows your actual position in the text. When you leave the EditMode with TAB , Blender fills the text-curve, so that you have a flat filled object that is renderable at once.

Now go to the EditButtons F9.

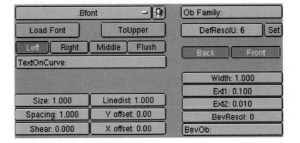

The buttons are described in detail in the reference section. As you can see in the MenuButton, Blender uses by default the ".Bfont" when creating a new text-object. Now click "Load Font" and, browsing what appears in the File-Window, go to a directory containing Postscript Type 1 fonts and load a new font (there are several free Postscript fonts provided on the CDROM). Try out some other fonts. After loading a font, you can use the MenuButton to switch the font for a TextObject.

For now we have only a flat object. To add some depth, we can use the "Ext1:" and "Ext2:" buttons in just the same way as we have done with curves.

With the "TextOnCurve:" option you can make the text follow a 2D-curve. Use the alignment buttons above the "Text-OnCurve:" textfield to align the text on the curve.

A powerful function is that a TextObject can be converted with ALT-C to a Curve, which allows you to edit the shape of every character. This is especially handy for creating logos or for custom lettering.

Special Characters

Normally, a Font Object begins with the word "Text". This can be deleted simply with SHIFT+BACKSPACE. In EditMode, this Object only reacts to text input. Nearly all of the hotkeys are disabled. The cursor can be moved with the arrow-keys. Use SHIFT+ARROWLEFT and SHIFT+ARROWRIGHT to move the cursor to the end of the lines or to the beginning or end of the text. Nearly all 'special' characters are available. A summary of these characters follows:

ALT+c: copyright
ALT+f: Dutch Florin
ALT+g: degrees
ALT+l: British Pound
ALT+r: Registered trademark
ALT+s: German S
ALT+x: Multiply symbol
ALT+y: Japanese Yen
ALT+DOTKEY: a circle
ALT+1: a small 1
ALT+2: a small 2
ALT+3: a small 3
ALT+%: promillage
ALT+?: Spanish question mark
ALT+!: Spanish exclamation mark
ALT+>: a double >>
ALT+<: a double <<

Many special characters are, in fact, a combination of two other characters, e.g. the letters with accents. First pressing ALT+BACKSPACE , and then pressing the desired combination can call these up. Some examples are given below.

AKEY, ALT+BACKSPACE, TILDE: ã
AKEY, ALT+BACKSPACE, ACCENT: à
AKEY, ALT+BACKSPACE, OKEY: å
EKEY, ALT+BACKSPACE, QUOTE: ë
OKEY, ALT+BACKSPACE, SLASH: ø

Complete ASCII files can also be added to a Text Object. Save this file as "/tmp/.cutbuffer" and press ALT+V.

Chapter 6
Special modelling techniques

6.2 **Dupliframes**

6.2.1 **Modelling with animation**

6.3 **Modelling with lattices**

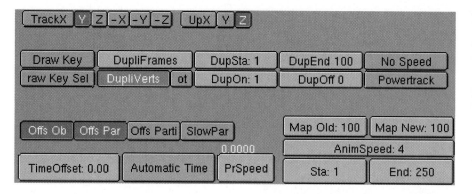

Dupliverts are an easy way to make arrangements of objects. In fact on every vertex of a mesh an instance of the base object is placed. The placed object can be of any object type which Blender supports.

Load the scene "Dupliverts00.blend". It contains a simple scene and a column. Switch to Layer 2 and create in the top-view (PAD_7) a mesh-circle with 12 vertices.

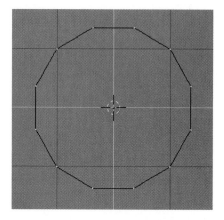

This circle will be our base for the arrangement. Now switch Layer 3 on with SHIFT-3KEY. The column appears in the middle of the circle. Select the column and then add the circle to the selection (hold SHIFT while selecting) and press CTRL-P to make the circle parent to the column.

Now select only the circle, switch the ButtonsWindow to the AnimButtons F7 and select here the option "DupliVerts".

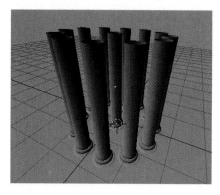

Note that the base column is still shown in the 3D-views, but it is not rendered. You now can select the column, change (scale, rotate, EditMode) it and all dupliverted objects will show the change. But the more interesting thing to note is that you also can change the parent object.

Select the circle and scale it. You can see that the columns are uniformly scaled with the circle. Now enter the EditMode TAB for the circle, select all vertices AKEY and scale about three times bigger. Leave EditMode and the dupliverted objects will update. This time they still have their own size but the distance between them is bigger. Not only can we scale in EditMode, but we can also delete or add vertices to change the arrangement of columns.

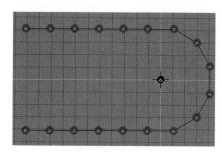

Try to delete the left four vertices of the circle in EditMode. Select the two on the left and extrude them to the left. Repeat this step a few times and then leave Edit-Mode. We now have an arrangement of columns similar to those which can be found in a temple or a big hall.

Rotating dupliverted objects

With the "Rot" option in the duplivert section of the AnimButtons, you can rotate the dupliverted objects according to the face-normals of the parent object.

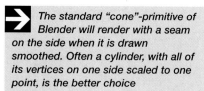

Add an Icosphere with two subdivisions. Next, add a cone and size it to a spike on your club.

→ *The standard "cone"-primitive of Blender will render with a seam on the side when it is drawn smoothed. Often a cylinder, with all of its vertices on one side scaled to one point, is the better choice*

Now, make the icosphere the parent of the spike. Select the icosphere alone and make it "Duplivert" in the AnimButtons. Note the effect of the option "Rot" when you click on it now.

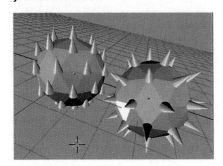

Depending on the orientation of the spike relative to the world, you may now need to rotate the vertices of the spike in EditMode to make all the spikes point outwards.

Again, the base mesh is not rendered.

The method of "Dupliframes" can be described as modelling with animation. Here are two illustrations of the technique.

Arrangements of dupliframed objects

This method is similar to the dupliverts method, but this time we can use curves and animation paths to arrange our objects.

| PathLen: 100 | CurvePath | CurveFollow | PrintLen | 0.0000 |

For a roller coaster animation, you start with a curve describing your tracks. A simple bevel will do your tracks ("Rollercoaster00.blend"), the curves are also reused for the camera path.

Add a cube that will act as sleeper for the track. Scale it so that it fits to the tracks. Now, select the sleeper, then extend the selection by the object "SleeperCurve" and make the Curve the parent of the sleeper (with CTRL-P).

Select the object "SleeperCurve" alone and activate the options "CurvePath" and "CurveFollow" in the AnimButtons F7. It maybe that the sleeper is now dislocated, in which case select the curve, then extend by the sleeper and press ALT-O to clear the origin. Then position the sleeper down under the tracks. Until now we have done little more than animate the sleeper along the curve. This can be verified by playing the animation with ALT-A.

Now, select the sleeper and go to the AnimButtons F7. Here, activate the option "DupliFrames". With the "DupSta:" and "DupEnd" NumButtons you can define the start and end of the duplication.

| DupliFrames | DupSta: 1 | DupEnd 100 | No Speed |

If the sleepers are too close to each other, you can adjust the number of objects using the "PathLen:" option of the sleeper-curve.

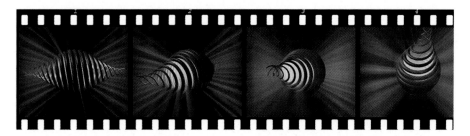

Modelling with dupliframes

With Dupliverts, not only can we create separate objects but we can also create one big object. Ideal for that purpose are NURBS-surfaces, because we can change the resolution easily after creation, and if we need to we can convert them to a mesh object. Also, the surface objects from Blender are ideal for "skinning".

Create a surface circle (ADD->Surface->Circle) in a front view. Don't leave Edit-Mode, just move the vertices of the circle until they are about 4 times the size of the circle diameter to the left.

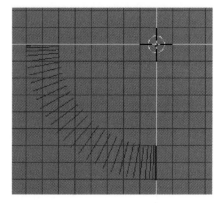

Switch to a TopView and insert a key using IKEY, then choose "Rotation" from the PopupMenu. Advance the frame slider by 30 frames (three times

CURSOR-UP). Now, rotate the circle 90 degrees and insert another keyframe.

Draw Key	DupliFrames	DupSta: 1	DupEnd 100	No Speed

Use F7 to open the AnimButtons and activate "DupliFrames". You can now see an arrangement of circles in your TopView. In the shaded 3DWindow you will see nothing so far, this we'll change at the end.

Switch one window to an IpoWindow using SHIFT-F6, and select the "RotZ" curve. Now, change the Ipo to "Extend Mode Extrapolation".

Switch off the "DupliFrames" option in the AnimButtons, and insert a keyframe-animation for the size of the circle. After that, animate the location of the circle with a keyframe animation along the

z-axis. Here you should also use the "Extend Mode Extrapolation" in the IpoWindow. You will get something that which is shown in the next picture after you have activated the "DupliFrames" option again.

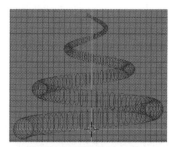

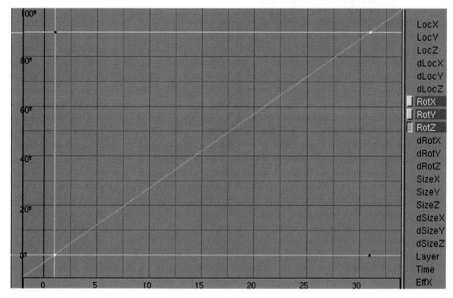

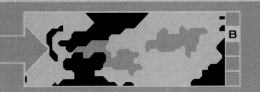
Making it real

To turn the structure into a real NURBS-object, select the base object and press CTRL-SHIFT-A. A PopupMenu will appear prompting "OK? Make Dupli's Real".

We now have a collection of NURBS forming the outline of our object, but so far they are not skinned, so we cannot see them in a shaded preview or in a rendering. To achieve this, we need to join all the rings to one object. Without deselecting any rings, press CTRL-J and confirm the PopupMenu request. Now, enter EditMode for the newly created object and press AKEY to select all vertices. Now we are ready to skin our object. Press FKEY and Blender will automatically generate the solid object.

When you leave EditMode, you can now see the object in a shaded view. But it is very dark. To correct this, enter EditMode and select all vertices, then press WKEY. Choose "Switch Direction" from the menu and leave EditMode. The object will now be drawn correctly.

The object we have created is a NURBS object. This means that you can still edit it. Even more interestingly, you can also control the resolution of the NURBS object via the EditButtons.

Make Knots	
Uniform U	V
Endpoint U	V
Bezier U	V
Order U: 3	V: 4
Resol U: 128	V: 20

Here you can set the resolution of the object using "ResolU" and "ResolV", so you can adjust it for working with the object in a low resolution, and then set it to a high resolution for your final render.

> NURBS objects are also very small in filesize for saved scenes. Compare the size of a NURBS scene with the same scene in which all NURBS are converted (ALT-C) to meshes.

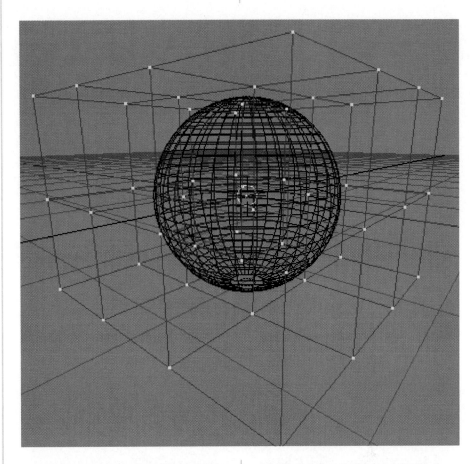

A Lattice consists of a three-dimensional grid of vertices. If the vertices are moved from their regular positions, this will cause a deformation of the child objects. Lattices only affect Meshes, Surfaces and Particles, and they can be used to give them a 'NURBS-like' flexibility. A Lattice does not affect the texture coordinates of a Mesh Surface. Subtle changes to mesh objects are easily facilitated in this way, and do not change the mesh itself.

A Lattice always begins as a 2 x 2 x 2 grid of vertices. Use the EditButtons->U,V,W settings to specify the desired resolution, then the Lattice can be deformed in EditMode. If there is a Child Object, the deformation is continually displayed and modified. Changing the U,V,W values of a Lattice returns it to a uniform starting position.

Lattices can be used as a modelling tool. They also allow you to make the deformation permanent. Use the SHIFT-CTRL+A command. A menu will ask: "Apply Lattice deform?".

Part C / Render

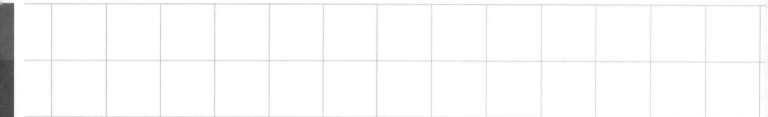

Materials and textures

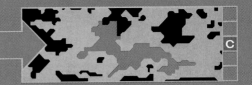

Chapter 7
Materials and textures

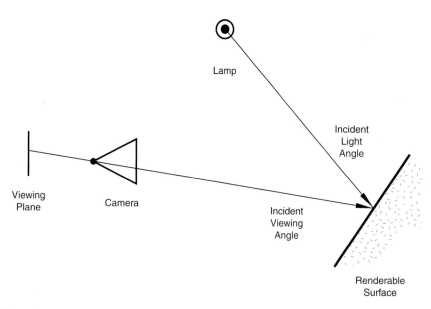

Figure 1

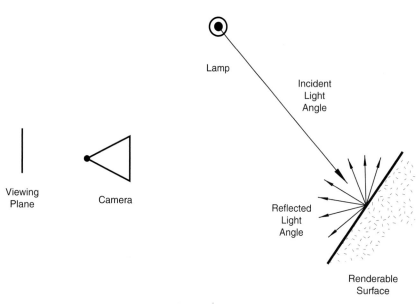

Figure 2

Effective material design requires some understanding of how simulated light and surfaces interact in Blender's rendering engine, how material settings control those interactions, and how to work around some limitations of the engine.

The viewing plane is the imaginary surface onto which the image is projected. It is similar to the film in a traditional camera, or the rods and cones in the human eye. It receives simulated light. To render an image of a scene, we answer this question: what light from the scene is arriving at each point on the viewing plane?

This question is answered by following a line (the simulated light ray) backward through that point on the viewing plane and a focal point (the location of the camera) to a renderable surface in the scene, then determining what light would strike that point. The surface properties and incident light angle tell us how much of that light would be reflected back along the incident viewing angle. See Figure 1.

There are two basic types of reflection which take place at any point on a surface: diffuse reflection and specular reflection. Diffuse reflection and specular reflection are distinguished from each other simply by the relationship between the incident light angle and the reflected light angle.

Diffuse Reflection

Light striking a diffuse surface will be scattered, i.e., reflected in all directions. This means that the camera will see the same amount of light from that surface point no matter the incident viewing angle. This quality is why diffuse light is called viewpoint independent. If most of the light striking a surface is being reflected diffusely, the surface will have a matt appearance. See Figure 2.

Specular Reflection

Specular reflection, on the other hand, is
viewpoint dependent. Light striking a
specular surface will be reflected at an
angle which mirrors the incident light
angle, so the viewing angle is very
important. Specular reflection forms tight,
bright highlights, making the surface
appear glossy. See Figure 3.

In reality, diffuse reflection and specular
reflection are exactly the same process.
Diffuse reflection is seen on a surface
which has so much small-scale
roughness in the surface that light is
reflected in many different directions by
many tiny changes in surface angle.
Specular reflection appears on a surface
with enough consistency in the angle of
the surface that the light is reflected in a
consistent direction, rather than being
scattered. It's just a matter of the scale of
the detail. An automobile's chrome fender
normally looks shiny, but from a
spacecraft it will appear as part of the
diffuse detail of the planet. Likewise,
sand has a matt appearance, but if you
look at it through a microscope you will
see smooth, shiny surfaces.

Blender allows us to easily control how
much of the incident light striking a point
on a surface is scattered, how much of it
is reflected as specularity, and how much
of it is not reflected at all. This determines in what directions (and in what
amounts) the light is reflected from a
given light source or, to look at it another
way, from what sources (and in what
amounts) the light is being reflected
toward a given point on the viewing
plane.

How these Concepts Work in Blender

Open the file "shinyball.blend" from the
CDROM. Go to the material buttons
(press F5) and look at how Blender
handles these concepts. Blender uses the
"Ref" slider to control how much diffuse
reflectivity a surface has. Blender uses
the "Spec" slider to control how much
specular reflectivity a surface has.

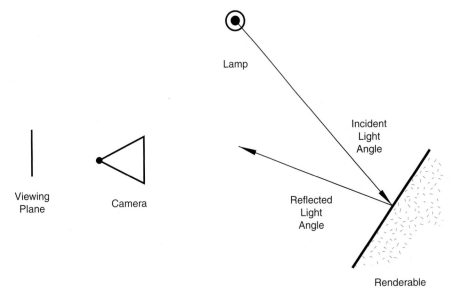

Figure 3

I like to make the sum of the "Spec"
setting and the "Ref" setting equal to 1.0,
assuming that 1.0 represents the total
light being received. I control the pigment,
which might absorb some of this light,
with the "Colour" RGB sliders. It's useful
to stick with a sensible system and use
several lights in your scene with whatever
level of brightness is necessary to get the
luminance you want in your scene.
See Figure 4.

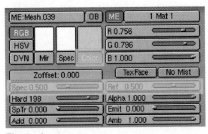

Figure 4

Press F12 to render the scene. This is
a very simple model of surface lighting.
It can be effective, but it is incomplete.
Images created using this model will
lack richness of lighting. Blender has
other settings that make this basic
lighting model more flexible.
See Figure 5.

Figure 5

The biggest deficiency of this model is
that it can only simulate light that travels
directly from a single-point lamp to a
surface to the camera. It does not take
into account light which is reflected by
more than one surface before reaching
the camera, or light emitting from an area
rather than a point. A fluorescent panel
is an example of a light source that
obviously emits light from an area.
In truth, every real-world light source
emits light from an area or a volume,
not a point.

The "Hard" slider lets you soften your specular highlights, making them appear more diffuse while maintaining independent control of purely diffuse reflection. See Figure 6.

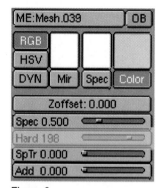

Figure 6

Adding an ambient component to the diffuse lighting model is a very "quick-and-dirty" way to simulate the diffuse interreflected light that bounces around in the scene before reaching the camera. The "Amb" slider controls how much ambient light each material will reflect. Every material in your scene should have the same ratio between "Amb" and "Ref". See Figure 6a.

Figure 6a

The "AmbR", "AmbG", and "AmbB" sliders in the world buttons control the actual amount of ambient light in the scene. The WorldButtons are accessed by clicking on the icon that looks like a tiny planet. If there is no World linked to your scene (in other words,

if no settings appear when you switch to the WorldButtons), you can add a world by selecting "ADD NEW" from the PullDownMenu. See Figure 6d.

Figure 6d

Their values should correlate to the amount and colour of ambient light that would likely be bouncing around, in accordance with the lamps and surfaces in the scene. Blender doesn't take the lamps in the scene into account when rendering this ambient light, so use your imagination to make this decision. This method creates the appearance of light of a single colour and intensity coming uniformly from all directions. The lighting tends to appear flat with this method, but it is simple to use and does not increase rendering time. See Figure 6b and 6c.

Figure 6b

Figure 6c

Materials and textures

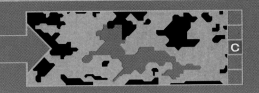

Additional soft lighting manually placed in the scene can create this illusion in a more subtle and varied way. "Hemi" lamps will produce a low-contrast effect throughout the scene and can be limited to specific parts of the scene using layers. "Lamp" lamps with the "Quad" setting create a very localised effect. These settings are found in the Lamp-ButtonsWindow (F4). See Figure 7.

A more accurate automated method to achieve this effect is a process called radiosity. The simulation of light that is reflected from very smooth, specular surfaces (such as polished metal) after traveling around in the scene before reaching the camera, can be achieved by a process called environment mapping. These techniques are replacements for diffuse and specular material settings. Both of these techniques extend the surface lighting model beyond the assumption that the light reflecting from a surface to the camera comes directly from zero-dimensional lamps.

First we will generate a radiosity model for the scene. Turn off layer 2, which contains the lights. We don't need them for anything else we will be doing. You can do this by clicking on the second layer in the 3DWindow while holding SHIFT or by pressing SHIFT-2. See Figure 7a.

Figure 7a

The only factors in Blender's radiosity engine are the "Colour", "Ref", and "Emit" values of the material settings. See Figure 8.

Switch to the RadiosityButtonsWindow (the one with the black and yellow radiation symbol). See Figure 8a.

Figure 8a

In Blender's radiosity engine, light is emitted not from a single point but from an area (or more likely, from several areas). Polygonal geometry is used to emit light, and the calculated luminance is stored in the polygonal geometry as vertex colours. Blender subdivides the geometry into smaller polygons called patches, which are in turn divided into even smaller polygons called elements. Blender's radiosity engine works by distributing light outward from any patches that have light to emit. Initially, this means patches created from geometry whose material has an "Emit" value greater than 0. The elements in the scene receive this luminance and reflect it by passing excess energy to their patches, which in turn distribute it further. This process continues until you press ESC, until the process has repeated as many times as the value of "Max Iterations", or until the amount of un-distributed energy in the scene is less than the value of "Convergence". See Figure 8b.

Figure 8b

To bring the mesh geometry into Blender's radiosity solver select all (AKEY) and click the "Collect Meshes" button.

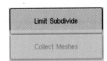

Figure 9

You will see some blue and white squares appear in front of the camera. The blue squares are the minimum and maximum element sizes, the white squares are the minimum and maximum patch sizes. The patch and element sizes determine how finely detailed the radiosity solution will be. Smaller patches increase accuracy of detail (especially for shadowing caused

Figure 7

Figure 8

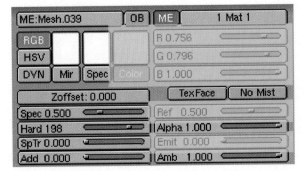

by intervening geometry), but they also increase the time required and are more likely to show artifacts. To get a preview of how finely subdivided your final mesh will be, select the blue "Wire" button to view the data as a wireframe. Then click "Limit Subdivide", followed by "Subdiv Shoot Element" and "Subdiv Shoot Patch". See Figure 9a.

In addition to controlling the amount of detail, the other buttons provide control over the completeness of the luminance distribution. In particular, the "Max Iterations" and "Convergence" buttons control how thoroughly the luminance is distributed through the scene. This time we're going to leave the settings at default.
Select the green "Gour" button so that as the solution progresses you can see how nice it looks. This is important because the speed of your processor and your level of patience may demand that the calculations be terminated as soon as they look good enough for the purpose at hand. The calculation process can be ended at any time by hitting ESC. Click "Go" to start the process. See Figure 10.

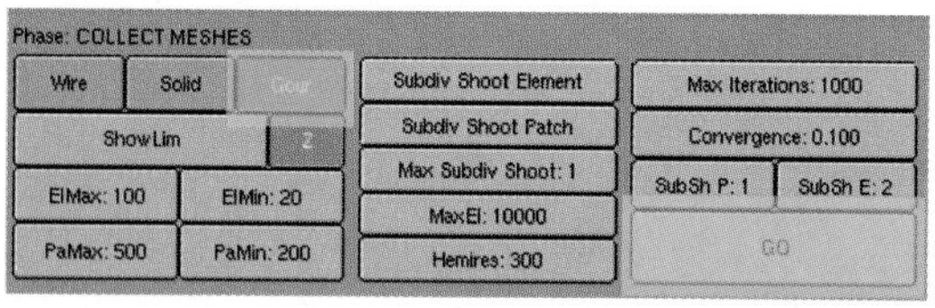

Now go enjoy a beer or a nice meal. Take a nap. Spend time with your loved ones. When the geometry in your scene is complex, the radiosity solution can take a very, very, long time. In a scene like this, you can take a shortcut in the radiosity solution by using low-resolution "proxy" versions of meshes that are complex but don't have much diffuse reflectivity, then swap them for the high-resolution versions for the final rendering. For example, you could model the car with NURBS surfaces so that you would have high- and low-polygon versions of it at your fingertips simply by changing the U and V resolution and converting them to meshes.
A very specular object doesn't show much diffuse light anyway, so you don't need an accurate solution for showing diffuse light on the car. If your smooth curvy object is very diffuse, you just have to put up with the long time necessary for the solution.

One benefit of a radiosity solution is that it only needs to be computed once. You can even adjust the luminance and luminance curve of the entire solution after it is calculated using the "Mult" and "quotGamma" buttons, as long as you are happy with the balance between the various light sources. This must be done before bringing the newly created mesh from the radiosity solver into the scene. For this scene, I used a "Gamma" value of 2.25 to adjust the luminance curve of the solution. If you know the gamma of

your monitor, try using that value as a starting point. To quickly get an idea of the overall look of the lighting, take just the room into the solution with the largest settings for patch and element sizes and run the solution for a very short while. Click the "Free Radio Data" button to remove all of the data from the radiosity solver, adjust your material settings, and try again. When you are happy you can bring all of the models back into the solver and let it work overnight. See Figure 11.

Figure 11

When you like the results, click the "Add New Meshes" button to copy the new radiosity-enhanced meshes from the radiosity solver into the scene, then click "Free Radio Data" to empty the solver. The new meshes will be added to the highest active layer (in this case, layer 6). Move the new mesh data (press M) to layer 3 so you can keep it separate from the old objects. In the 3DWindow, turn off layer 1 and turn on layer 3.

Blender has created the radiosity solution as a single mesh. In order to re-apply your materials to the models, you will need to either separate the mesh into a number of separate objects, or to create a discrete material index for the section of the mesh corresponding to each material. I like to separate the mesh into objects so that I can easily place them on different layers. This will be useful when we come to the environment mapping section. We will go through the separation process now.

With the new mesh selected, enter edit mode (TAB). Holding your mouse over a vertex of the first section you want to separate, select the vertices linked to it by pressing LKEY.

Figure 9a

Figure 10

Any groups of polygons that were not "Set Smooth" in the edit buttons before being brought into the radiosity solver and are not planar with neighbouring faces will be split from their neighbours. Separate the selected vertices using P ->SEPARATE. Continue this process for each part you want to separate.

Create a discrete object for each material. We need to be able to link the materials to these new objects, and using material indices is too difficult with so many vertices. With curved meshes (such as the ball), go to the edit buttons (F9) and click "Set Smooth" after you have separated them from the large mesh. Now link the materials to the new objects as usual. Finally, make sure that your materials all have "VCol Light" selected (but not "VCol Paint"), so that the rendering engine treats the vertex colours as precalculated light. At this point, you should be able to go into textured preview mode (ALT-Z) and see your scene with the diffuse lighting, and also render the scene (F12) and see everything lit with diffuse lighting, even though you have turned off the layer with all of the lights! The file "shinyball_rad.blend" is how your scene should look with radiosity. See Figure 12.

Figure 12

The important thing to remember is that light should function the same whether it comes directly from a lamp or is being reflected from another object, and no light source could really be a single point. Therefore light will behave better if it's being emitted from some geometry. We've already addressed these issues for simulating diffuse light, and now we will do the same thing for specular highlights.

Environment Maps

Now on the shiny surfaces we will put some highlights that are a bit visually richer than the standard Phong specular highlights. The ironic thing about Phong surfaces is that they are like mirrors that show you things you ordinarily can't see, but none of what you ordinarily can see. What I mean by this is that Phong surfaces show you a bright spot as a mirror-like reflection of a lamp. This makes sense, except that if you turn the camera directly toward the lamp, you won't see it! The camera sees this light only if it is being reflected by a Phong surface, not directly. On the other hand, objects that appear very bright in your scene (i.e. they reflect a lot of light to the camera) don't show up in these highlights. This looks especially strange when some of the bright objects should throw more light than some of lamps, but in the specular highlights only the lamps are visible. It is easy enough to make a lamp which is directly visible to the camera by placing some renderable object in the scene which looks like some appropriate sort of lamp fixture, flame, sun, etc. However, wide light sources should appear as wide highlights when reflected, but the shinier the Phong surface is, the smaller the specular highlight will be. This is the sort of problem we will address using the technique of environment mapping.

Just as we render what light is reaching the viewing plane using the camera to define a viewpoint, we can render what light is reaching the surface of an object (and hence, what light might ultimately be reflected to the camera). Blender's environment mapping renders a cubic image map of the scene in the six cardinal directions from any point. When the six tiles of the image are mapped onto an object using the "Refl" input coordinates, they create the visual complexity that the eye expects to see from shiny reflections. It's useful to remember here that the true goal of this technique is believability, not accuracy. The eye doesn't need a physically accurate simulation of the light's travel;

it just needs to be lulled into acceptance by seeing the complexity it expects. The most unbelievable thing about most rendered images is the sterility, not the inaccuracy.

The first step for creating an environment map is to define the viewpoint for the map. Add an empty to the scene and place it in the center of the ball. Ideally, the location of the empty would mirror the location of the camera across the plane of the polygon onto which it is being mapped. It would be ridiculously difficult to create a separate environment map for every polygon of a detailed mesh, so we take advantage of the fact that the human eye is very gullible. The decision about where to place the empty is more critical when the reflective geometry is more or less a large flat surface, such as water. Since the ball bears little resemblance to a large flat surface, we can get away with simply placing the empty near the center. Name the empty "env" so we can refer to it by name in the environment map settings.

Select the ball and go to the material buttons. Add a new texture by selecting "Add New" from the texture PullDownMenu. See Figure 12a.

Figure 12a

Go to the texture buttons with F6. Select "EnvMap" as the texture type. In the "Ob:" button, type "env". The "ClipSta" and "ClipEnd" settings work just like the similarly named settings for a camera. If the objects you want to see in the environment map do not fall within that range of distances from the empty's location, increase this value. The default range of 0.1 to 100.0 works well for the demo file.

Move the ball to layer 4, and turn on layer 4 in the 3DWindow. The buttons marked "Don't render layer" determine what layers are not rendered as part of the environment map. This is very important, because it's necessary to prevent the object to which the environment map will be applied from being rendered in the map. Otherwise, instead of reflecting the environment around the ball, the ball will reflect its own interior. Select the fourth layer, which contains the ball, from among these buttons. See Figure 13.

If you want the environment map to be re-rendered every time you render the scene, select the green "Anim" button. In an animation, this setting causes the environment map to be re-rendered for every frame of the animation so that it looks correct. If you select the "Static" button instead, the environment map will only be created the first time the scene is rendered. This will speed up subsequent renderings of the scene and will save time if you are making lots of test-renderings. However, any changes you make to the scene will not show up in the environment map after the first time you render. If you make changes to the scene and you want the environment map to be re-rendered, press "Free Data". You can save the environment map to a file with the "Save EnvMap" button so that it can later be re-used by loading it with the "Load" button. See Figure 13a.

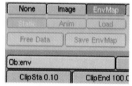

Figure 13a

Go back to the material buttons. Change the input coordinates for the environment map texture from "Orco" to "Refl". If we were using standard lamps to provide the diffuse light in this scene, we could select the "Cmir" texture output button and deselect the "Col" button. We would set the "Col" slider at the bottom of the texture output buttons to 0.7, because

the "Ref" setting is 0.3 (using the formula Spec + Ref = 1). However, Blender's vertex light has an idiosyncracy that we must circumvent: Textures mapped to "Cmir" do not behave well with vertex light. The solution is to add the texture's output to the material's colour and emit values. To do this, select the "Col", "Emit", and "Add" texture output buttons. Set the "Col" slider at the bottom of the texture output buttons to 0.2 (this controls how much "Col" is added) and set the "Var" slider to 0.1 (this controls how much "Emit" is added). Render the scene. The finished product will look something like "shinyball_env.blend". See Figure 14.

Figure 13

Figure 14

7.3
Solid and hollow
glass by Randall Rickert

We've looked at how we can create a better reflection of an object's environment. Now let's look at another use for environment maps: simulating refraction.

Open the file "glass.blend". We will make the blue sphere look like a solid ball of glass, so we need to create the appearance that light is bending as it passes through. We expect to see the objects behind the sphere heavily warped, as if through a very thick lens. Blender lets us achieve this effect by inverting the environment map and doing some wacky tricks with transparency and procedural textures.

Faking Refracted Transparency

Set up an environment map for the sphere's material the same way we did for the ball in the last tutorial, with an empty to locate the environment map's perspective at the center of the sphere. This time, however, we will use the "Cmir" output button with "Mix", as the vertex colour light which was problematic in the radiosity tutorial is not present in this one. We make some changes to the output mapping with the "ofsZ", "sizeX", "sizeY", "sizeZ" and "Col" sliders to warp the map in a way that looks like refraction. Use the following settings for the texture output: See Figure 15.

You now have a blue-tinted refraction of the environment. Shiny glass also needs a reflection map, so place the same texture into another texture channel. Press the "Add", "Col", and "Emit" buttons, and use the "Refl" button for the coordinates. Make the material "Colour" black and turn "Emit" all the way up. Don't ask any questions - just trust me! See Figure 17.

Finally, in order to get the refraction texture back to a nice blue tint again, we have to add a new texture, leaving the texture type set to "None". Select the "Mix" and "Cmir" buttons, and set the "Col" slider about halfway up. Click the "Neg" button and set the texture input RGB sliders to a dark blue. See Figure 18.

Figure 15

Figure 16

Figure 18

Select the "Mir" RGB material sliders and lower the "R" and "G" a bit to give a blue tint to the texture. Experience with the idiosyncrasies of Blender's handling of mirror colours dictates this unintuitive approach when combining environment-mapped reflections and refractions in a single material. Turn the "Ref" slider all the way down. See Figure 16.

Figure 17

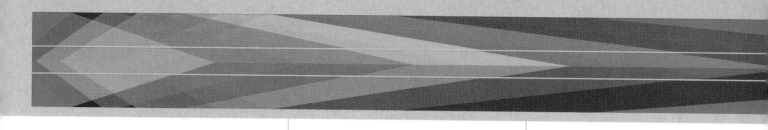

The result should look like "solidglass.blend". The refraction effect is most noticeable when the scene is animated. Render and enjoy. See Figure 19.

Figure 19

That's fine for a solid lump of glass, but how do we go about making hollow-looking glass such as you might need for making a vase? Thin glass has strong refraction only where it slopes away from the eye at a steep angle. We can easily mimic this effect by using Blender's "Blend" texture to control the object's transparency, plus another transparency texture to keep the bright highlights visible.

Procedural Transparency Mapping for Hollow Glass

Add a new texture to the material. Select "Blend" as the type and select the green "Sphere" option. Go back to the material buttons, select "Nor" as the mapping type, and disable the X and Y axes in the input coordinates. "Mix" the texture with "Alpha". Move the "Alpha" material slider to 0.0 and set the blue "ZTransp" option. See Figure 20.

This gives nice transparency as the surface angles toward the eye, but we want the bright environment-mapped reflections to show up on those otherwise-transparent areas. If you look at glass windows, you will see that bright light reflecting from the surface will be visible and prevent you from seeing through a pane that is ordinarily transparent. We can do this easily by selecting the environment-mapped reflection texture in the material window and enabling the "Alpha" option. See Figure 21.

That's all there is to it. The result should look like "hollowglass.blend". See Figure 22.

Figure 22

Figure 21

Figure 20

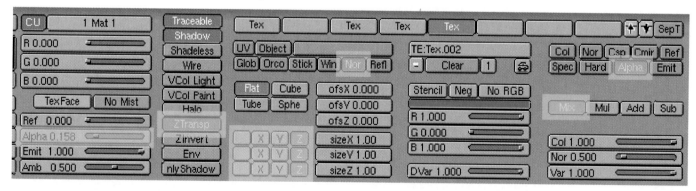

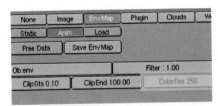

Creating an environment map for an object that is planar or roughly planar requires us to modify our approach to locating the perspective of the map. Open the file "water.blend", and we will go through the steps for making a plane look like water. The scene is similar to "glass.blend".

Locating Planar Environment Map Perspective

Add an environment map texture to the material of the green plane just as in the previous tutorials. Give the texture a descriptive name, such as "envMap". In fact, it is good practice to name all of your textures descriptively so that you can easily identify them. Once again, select layer 2 in the "Don't Render Layer" section in the texture buttons. This time, we will place an empty in a position that mirrors the position of the camera across the green plane. Now enter the name of the empy in the "Ob:" textfield

Switch to front view in the 3DWindow (NUMPAD_1). Select the camera and snap the cursor to the location of the camera by pressing SHIFT-S 4KEY. Add an empty. It will be created at the camera's location. Name the empty "env". Select the green plane and snap the 3DCursor to it (as above).

We want to use the 3DCursor as the pivot point for our next operation. This can be done by pressing PERIOD. Select the empty. Take your hand off of your mouse so that it doesn't move at all. This is necessary for creating the environment map accurately. Press SKEY to use the scale tool, then YKEY to mirror the empty across the 3DCursor along the Y-axis of the current view. Before touching your mouse again, press ENTER. At this point you should see the empty below the plane, mirroring the position of the camera that is above the plane. See Figure 22a.

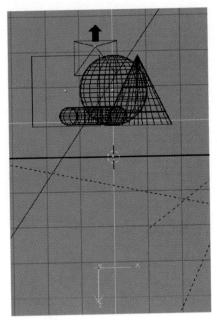

Figure 22a

Select the green plane again. Switch back to the camera view (NUMPAD_0). In the material buttons window, use the "Refl" and "Cmir" texture mapping buttons (deselect the "Col" button). See Figure 23.

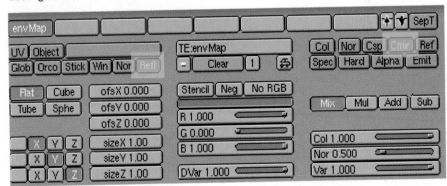

Figure 23

If you render the scene, you will see that the environment map makes the plane look like a blurry mirror. Let's get rid of some of the blur by turning up the value in the "Cube Res" number button in the texture buttons window. See Figure 24.

Figure 24

Go back to the material buttons window. Lower the "Col" texture output slider so that the environment map won't be the only colour visible. See Figure 25.

Figure 25

Lower the "Ref" material slider. Raise the "Spec" and "Hard" sliders. See Figure 26.

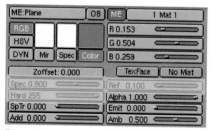

Figure 26

Finally, let's turn on the "Mist" setting in the world buttons window to make the plane fade out toward the horizon, instead of ending abruptly. The "Sta" and "Di" settings determine how far from the camera the mist starts and ends, respectively. The "Qua" button means that the mist will have a quadratic progression, appearing very dense very quickly near the limit of the mist distance (the value of "Di"). See Figure 27.

Figure 27

The result should look like the file "water_env.blend". See Figure 28.

Figure 28

It certainly looks like a large reflective surface of some sort, but it needs some ripples in order to be convincing. We don't need to change the actual geometry of the surface to create the illusion of ripples. We can accomplish the effect using bump mapping. Blender has a procedural texture that is designed for this.

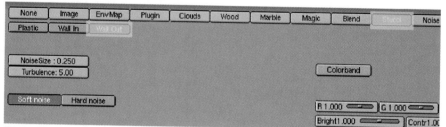

Figure 29

Switch back to the MaterialButtons window. Select the "Glob" and "Nor" texture output buttons, and de-select "Col". See Figure 30.

Figure 30

Procedural Bump-Map Ripples

With the plane selected, go to the MaterialButtons window again. Add a new texture, and in the texture buttons window, select "Stucci" as the type. Select the "Wall Out" button to create somewhat "pointy" ripples. See Figure 29.

Render the scene. If you created the environment map texture in the first slot of the material's texture list and the bump map texture in the second slot (as I did), you will see that the bump map is visible in the specular highlights, but it is not affecting the environment map. This is because the textures are calculated in the order in which they appear in the MaterialButtons window (from left to right). We have to make the environment map follow the bump map. Fortunately, Blender has a facility for just such texture manipulation. We can easily copy the texture link and all of the settings associated with it to a different slot in the material's texture list.

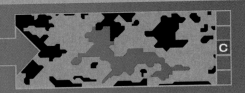

Select the environment map texture. Click the button with the upward arrow at the right end of the texture list. The button which pops up informs you "copied!". You can click the button to dismiss it, or just hit ESC or move your mouse. It doesn't matter what you do with the button. It's just there to inform you. With the environment map texture still selected in the texture list, unlink the texture from the material by clicking the "Clear" button in the texture linking buttons. See Figure 31.

Figure 31

Now select a slot to the right of the bump texture and click the button with the downward arrow at the right end of the texture list. You will see another confirmation button, this time informing you that the texture and its settings have been pasted into the selected slot in the texture list. See Figure 32.

Figure 32

It's giving us the right effect now, so let's fine-tune the bump texture settings to make it look a bit nicer. Select the bump texture again in the list. Push the "Nor" slider up to 2.0 and change the "SizeX" and "SizeY" number buttons to a value of 0.5. See Figure 33.

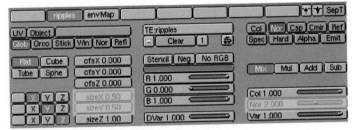

Figure 33

The result should look like "water_bump.blend". See Figure 34.

This makes a nice still image, but it's much more fun when animated. One of the benefits of procedural textures is that they can be easily animated.

Animating the Procedural Texture

Go to frame 1. If you are not on it, you can jump to it by pressing SHIFT+LEFT_ARROW. You can see the current frame number in the frame number button.
See Figure 35.

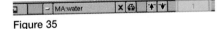

Figure 35

Figure 34

The first thing we will do is to insert a material key on this frame. With the bump map texture selected and with your mouse somewhere over the Material-Buttons window, press IKEY >Ofs. See Figure 36.

Figure 36

We will now insert a material key on the last frame. Switch to the last frame by pressing SHIFT-ARROW_RIGHT. In the demo file, the last frame is 31. Change the value in the "OfsX" number button to 0.8 and the value in the "OfsZ" number button to 0.2. The "OfsX" change will make the ripples appear to drift side-ways, and the "OfsZ" change will make the ripples change shape, so it doesn't look like the entire water surface is simply sliding sideways. The "OfsZ" change works because the "Stucci" texture varies in the Z direction as well as in the X and Y directions. See Figure 37.

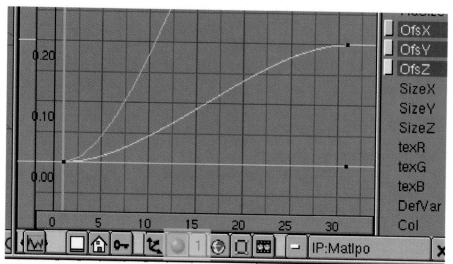

Figure 38

Figure 37

Insert a keyframe exactly as above. If you don't set a keyframe, the changes you made to the texture output values will be lost.

Blender smoothly interpolates between these two keys by using a Bezier equation. To see the curve described by this equation, click the material icon in the IPO window. Next to it a number button will appear, which correlates to the position of the texture in the material's texture list. It probably says "0". Change the number to 1. See Figure 38.

Press HOME with your mouse over the IPO window to see the best view of the curves. You will see that the translation of the texture will start and end smoothly. In contrast, what we want is for the texture to show a constant (linear) change, with the slope defined by the two keys we set. This is accomplished with the constant slope button at the base of the IPO

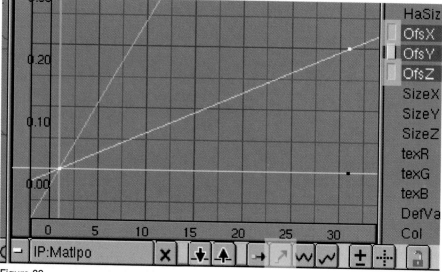

Figure 39

window. To find this button, you may need to move the header at the bottom of the window to the left by dragging it with the middle mouse. SHIFT+LEFT_CLICK the coloured buttons next to "OfsX" and "OfsZ" in the list of keyable attributes on the right side of the IPO window, then click the constant slope button. Your curves should straighten out. See Figure 39.

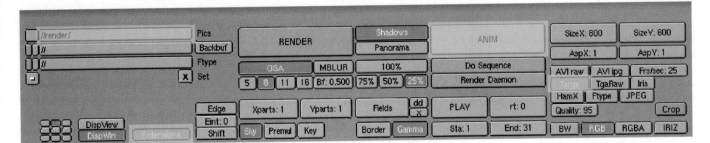

Figure 40

Your scene file should now look like "water_anim.blend". Click the "Anim" button in the render buttons window to render the entire animation. Make sure that the render directory is valid and that you have selected a file type that your system can play back. The "Extensions" button will ensure that the names of your rendered files have file type extensions in them, in case your system or your other applications use the extensions to determine file types. See Figure 40.

The resulting animation should look like "water_anim.mpg".

Halomaterial

Halomaterials are most often used for particle systems (see that section). But they are also good for creating some special effects, e.g. to make an object glow, or to make a viewable light source. Here I will show you how to use a halomaterial to make a dotmatrix display.

Add a grid with the dimensions 32 x 16. Add a camera and adjust your scene in such a way that you have a nice view of our billboard. Now use a 2D image program to create some red text on a black background, and use a simple and bold font. I created an image 512 pixels in width by 64 pixels in height, with some black space at both sides.

Now add a material for the billboard, and set it to the type "Halo". Set the HaloSize to 0.06 and render, you will see a grid of white spots. Now switch to the Texture-Buttons and add a new image texture. Load your picture and render again, you will see some red tinted dots in the grid. Go back to the MaterialButtons and adjust the "sizeX" parameter to about 0.5 and do a render again, the text should now be centered on the Billboard.

To get rid of the white dots, adjust the material colour to a dark red and render again. We have now only red dots, but it is still too dark. We can fix this by entering EditMode for the board and by copying all vertices using the SHIFT-D shortcut. We can now adjust the brightness with the "Add" value in the MaterialButtons.

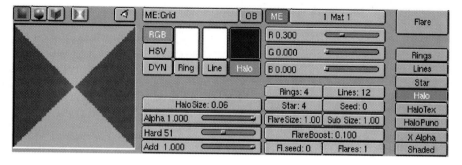

You can now animate the texture to move over the billboard, with the "ofsX" value in the MaterialButtons. An example is located in the file "DotMatrix.blend" on the CDROM. Of course, you can also use a higher resolution for the grid, but then you will have to adjust the size of the halos (HaloSize).

→ We have not used the "HaloTex" option here. This option will map the whole image to every halo. This is very usefull when you want to create a realistic rain effect using particle systems, or similar.

Lens flares

Our eyes have been trained to believe an image if it shows familiar artifacts from the mechanical process of photography. 'Motion blur' and 'lens flares' are just two examples of these artifacts. A simulated lens flare tells the viewer that the image was created with a camera, and it is therefore 'authentic'.

In Blender, a lens flares is created from a mesh object using the "Halo" and "Flare" options in the material settings. Try turning on "Rings" and "Lines", though I would recommend that you keep the colours for these settings fairly subtle. Play with the "Flares" and "Fl.seed" settings until you arrive at something that is pleasing to the eye. This tool does not simulate the physics of photons traveling through a glass lens; it's just a eye candy. See Figure 1.

An example of this technique can be seen in "lensflare.blend". See Figure 2.

Figure 1

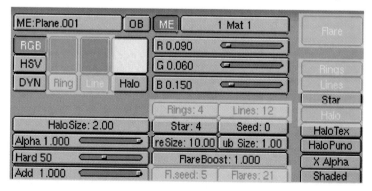

Figure 2

Blender's lens flare looks nice in motion, and disappears when another object occludes the flare mesh. Look at "lensflare.mpg" on the CD.

Most objects are assembled so that they can be modelled in parts, which then will be attached to each other. Some objects need more materials, but at least it is easier to have two or more materials on one mesh. With textures this facility is even more important.

A simple example is a dice with six different textures that show the points. Make a cube and add a material to it. Make the mapping "Cube". If you want to use the textures from the CDROM, then switch on "Neg" in the texture colour settings and activate also "Nor" for the texture mapping output. Now, add an image texture to the material and choose the image with the one point. A rendering should give you a dice with only one point on every side.

Now switch one 3DWindow to a side view and enter EditMode for the dice. Go to the EditButtons F9 and look at the Multi-MaterialButtons. They show the name of the actual material ("Dice1"), and the "1 Mat 1" means that you have selected the first material from a total number of one materials.

Now click on "New" and the buttons changes to "2 Mat 2". Now select the top vertices of the cube with the Border-Select (BKEY) and click on "Assign". This will assign material number two to the selected vertices.

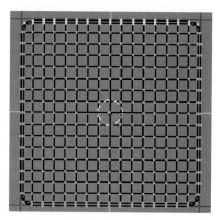

"Select" and "Deselect" allowing you to select all vertices with the indicated material.

Leave the EditMode and go back to the MaterialButtons. Here you will find a similar "2 Mat 2" button. The material has now two users, indicated by the blue colour in the name of the material and the number button showing "2".

Click on the "2" and confirm the "OK? Single user" question, then rename the material to "Dice2". Now go to the TextureButtons for that material and make the texture single user as well. Load the texture with the two points on it. When you render, you will see that the top of the dice has the new texture assigned. The other sides will have remained unchanged.

Repeating the steps you can now assign every side a different material and texture.

In Blender, the Materials and Textures form separate blocks. This approach was chosen to keep the interface simple and to allow universal integration between Textures, Lamps, and World blocks. The relationship between a Material and a Texture is called the 'mapping'. This relationship is two-sided. First, the information that is passed on to the Texture must be specified. Then the effect of the Texture on the Material is specified. The MaterialButtons on the right-hand side (and the Lamp and World buttons) are reserved for the mapping. The buttons are organized in the sequence in which the 'texture pipeline' is performed.

1

Texture channels. Each Material has eight channels to which Textures can be linked. Each channel has its own individual mapping. By default, textures are executed one after another and then superimposed. A second Texture channel can completely replace the first one.

2

Coordinates input. Each Texture has a 3D coordinate (the texture coordinate) as input. The starting point is usually the global coordinate of the 3D punt that can be seen in the pixel to be rendered. A Material has a number of options for this, allowing you to create animated or reflecting textures.

3

3D to 2D conversion. Only for Image Textures; this indicates the way in which the 3D coordinate is converted to 2D. The options include flat, spherical and cubical methods.

4

Coordinates switch. Switches between the X, Y or Z coordinates, or turns them off.

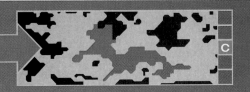

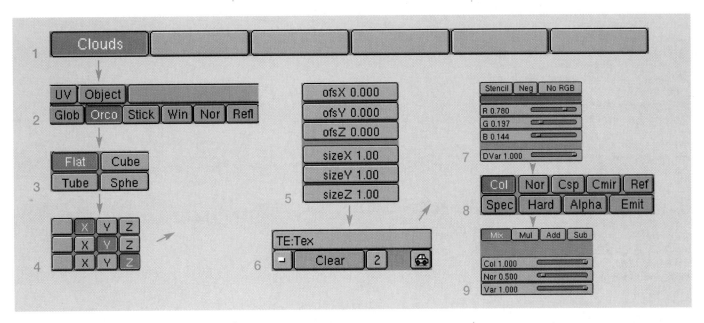

5

Coordinates transform. The texture coordinate can be given an extra translation or scaling.

6

The Texture itself. Only the name of the Texture block must be specified.

7

Texture input settings. A number of standard settings for the Texture, plus specification of the effect of the current Texture on the next one.

8

Mapping: output to. All prior data is used to change parts of the Material. Textures can therefore have an effect not only on colour, but on the normal (bump mapping) or the "Alpha" value as well.

9

Output settings Indicates the strength of the effect of the Texture output. Mixing is possible with a standard value, addition, subtraction or multiplication.

Textures give three types of output:

Intensity textures: return a single value. This intensity can control "Alpha", for example, or determine the strength of a colour specified using the mapping-buttons.
RGB textures: return three values, they always affect colour.
Bump textures: return three values, they always affect the normal vector. Only the "Stucci" and "Image" texture can give normals.

A distinction is also made between 2D textures and 3D (procedural) textures. "Wood", for example, is a procedural texture. This means that each 3D coordinate can be translated directly into a colour or a value. These types of textures are 'real' 3D, they fit together perfectly at the edges and continue to look like what they are meant to look like even when cut; as if a block of wood has really been cut in two. Procedural textures are not filtered extra or anti-aliased. This is hardly ever a problem: the user can

easily keep the specified frequencies within acceptable limits.

Colourband

The colourband is an often-neglected tool in the TextureButtons window (F6). It gives you an impressive level of control over how procedural textures are rendered.
Instead of simply rendering each texture as a linear progression from 0.0 to 1.0, you can use the colourband to create a gradient which progresses through as many variations of colour and transparency (alpha) as you like.

To use it, select a procedural texture, such as "Wood". Click the "Colourband" button. The "Colourband" is Blender's gradient editor. Each point on the band can be placed at any location and can be assigned any colour and transparency. Blender will interpolate the values from one point to the next.

Select the point you want to edit with the "Cur:" number button. Add and delete points with the "Add" and "Del" buttons. The RGB and Alpha values of the current point are displayed, along with the point's location on the band. Dragging with the left mouse can change the location of the current point. See Figure 1.

In the file "colourband.blend", I am using two "Wood" textures to make ring patterns in two different scales which have different effects on the appearance of the wood. The "Wood" textures are identical except for the way they are mapped in the MaterialButtons window, and the different colour bands used. I am also using a "Clouds" texture to make a grain pattern. To see the result of just one texture, isolated from the others, select the "Sept" button. See Figure 1a.

Here you can see the three individual textures which, when combined in a single material and mapped to various material parameters, creates a nice wood texture.

The "bigRings" texture...
(see Figure 1b)

plus the "smallRings" texture...
(see Figure 1c)

plus the "grain" texture...
(see Figure 1d)

produces the wood material.
(see Figure 2)

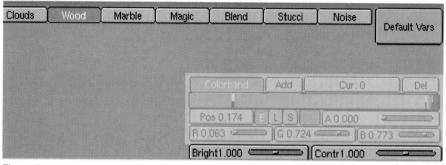

Figure 1

Figure 1a

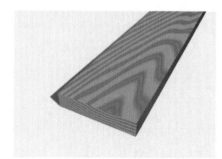

Figure 1c

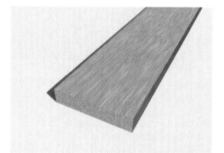

Figure 1d

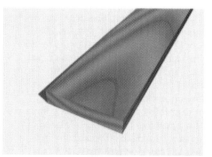

Figure 1b

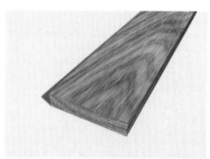

Figure 2

The ImageTexture is the only 2D texture and is the most frequently used and most advanced of Blender's textures. The standard, built-in bump mapping and perspective-corrected mip mapping, filtering and anti-aliasing guarantee outstanding images (set DisplayButtons->OSA to ON for this). Because pictures are two-dimensional, the way in which the 3D texture coordinate is translated to 2D must be specified in the mapping buttons.

There are four types of mapping "Flat", "Cube", "Tube" and "Sphere". Depending on the overall shape of the object, one of these types is most useful.

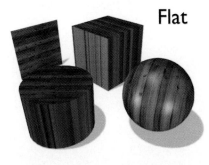

Flat

The Flat mapping gives best results on single planar faces, it also gives an at least interesting effect on the sphere, but compared to a sphere-mapped sphere it looks flat. On faces not in the mapping plane the last pixel of the texture is repeated, this results in the stripes on the cube and cylinder.

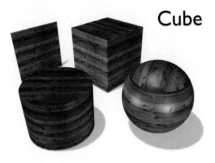

Cube

The cube-mapping gives often the most useful results when the objects are not too curvy and organic. But notice the seams on the sphere.

Tube

The tube-mapping maps the texture around an object like a label on a bottle. The texture is therefore more stretched on the cylinder. This mapping is of course very good for making the label on a bottle or assigning stickers to rounded objects. This is not a cylindrical mapping so the ends of the cylinder are undefined.

Sphere

The sphere-mapping is understandably the best type for mapping a sphere, it is perfect for making a planet and similar stuff. Often it is also very useful for organic objects. It also gives an interesting effect on the cylinder.

As described in the previous section you can manipulate the texture in the texture part of the MaterialButtons. There is one important feature to manipulate the textures.

When you select an object and press TKEY, you get the option to visually scale and move the texture space.

But you cannot rotate the texture here. Besides this shortcut, we also have an even more powerfull function for manipulating our textures.

You can use every object to deliver the size, location and rotation for other objects textures! Empties are very good for that. I often use cubes as input for the textures of a collection of objects. This way I can have a renderable preview of my textures, and use the same mapping on many different surfaces, e.g. the walls inside a building.

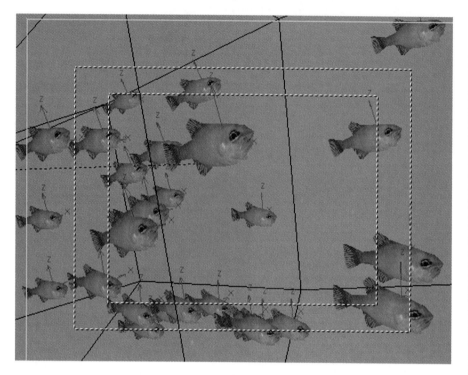

The UV-Editor allows you to map textures directly on the faces of Meshes. Each face can have an individual image assigned to it. These textures can be combined with vertexcolours to tint the texture or to make it brighter or darker. It gives you the absolute control over the mapping, but it does involve more work than the automatic mapping described in the previous section. A UV-textured example of that scene can be found in layer six in the file "Mapping.blend".

For each face, the use of the UV-Editor adds two extra features:
1. Four UV coordinates. These define the way an image or a Texture is mapped on the face. They are 2D coordinates, which is why it is called UV to distinguish it from XYZ coordinates. These coordinates can be used for rendering, and for the realtime OpenGL display for previewing and the game engine.
2. A link to an image. Every face in Blender can have a link to a different image. The UV coordinates define the way in which the image is mapped to the face. The image can then be rendered or displayed for preview and the game engine.

Assigning images to faces

Add a mesh object to your scene. This can be a simple cube or a model created with the help of the texture which we want to use later for texturing. Take a look at the "A Logo with Curves" tutorial to see how to use images as a modelling helper. Here I am using a simple (low poly) mesh of a fish (the fish is on the CDROM and is entitled: "UVTexFish00.blend"). We can use that object later as an object for particle effects, or as an object for gameBlender.

Select the mesh object and press FKEY. Blender now enters the face select mode for the active 3DWindow. Alternatively, you can use the icon in the 3DWindow header.

Your mesh will now be drawn z-buffered. When you enter the textured draw mode, with ALT-Z, you see that your object will be drawn in purple. This colour indicates that currently there is no texture assigned to our mesh. It also helps to find untextured faces in complicated objects. All selected faces have a dotted outline, so when you now press AKEY, all the faces will be selected.

Change one window to a ImageWindow using SHIFT-F10. Click on "Load" to get an ImageWindow, then browse for the texture "Fish_a.rgb" on the CDROM and load it with MMB.

All of the supported image formats that Blender can read are suitable for the UV-texturing, just so long as the size is to a power of 64. This is a limitation from OpenGL.

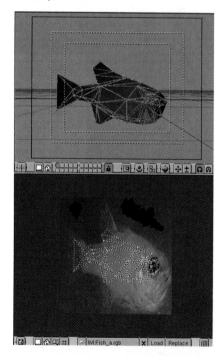

The object will now look a little odd, but that's because the initial mapping of the image has mapped the image on to every single face.

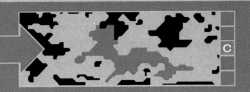

To give you a start for the texturing, move the mouse over the big 3DWindow (a front view), select all faces with AKEY (if there are still some faces selected you will have to press AKEY twice) and then press UKEY to call up the "UV Calculation" menu.

UV Calculation

UV Calculation
Cube
Cylinder
Sphere
Bounds to 64
Bounds to 128
Standard 64
Standard 128
Standard 256
From Window

Choose "From Window" and the vertices with the shape of the fish will appear in the ImageWindow. Here you can select vertices with the right mouse button and move, scale, and rotate them. Every point consists of at least two vertices because we shall want to texture both sides of the fish. So, it's best to use the rectangle selection (BKEY) to select vertices.

Begin by selecting select all vertices and use the move (GKEY), rotate (RKEY) and scale (SKEY) to fit the fish roughly to the image. Then select individual corners to fit it perfectly to the image. It helps here to switch the front view into the textured drawmode using ALT-Z. Click on the lock-icon to get instant feedback in the 3DWindows when you move vertices in the ImageWindow.

We also can use VertexPainting to adjust the brightness of the fish, or even to tint the colour of the texture. For this, switch to VertexPaintMode with VKEY, or use the icon in the 3DWindow-header. Switch to the Face/PaintButtons , choose a colour with the colour sliders, and then fill the mesh with SHIFT-K.

→ *Use the VertexPainting to adjust the brightness of the texture, or to match the lighting of the texture to your scene lighting.*

The image also contains some Alpha-channel information, but we will need to tell Blender to use it. Select all of the faces that build up the fins of the fish. You will need to switch to a back-view to make the selection of faces on the back side of the fish.

In the Face/PaintButtons, activate "Alpha" and press the "Copy DrawMode" button to copy the draw mode from the active to all selected faces. You should now immediately see the effect in the textured views; the fins will now be partially transparent.

→ *You can switch from face select mode to EditMode by using TAB. Do your selection here and, after leaving EditMode, you will see the faces build up by the vertices that have been selected.*

→ *The OpenGL realtime preview draws only one-sided faces, so depending on the direction of the view, faces can disappear. This does not affect a rendering, but for the realtime view, choosing the option "Twoside" will solve this.*

Rendering and UV coordinates

Even without an image assigned to faces, you can render textures utilizing the UV coordinates. For this, use the green "UV" button in the MaterialButtons. If you want to render the assigned texture as well, press the "TexFace" button. Of course, you can combine that with the "VertexCol" option in order to use vertex colours.

→ *Often a material with the "Shadeless" option works best for image textures, when the lighting in it does not differ too much from the scene lighting.*

With the "UV" button, you can also use the UV coordinates to map Nor and Alpha maps on a object. For more detail refer to the material settings in the file "UVTexFish07.blend".

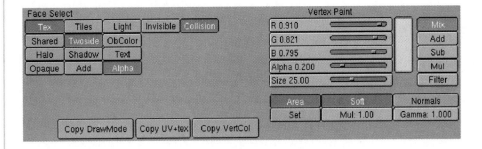

Chapter 8
Lighting

Lighting is just as important as the models and textures are in a 3D scene. The first thing to realise is that one light will never be enough to properly illuminate a scene, or even a single object. Many people misuse lighting trying to duplicate nature, like using a single light to mimic the Sun or a lamp on a desk, but end up with an unrealistic result. In this chapter we shall overcome this problem and with the use of a classic lighting style known as the 'three light setup', with emphasis on the use of the spot light to cast shadows.

Blender offers four basic lights. The Lamp is a point light that shines in all directions from a single point. The Spot is a cone-shaped spot light which is the only light that can cast shadows. A Sun lamp is a light source that shines from a constant direction, and the Hemi light is similar to the Sun except that the light is shed in the form of a half sphere. At the end of the chapter we will cover advanced lighting techniques, such as the use of light gels and volumetric lighting.

You will see how lighting can play an important part in any scene, and getting it right can be very challenging, even in the simplest of scenes. Blender provides us with a variety of lamp types and options to meet most situation requirements. With practice, and this chapter as your starter, you will learn how to use these many types of lights in a variety of ways in order to achieve the result you are seeking.

The only type of light that can cast a shadow is the Spot Light. Before a spot light can cast shadows, a few things must be set up in the scene. Load the file "no_lights.blend" in Blender. The scene contains a ground plane, a model of a woman, and a camera. Verify that shadows are enabled in the rendering engine by pressing the ShadowsButton in the DisplayButtons Window (Fig. 1).

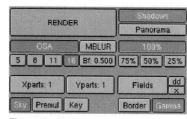

Figure 1

Select the ground plane and press F5 to display the MaterialButtons. Make sure that the Shadow and Traceable buttons are pressed (Fig. 2). Both of these buttons are set by default. The Shadow button will ensure that the object with this material (the ground plane) will receive shadows. The Traceable button needs to be set for the material of any object that needs to cast shadows.

Figure 2

Figure 3

The first light in a standard three-light set up will be a spot light known as the Key Light. In top view add a Lamp and press F4 to display the Lamp Edit Buttons. Press the Spot button and make sure that the Shadows button is also pressed. Compare your settings with the rest of the buttons in Fig. 3. The Energy slider button determines the brightness of the light, the SpotSi slider button sets the size of the spot light's cone, and the SpotBl sets the amount that the edge of the lamp's light blends within the area not lit by the lamp.

Now that the spot light has been added to the scene and all the basic necessities have been put into place, the spot light needs to be positioned and rotated. Place the light in front, above, and to the right of the main object of focus (the model of the woman). The easiest way to point the spot light is to make it track an empty. In top view add an empty directly below the spot light. Select the spot light, hold down SHIFT and select the empty. Press CTRL+T to make the spot light track the empty (Fig. 4).

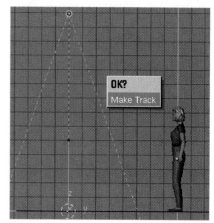

Figure 4

We can actually look through the spot light as if it were a camera while positioning the empty to point to the spot light. This is done by selecting the spot light and pressing CTRL-NUMPAD_0. Move the empty in camera view and in the other view ports until the subject

is centred as in Fig. 5. You can always return to the real camera view by pressing ALT-NUMPAD_0. There are still a few more settings that must be adjusted to achieve nice shadows.

Blender uses something known as clipping to determine which parts of the scene will be included in the shadow calculations during rendering. All objects contained within the ClipSta and ClipEnd values will cast and receive shadows. Fig. 6 is a demonstration of a high Clip-Sta value. The value is so high that the top part of the model cannot be seen in the spot lights view when used as the camera.

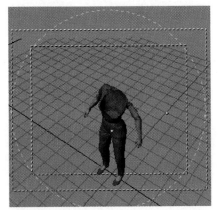

Figure 6

Adjust the clipping values so that the model of the woman and the ground plane fall inside of the visible boundaries of the spot light (Fig. 7).

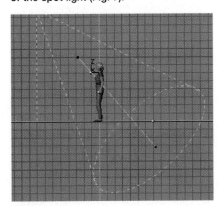

Figure 7

Before we test render, increase the values of the BufSi, Samples, and Bias buttons (Fig. 8). These settings will increase the quality of the shadows but will also increase render time. BufSi sets the size of the shadow buffer in pixels and Samples determines how many samples of the shadow buffer are sampled to reduce aliasing. The best way to see the effect of these values is to make many test renders while adjusting the values and comparing the renders to each other.

| BufSi 512 | 768 | ClipSta: 9.00 | |
| 1024 | 1536 | 2560 | ClipEnd: 30.00 | |

| | Samples: 5 | Bias: 5.000 | |
| | Halo step: 0 | Soft: 3.00 | |

Figure 8

In order to do a test render we need to return the view from the spot light back to the camera. Select the camera and press ALT+ZERO and then F12 to render. The result of all this hard work so far can be seen in Fig. 9. Compare your settings with those in the "spot.blend" file on the CDROM. Although we have a nice shadow, our scene still needs a great deal of more work and more lighting.

Figure 9

Flood Fill and Back Lighting

The next light in a standard three-light setup is the Back Lighting. The Back Light is not only used to illuminate the back of the object but to also separate the foreground objects from the background and add overall depth to the scene. The positioning is usually above and behind the main subject and offset opposite from the position of the Key (Fig. 10).

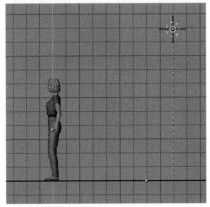

Figure 10

The default lamp settings will work well for back lighting. If only one lamp is used then the energy value should be greater than or equal to the key light. If needed increase the Dist setting as seen in Fig. 11.

Test render the scene with just the back lighting in place. This can be done by moving the other lights in the scene to an inactive layer or adjust their energy values to zero. Notice how a nice silhouette of the model can be seen separated from the background (Fig. 12).

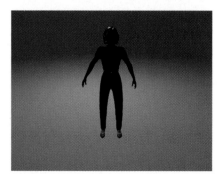

Figure 12

The third and final style of light needed to complete our scene is the Fill Light. The fill light is usually placed behind the camera and is used to soften shadows from the Key and to add to the overall ambience of a scene (Fig. 13). The intensity, or energy of the light is usually slightly less than that of the key and back lights.

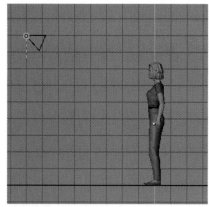

Figure 13

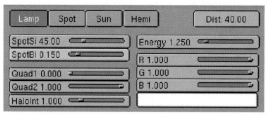

Figure 11

After test rendering the scene with just the fill light, we see that parts of the model, not visible with the other two styles, can now be seen. It is also noticeable that without a shadow there are no visible clues available and the model seems to be floating off the floor. This is one reason why shadows are so important in a lighting solution (Fig. 14).

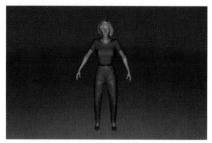

Figure 14

Add all 3 lights to the scene and compare their settings to those in the file "three_lights.blend" and render the scene. Not one of the renders from the single lights was enough to properly render the scene, but notice how rich the result is when all three lights are used together, complimenting each other as a whole (Fig. 15).

Figure 15

Shadow-Only Spots

Sometimes it is necessary to cast shadows without the need for the bright, hard-edged light that a spot light casts, or you may just want greater control over the intensity of the shadow itself. This is just what the shadow-only spot light is for. Select the spot light in our scene and duplicate it with SHIFT-D. Turn one of the spot lights into a standard lamp by clicking the Lamp button in the Lamp Edit Buttons. Select the other spot light and click the OnlyShadow button (Fig. 16).

Reduce the energy of the shadow-only spot light and render the scene. Notice the softer mood that is achieved in Fig. 17 than that of Fig. 15. Compare your settings with the settings in the file "shadow_only.blend" on the CDROM.

Figure 17

Light Gels

A light gel in real life is when you place a coloured piece of film over a stage light or a slide with an image on it. The colour or image is then cast on the scene with the light. In Blender, this is as simple as assigning a texture to a lamp. If you wanted to simulate the shadow cast

Figure 16

by a latticed windowpane, but without having to model the architecture, you could use an image similar to Fig. 18. Add a new image texture to your three light scene and use the window.jpg image on the CDROM. If you are not familiar with adding an image texture please review the chapters covering the use of materials and textures in Blender.

Figure 18

With the spot light selected open the Lamp Edit Buttons and activate the Add New menu to add the texture in the same way you would add a texture to a material. Press the View button so that the spot light will project the image properly (Fig. 19). Make sure you return the spot light back to its default setting by removing the OnlyShadow option.

Figure 19

The last step to take on the spot light is to change it to a square spot light. Press the Square button next to the light preview window. This is necessary so that the corners of the image don't get cropped off.

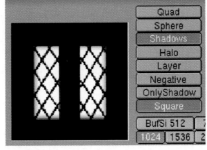

Figure 20

The final result is quite convincing (Fig. 21). Colour images can also be used to simulate light from a stained glass window, and even animated images and textures can be used for special effects.

Figure 21

The term Volumetric Lighting refers to light with some type of volume perceived. Usually this is in the form of light rays because of dust in the air, fog, mist, or under water effects. This is best seen when a volumetric light is obstructed by something and casting shadows. Load the file "volumetric1.blend" from the CDROM. Our scene consists of only a pre-calculated radiosity solution (Fig. 22).

Figure 22

A volumetric light (or halo spot) must start out as a spot light and all the rules of a spot that cast shadows must also apply to a volumetric light, including clipping. Use Fig. 23 as a reference when placing your spot light. Adjust the clipping as needed.

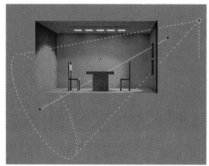

Figure 23

There are three areas of interest when converting a spot light to a volumetric light (Fig. 24). First, the Halo step value must be changed from the default value of zero. The values range from 1 to 12, the lower the number the higher the quality and the longer the render time. A setting of zero makes the halo rendering inactive. Next press the Halo button to activate volumetric lighting.

This is where the name halo spot comes from. The intensity of the light rays are adjusted with the HaloInt slider button.

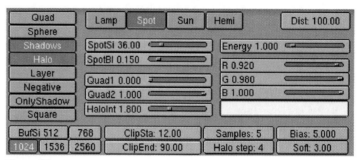

Figure 24

In the final render, the colour of the halo spot was changed to a light blue to help give the look of daylight (Fig. 25). This use of colour is used to suggest the time of day. It can easily be changed by rotating the angle of the light rays and the colour of the lamp. In Fig. 26 the angle was lowered and the colour of the lamp was changed to a reddish-orange, to suggest a sunset mood (see "volumetric2.blend").

Figure 25

Figure 26

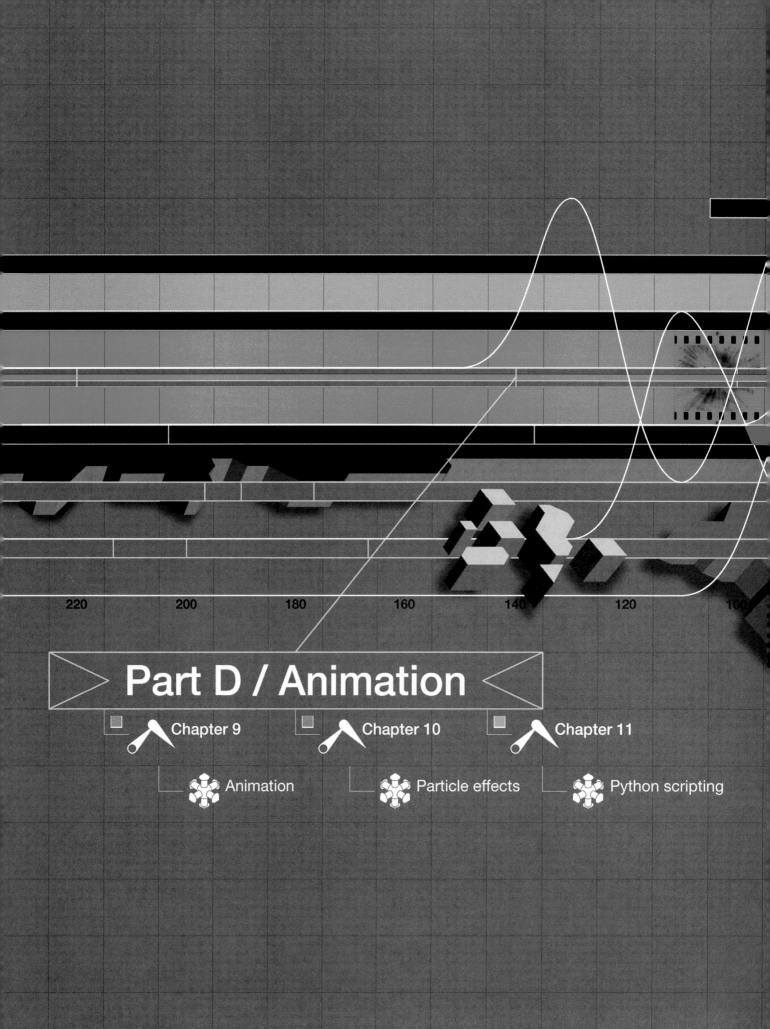

220 200 180 160 140 120 100

Part D / Animation

Chapter 9 Chapter 10 Chapter 11

Animation Particle effects Python scripting

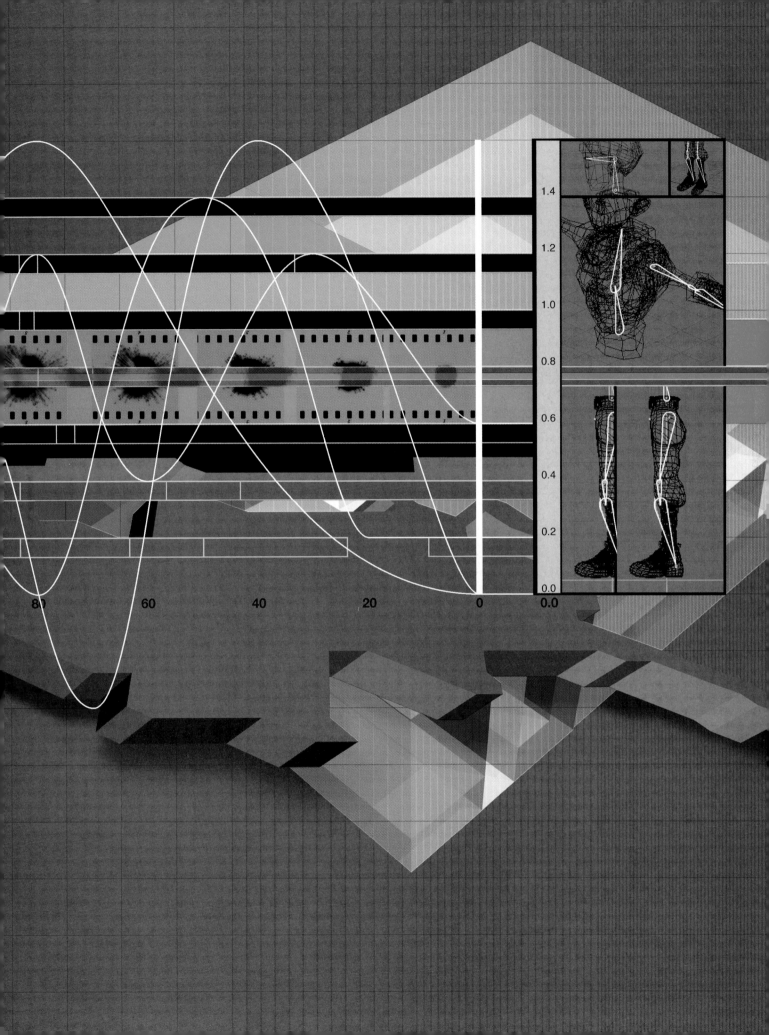

Chapter 9
Animation

Two methods are normally used in animation software to make a 3D object move.

Key frames

Complete positions are saved for units of time (frames). An animation is created by interpolating an object fluidly through the frames. The advantage of this method is that it allows you to work with clearly visualised units. The animator can work from one position to the next and can change previously created positions, or move them in time.

Motion Curves

Curves can be drawn for each XYZ component for location, rotation, and size. These form the graphs for the movement, with time set out horizontally and the value set out vertically. The advantage of this method is that it gives you precise control over the results of the movement.

Both systems are completely integrated in Blenders "Ipo" system. Fundamentally, the Ipo system consists of standard motion curves. A simple press of a button changes the Ipo to a key system, without conversion, and with no change to the results. The user can work anyway they choose to with the keys, switching to motion curves and back again, in whatever way produces the best result or satisfies the user's preferences.

This section describes the basic principles of the Ipo block, working with motion curves and the "IpoKey" system.

Ipo Block

The Ipo block in Blender is universal. It makes no difference whether an object's movement is controlled or the material settings are set. Once you have learned to work with object Ipos, how you work with other Ipos will become obvious. Blender does distinguish between different types of Ipos. Blender concerns itself only with the type of blocks on which Ipos can work. It is better not to link object Ipos with a

material as the user does not need to think about this. The interface keeps track of it automatically.

Every type of Ipo block has a fixed number of available channels. These each have a name (LocX, SizeZ, etc.) that indicates how they can be applied. When you add an IpoCurve to a channel, animation begins immediately. At your discretion (and there are separate channels for this), a curve can be linked directly to a value, or it can affect a variance of this relationship. The latter enables you to move an object as per usual, with the Grabber, while the actual location is determined by IpoCurves relative to it.

The Blender interface offers many options for copying Ipos, linking Ipos to more than one object (one Ipo can animate multiple objects), or deleting Ipo links. The IpoWindow Reference section gives a detailed description of this. This chapter is restricted to the main options for application.

Making Ipos in the 3DWindow

Insert Key
- Loc
- Rot
- Size
- LocRot
- LocRotSize
- Layer
- Avail

The most simple method for creating an object Ipo is with the "Insert key" (IKEY), command in the 3DWindow. A Popup-Menu provides a wide selection of options. We will select the topmost option: "Loc". Now the current location X-Y-Z, is saved and everything takes place automatically:

If there is no Ipo block, a new one is created and linked to the object.
If there are no IpoCurves in the channels "LocX", "LocY" and "LocZ", these are created.
Vertices are then added in the IpoCurves with the exact values of the object location.

We go 30 frames further on (3 x UPARROW) and move the object. Again we use IKEY and immediately press ENTER. The new position is inserted in the IpoCurves. We can see this by slowly paging back through the frames (LEFTARROW). The object moves between the two positions.

In this way, you can create the animation by paging through the frames, position by position. Note that the location of the object is directly linked to the curves. When you change frames, the Ipos are always re-evaluated and re-applied. You can freely move the object within the same frame, but since you have changed frame, the object 'jumps' to the position determined by the Ipo.

The rotation and size of the object are completely free in this example. They can be changed or animated with the "Insert key".

The IpoWindow

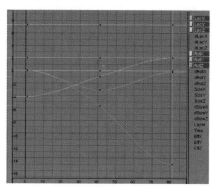

Now we want to see exactly what happened. The first Screen for this is initialised in the standard Blender start-up file. Activate this Screen with (ALT-)CTRL+LEFTARROW. At the right we see the IpoWindow displayed. This shows all the IpoCurves, the channels used and those available. You can zoom in on the IpoWindow and translate, just as everywhere else in Blender with (CTRL+MiddleMouse.

In addition to the standard channels, you have the 'delta' options,

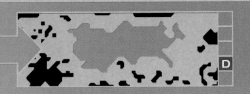

such as "dLocX". These channels allow you to assign a relative change. This option is primarily used to control multiple objects with the same Ipo. In addition, it is possible to work in animation 'layers'. You can achieve subtle effects this way without having to draw complicated curves.

Each curve can be selected individually with the RMB. In addition, the Grabber and Size modes operate here just as in the 3DWindow. By selecting all curves (AKEY) and moving them to the right (GKEY), you can move the complete animation in time.

Beziers

Each curve can be placed in EditMode individually, or it can be done collectively. Select the curves and press TAB. Now the individual vertices and handles of the curve are displayed. The Bezier handles are coded, just like the curve object:

Free Handle (black). This can be used any way you wish. Hotkey: HKEY (switches between Free and Aligned). Aligned Handle (pink). This arranges all the handles in a straight line. Hotkey: HKEY (toggles between Free and Aligned). Vector Handle (green). Both parts of a handle always point to the previous or next handle. Hotkey: VKEY

Auto Handle (yellow). This handle has a completely automatic length and direction. Hotkey: SHIFT+H.

Handles can be moved by first selecting the middle vertex with RMB. This selects the other two vertices as well. Then immediately start the Grab mode with RMB -hold and move. Handles can be rotated by first selecting the end of one of the vertices and then use the Grabber by means of the RMB -hold and move action.

As soon as handles are rotated, the type is changed automatically:

Auto Handle is Aligned.
Vector Handle becomes Free.

"Auto" handles are placed in a curve by default. The first and last Auto handles always move horizontally, which creates a fluid interpolation.

IpoCurves

The IpoCurves have an important feature that distinguishes them from normal curves: it is impossible to place more than one curve segment horizontally. Loops and circles in an Ipo are senseless and ambiguous. An Ipo can only have 1 value at a time. This is automatically detected in the IpoWindow. By moving part of the IpoCurve horizontally, you see that the selected vertices move 'through' the curve. This allows you to duplicate parts of a curve (SHIFT+D) and to move them to another time frame.

It is also important to specify how an IpoCurve must be read outside of the curve itself. There are three options for this in the IpoHeader.

Extend mode Constant (IconBut)

The ends of selected IpoCurves are continuously (horizontally) extrapolated.

Extend mode Direction (IconBut)

The ends of the selected IpoCurves continue in the direction in which they ended.

Extend mode Cyclic (IconBut)

The complete width of the IpoCurve is repeated cyclically.

Extend Mode Cyclic Extrapolation (IconBut)

The complete width of the IpoCurve is extrapolated cyclic.

In addition to Beziers, there are two other possible types for IpoCurves. Use the TKEY command to select them. A PopupMenu asks what type the selected IpoCurves must be:

"Constant" - after each vertex of the curve, this value remains constant. No interpolation takes place.
"Linear" - linear interpolation occurs between the vertices.
"Bezier" - the standard fluid interpolation.

Draw IpoCurves

The IpoCurves can also be drawn 'by hand'. Use the CTRL+LMB command. Here are the rules:

There is no Ipo block yet (in this window) and one channel is selected: a new IpoBlock is created along with the first IpoCurve with one vertex.
There is already an Ipo block, and a channel is selected without an IpoCurve: a new IpoCurve with one vertex is added Otherwise only a new point is added to the selected IpoCurve.
This is not possible if multiple IpoCurves are selected or in EditMode.

This is the best method for specifying axis rotations quickly. Select the object. In the IpoWindow, press one of the "Rot" channels and use CTRL+LMB to insert two points. If the axis rotation must be continuous, you must use the button IpoHeader->"Extend mode Directional".

Rotations and Scaling

One disadvantage of working with motion curves is that the freedom of transformations is limited. You can work quite intuitively with motion curves, but only if this can be processed on an XYZ basis. For a location, this is outstanding, but for a size and rotation there are better mathematical descriptions available: matrices (3x3 numbers) for size and quaternions (4 numbers) for rotation. These could also have been processed in the channels, but this can quite easily lead to confusing and mathematically complicated situations.

Limiting the size to the three numbers XYZ is obvious, but this limits it to a rectangular distortion. A diagonal scaling such as 'shearing' is impossible. Simply working in hierarchies can solve this. A non-uniform scaled Parent will influence the rotation of a Child as a 'shear'.

The limitation of the three number XYZ rotations is less intuitive. This so-called Euler rotation is not uniform - the same rotation can be expressed with different numbers - and has the bothersome effect that it is not possible to rotate from any position to another, the infamous gimbal lock. While working with different rotation keys, the user may suddenly be confronted with quite unexpected interpolations, or it may turn out to be impossible to force a particular axis rotation when making manual changes. Here, also, a better solution is to work with a hierarchy. A Parent will always assign the specified axis rotation to the Child. (It is handy to know that the X, Y and Z rotations are calculated one after the other. The curve that affects the "RotX" channel, always determines the X axis rotation).

Fortunately, Blender calculates everything internally with matrices and quaternions. Hierarchies thus work normally, and the Rotate mode does what you would expect it to. Only the Ipos are a limitation here, but in this case the ease of use prevails above a not very intuitive mathematical purity.

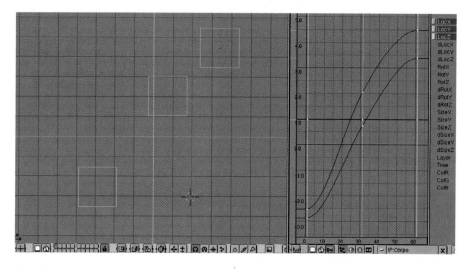

IpoKeys

The easiest way to work with motion curves is to convert them to IpoKeys. We return to the situation in the previous example: we have specified two positions in an object Ipo in frame 1 and frame 31 with "Insert Key". At the right of the screen, you can see an IpoWindow. We set the current frame to 21.

Press KKEY while the mouse cursor is in the 3DWindow. Two things will happen now:

The IpoWindow switches to IpoKey mode.
The selected object is assigned the "DrawKey" option.

The two actions each have separate meanings.

The IpoWindow now draws vertical lines through all the vertices of all the visible IpoCurves. Vertices with the same 'frame' value are linked to the vertical lines. The vertical lines (the "IpoKeys") can be selected, moved or duplicated, just like the vertices in EditMode. You can translate the IpoKeys only horizontally. The position of the object for each IpoKey is drawn in the 3DWindow.

In addition to now being able to visualise the key positions of the object, you can also modify them in the 3DWindow. In this example, use the Grab mode on the object to change the selected IpoKeys.

Below are a number of instructions for utilising the power of the system:

You can only use the RMB to select IpoKeys in the IpoWindow. Border select, and extend select, are also enabled here. Select all IpoKeys to transform the complete animation system in the 3DWindow. The "Insert Key" always affects all selected objects. The IpoKeys for multiple objects can also be transformed simultaneously in the 3DWindow. Use the SHIFT+K command: "Show and select all keys" to transform complete animations of a group of objects all at once.
Use the PAGEUP and PAGEDOWN commands to select subsequent keys in the 3DWindow.
You can create IpoKeys with each arrangement of channels. By consciously exluding certain channels, you can force a situation in which changes to key positions in the 3DWindow can only be made to the values specified by the visible channels. For example, with only the channel "LocX" selected, the keys can only be moved in the X direction. Each IpoKey consists of the vertices that have exactly the same frame value.

If vertices are moved manually, this can result in large numbers of keys, each having only one curve. In this case, use the JKEY ("Join") command to combine selected IpoKeys. It is also possible to assign selected IpoKeys vertices for all the visible curves: use IKEY in the Ipo-Window and choose "Selected keys". The DrawKey option and the IpoKey mode can be switched on and off independently. Use the button Edit-Buttons->DrawKey to switch off this option or object. You can switch IpoKey mode on and off yourself with KKEY in the IpoWindow. Only KKEY in the 3DWindow turns on/off both the DrawKey and IpoKey mode.

There are three ways to create an animated Material:

1 Material Ipos. Just as with objects, IpoCurves can be used to specify 'key positions' for Materials. With the mouse in the ButtonsWindow, the command IKEY calls up a PopupMenu with options for the various Material variables. Per Material, the mapping for all 8 channels can be controlled with IpoCurves. A continuously rising curve can be placed in the channel "OffsZ", for example, to create a waterlike effect in an X-Y face.
2 Objects that give texture coordinates. Each object in Blender can be used as a source for texture coordinates. To do this, the option "Object" must be selected in the green "Coordinates input" buttons and the name of the object must be filled in. An inverse transformation is now performed on the global render coordinate to obtain the local object coordinate. This links the texture to the location, size, and rotation of the object.
3 Animated Images. Per frame, Blender can load another (numbered) Image as a texture map. It is also possible to use SGI movie files or AVI files for this.

©2000 Michael Hein

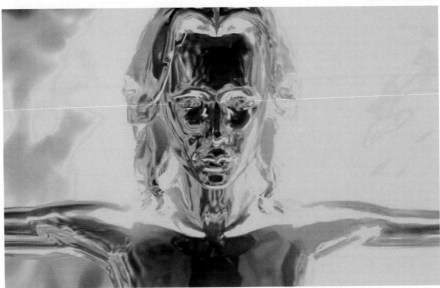

Often objects need to follow a path, or it is too hard to animate a special kind of movement with the keyframe method. Think of a planet following its way around the sun. Animating that with keyframes is virtually impossible.

Curve objects can be used for the 3D display of an animation path. Only the first curve in the object is then used. Each Curve becomes a path by setting the option AnimButtons->CurvePath to ON. All Child objects of the Curve move along the specified path. It is a good idea to set the option EditButtons->3D to ON so that the paths can be freely modelled. In the ADD menu under Curve->Path, a primitive with the correct settings is available. This is a 5th order Nurbs spline, which can be used to create very fluid, continuous movements.

Curves that are used as paths always get the correct number of interpolated points automatically. The button EditButtons->ResolU has no effect here.

Speed Ipo

The speed along a path is determined with a curve in the IpoWindow. To see it, the Header button with the 'arrow' icon must be pressed in. The complete path runs in the IpoWindow between the vertical values 0.0 and 1.0. Drawing a curve between these values links the time to the position on the path. Backward and pulsing movements are possible with this. For most paths, an IpoCurve must run precisely between the Y-values 0.0 and 1.0. To achieve this, use the Number menu (NKEY) in the IpoWindow. If the IpoCurve is deleted, the value of AnimButtons->PathLen determines the duration of the path. A linear movement is defined in this case.

Using the option AnimButtons->Curve-Follow, a rotation is also given to the Child objects of the path, so that they permanently point in the direction of the path. Use the "tracking" buttons in the AnimButtons to specify the effect of the rotation:

TrackX, Y, Z, -X, -Y, -Z (RowBut)

This specifies the direction axis, i.e. the axis that is placed on the path.

UpX, UpY, UpZ (RowBut)

Specifies which axis must point 'upwards', in the direction of the (local) positive Z axis. If the "Track" is the "Up" axis, it is deactivated.

Curve paths cannot be given uniform rotations that are perpendicular to the local Z axis. That would make it impossible to determine the 'up' axis.

To visualise these rotations precisely, we must make it possible for a Child to have its own rotations. Erase the Child's rotation with ALT+R. Also erase the "Parent Inverse": ALT+P. The best method is to 'parent' an unrotated Child to the path with the command SHIFT-CTRL+P: "Make parent without inverse". Now the Child jumps directly to the path and the Child points in the right direction.

3D paths also get an extra value for each vertex: the 'tilt'. This can be used to specify an axis rotation. Use TKEY in EditMode to change the tilt of selected vertices in EditMode, e.g. to have a Child move around as if it were on a roller coaster.

With the Timelpo curve you can manipulate the animation time of objects without changing the animation or the other Ipos. In fact, it changes the mapping of animation time to global animation time.

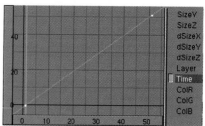

Make a simple keyframe-animation of a moving object and create a Timelpo in the IpoWindow. In frames where the slope of the Timelpo is positive, your object will advance in its animation. The speed depends on the value of the slope. A slope bigger than 1 will animate faster than the base animation. A slope smaller than 1 will animate slower. A slope of 1 means no change in the animation, negative power slopes allow you to reverse the animation.

The Timelpo is especially interesting for particle systems, allowing you to "freeze" the particles or to animate particles absorbed by an object instead of emitted. Other possibilities are to make a time lapse or slow motion animation.

→ *You need to copy the Timelpo for every animation system to get a full slow motion. But by stopping only some animations, and continue to animate, for example, the camera can give some very nice effects (like those used to stunning effect the movie "The Matrix").*

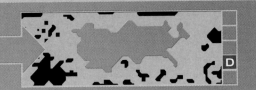

You can use Lattices for two kinds of animation:

Animate the vertices with vertex keys (or relative vertex keys)
Move the lattice or the child object of the lattice.

With the second kind you can create animations that squish things between rollers, or achieve the effect of a well-known space ship accelerating to "warp"-speed.

Make a space ship and add a lattice around the ship. I made the lattice with the following parameters:

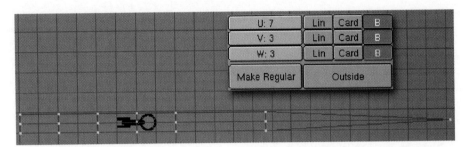

I put the lattice into EditMode for this picture, so you can see the vertices. For working with lattices it is also good to switch on the "Outside" option in the EditButtons for the Lattice, as this will hide the inner vertices of the lattice.

Select the ship, extend the selection to the lattice (holding SHIFT while selecting), and press CTRL-P to make the lattice the parent of the ship. You should not see any deformation of the ship because the lattice is still regular.

For the next few steps it is important to do them in EditMode. This causes a deformation only if the child object is inside the Lattice. So now select the lattice, enter EditMode, select all vertices (AKEY), and scale the lattice along its x-axis (press MMB while initiating the scale) to get the stretch you want. The ship's mesh shows immediately the deformation caused by the lattice.

Now I edited the lattice in EditMode so that the right vertices have an increasing distance from each other. This will increase the stretch as the ship goes into the lattice. The right ends vertices I have scaled down so that they are nearly at one point; this will cause the vanishing of the ship at the end.

Select the ship again and move it through the lattice to get a preview of the animation. Now you can do a normal keyframe animation to let the ship fly through the lattice.

→ With this lattice animation, you can't use the pivot point of the object for tracking or parenting. It will move outside the object. You will need to vertex-parent an Empty to the mesh for that. To do so, select the Empty, then the mesh, enter EditMode and select one vertex, then press CTRL-P.

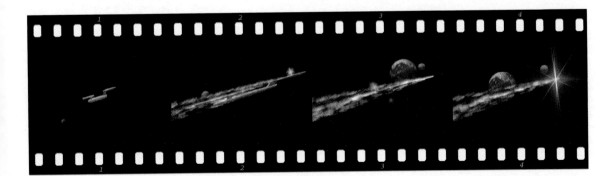

VertexKeys, which should not be confused with "Object keys", the specified positions of objects, can also be created in Blender; VertexKeys are the specified positions of vertices in ObData. Since this can involve thousands of vertices, separate motion curves are not created for each vertex, but the traditional Key position system is used instead. A single IpoCurve is used to determine how interpolation is performed and the times at which a VertexKey can be seen.

VertexKeys are part of ObData, not of an object. When duplicating ObData, the associated VertexKey block is also copied. It is not possible to permit multiple users to use VertexKeys in Blender, since it would not be very practical.

The Key block is also universal and understands the distinction between a Mesh, a Curve, a Surface or a Lattice. Their interface and use are therefore identical. Working with Mesh VertexKeys is explained in detail in this section, which also contains a number of brief comments on the other ObData.

The first VertexKey position that is created is always the reference Key. This key defines the texture coordinates. Only if this Key is active can the faces and curves, or the number of vertices, be changed. It is allowed to assign other Keys a different number of vertices. The Key system automatically interpolates this.

Mesh VertexKeys

Creating VertexKeys in Blender is very simple, but the fact that the system is very sensitive in terms of its configuration, can cause a number of 'invisible' things to happen. The following rule must therefore be taken into consideration:

> **As soon as a VertexKey position is inserted it is immediately active.** All subsequent changes in the Mesh are linked to this Key position. It is therefore important that the Key position be added before editing begins.

A practical example is given below. When working with VertexKeys, it is very handy to have an IpoWindow open. Use the first Screen from the standard Blender file, for example. In the IpoWindow, we must then specify that we want to see the Vertex-Keys. Do this using the Icon button with the vertex square. Go to the 3DWindow with the mouse cursor and press IKEY. With a Mesh object active, this key gives us the "Insert Key" menu with the "Mesh" option at the bottom. As soon as this has been selected, a yellow horizontal line is drawn in the IpoWindow. This is the first key and thus the reference Key. An Ipo-Curve is also created. Go a few frames further and again select: IKEY, ENTER (in the 3DWindow). The second Key is drawn as a light blue line. This is a normal Key; this key and all subsequent Keys affect only the vertex information. Press TAB for EditMode and translate one of the vertices in the Mesh. Then browse a few frames back: nothing happens! As long as we are in EditMode, other VertexKeys are not applied. What you see in Edit-Mode is always the active VertexKey. Leave EditMode and browse through the frames again. We now see the effect of the VertexKey system. VertexKeys can only be selected in the IpoWindow. We always do this out of EditMode: the 'contents' of the VertexKey are now temporarily displayed in the Mesh. We can edit the specified Key by starting Editmode. There are three methods for working with Vertex Keys:

1 The 'performance animation' method.
  This method works entirely in
  EditMode, chronologically from position to position.
  Insert Key. The reference is specified.
  A few frames further: Insert Key. Edit the Mesh for the second position.
  A few frames further: Insert Key. Edit the Mesh for the third position.
  Continue the above process...
2 The 'editing' method.
  We first insert all of the required Keys, unless we have already created the Keys using the method described above.
  Blender is not in EditMode.

Select a Key. Now start EditMode, change the Mesh and leave EditMode. Select a Key. Start EditMode, change the Mesh and leave EditMode. Continue the above process...
3 The 'insert' method.
  Whether or not there are already Keys and whether or not we are in EditMode does not matter in this method.
  Go to the frame in which the new Key must be inserted.
  Insert Key.
  Go to a new frame, Insert Key.
  Continue the above process...

While in EditMode, the Keys cannot be switched. If the user attempts to do so, a menu appears: "Copy Key". This method can be used to copy the current key to the newly selected Key.

The IpoCurve and VertexKey lines

Both the IpoCurve and the VertexKey lines are drawn in the IpoWindow. They can be separately selected with RMB. Since it would otherwise be too difficult working with them, selection of the Key lines is switched off when the curve is in EditMode. The channel button can be used to temporarily hide the curve (SHIFT+LMB on "Speed") to make it easier to select Keys.

The Key lines in the IpoWindow can be placed at any vertical position. Select the line and use Grab mode to do this. The IpoCurve can also be processed here in the same way as described in the previous section.
Instead of a 'value', however, the curve determines the interpolation between the Keys, e.g. a sine curve can be used to create a cyclical animation.

With a Key line selected, three interpolation types can be specified. Press TKEY to open a menu with the options:

"Linear": interpolation between the Keys is linear. The Key line is displayed as a dotted line.
"Cardinal": interpolation between the

Keys is fluid, the standard setting. "BSpline": interpolation between the Keys is extra fluid and includes four Keys in the interpolation calculation. The positions are no longer displayed precisely, however. The Key line is drawn as a broken line.

Tips

Key positions are always added with IKEY, even if they are located at the same position. Use this to copy positions when inserting. Two key lines at the same position can also be used to change the effect of the interpolation.

If no Keys are selected, EditMode can be invoked as usual. However, when you leave EditMode, all changes are undone. Insert the Key in EditMode in this case. For Keys, there is no difference between selected and active. It is therefore not possible to select multiple Keys. When working with Keys with differing numbers of vertices, the faces can become disordered. There are no tools that can be used to specify precise sequence of vertices. This option is actually suitable only for Meshes that have only vertices such as Halos. Editbuttons->Slurph is an interesting option. The "Slurph" number indicates the interpolation of Keys per vertex with a fixed delay. The first vertex comes first and the last vertex has a delay of "Slurph" frames. This effect makes it possible to create very interesting and lively Key framing. Pay special attention to the sequence of the vertices for Meshes. They can be sorted using the command EditButtons->Xsort or made random using the command EditButons->Hash. This must of course be done before the VertexKeys are created. Otherwise, unpredictable things can and will happen (this is great for Halos though!).

Curve and Surface Keys

As mentioned earlier in this guide, Curve and Surface Keys work exactly the same way as Mesh Keys. For Curves, it is particularly interesting to place Curve Keys in the bevel object. Although this animation is not displayed realtime in the 3DWindow, but it will be rendered.

Lattice Keys

Lattice Vertex Keys can be applied in a variety of ways by the user. When combined with "slurping", they can achieve some interesting effects. As soon as one Key is present in a Lattice, the buttons that are used to determine the resolution are blocked.

Relative VertexKeys

Face by Jason Nairn

Relative VertexKeys simplify the creation of facial and character animation by blending sets of VertexKeys. While traditional vertex keys are controlled with only one interpolation curve, relative vertex keys are controlled by one interpolation curve for every key position, thus relative keys can be mixed (added, subtracted, etc.).

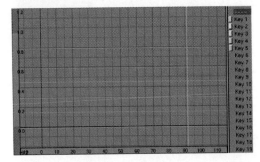

For facial animation, the base position might be a relaxed position with a slightly open mouth and eyelids half open. Then keys would be defined for left/right eye-blink, happy, sad, smiling, frowning, etc.

The trick with relative vertex keys is that only the vertices that are changed between the base and the key affect the final output during blending. This means it is possible to have several keys affecting the object in different places all at the same time.

For example, a face with three keys: smile, and left/right eye-blink could be animated to smile, then blink left eye, then blink right eye, then open both eyes and stop smiling - all by blending 3 keys. Without relative vertex keys 6 vertex keys would have needed to be generated, one for each target position.

The Relative VertexKey buttons

Relative Keys

The "Relative Keys" button (AnimButtons, F7) toggles the VertexKey system for the selected object between traditional and relative mode. It only becomes active after the first ('base') key has been inserted.

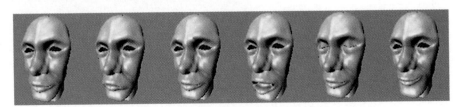

Relative keys are defined by inserting normal vertex keys. The vertical order of the vertex key determines its corresponding Ipo curve, i.e. the lowest blue key line will be controlled by the "Key1" curve, the second lowest will be controlled by the "Key2" curve, and so on.

The "Relative Keys" button in the Anim-Buttons must be active for the Key curves to be displayed. When "Relative Keys" is active the speed curve no longer affects the mesh position and can be removed.

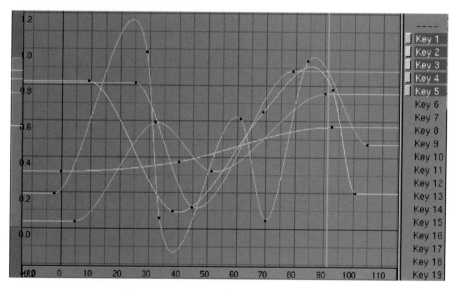

The Ipo curve for each key controls the blending between relative keys. These curves should be created in the typical fashion. The final position is determined by adding all of the affects of each individual Ipo curve.

An important part of relative keys is the use of additive or extrapolated positions. For example, if the base position for a face is with a straight mouth, and a key is defined for a smile, then it is possible that the negative application of that key will result in a frown. Likewise, extending the Ipo Curve above 1.0 will "extrapolate" that key, making an extreme smile.

Setting up Character Animation

In this tutorial we will walk through the steps involved in preparing a character model for animation. This involves adding the bones and controls that will be used to deform the mesh.

You can either use a character of your own, or you can load the "KNIGHT.BLEND" file from the CDROM.

When designing your character, model it up so that the arms are stretched out to the sides, with the palms facing down. The legs should be straight with the feet flat on the floor (Fig. 1).

Figure 1

There are three main sets of components involved in the character animation setup process. The mesh, the skeleton, and the controls.

The mesh is the actual model geometry that is rendered. The mesh is deformed by the skeleton that is composed of the IKAs and Empties that define the deformation envelope. To simplify the animation process, the skeleton is often manipulated indirectly with a series of control objects.

→ It is a good idea to separate the different objects involved in the animation onto layers based on their functions. Consider the following layout for example:
Deformed Mesh Layer
Reference Mesh Layer
Primary IKA skeleton
Secondary IKA elements (bones that are a part of the control system but which do not directly contribute to the skeleton's deformation)
Control Empties / Effector targets
Deformation objects
This makes it easy to show or hide layers to reveal just the mesh or the skeleton, to easily locate the control empties or to hide the deformation objects. Depending on the complexity of your skeletal system you may want more or fewer layers. Putting a character's finger IKAs on a layer of their own would it much easier to select and focus on the small bones without accidentally selecting items in the rest of the character's skeleton.

Working with IKAs

IK vs. FK

The TAB key toggles IKA chains between Forward Kinematics (FK) and Inverse Kinematics (IK) mode. In FK mode, manipulating the IKA chain affects the root, or base of the system. In IK mode, the end or effector is controlled. Once the effector has been placed, the IKA chain will constantly try and adjust itself to that it touches the effector. You can tell which mode is active by looking at the position of the yellow dot present on the chain when it is selected. If the dot is at the base, the IKA is in FK mode. If it is at the tip, the limb is in IK mode.

In a character setup, most of the major IKA chains will be left in IK mode.

→ Note: you cannot toggle between IK mode and FK mode in the course of an animation.

Effector Parents

Unlike other objects in Blender, IKA chains can have two parents. In addition to normal parenting relationship, an IKA can have an effector parent. An IKA chain with an effector parent will attempt to solve itself so that the tip of the chain touches the parent. If this can't be done – if, for example the effector parent (or target) is too far away to reach – the solver tries to get as close as possible. Note that moving the effector parent will never change the position of the start of the chain (Fig. 2).

Figure 2

Though it is possible to directly manipulate the location of an IKA chain's effector, it is often better to use an empty as an effector parent and move that instead. This way it is possible to see where the IKA chain is trying to go, and to set targets that would not normally be reachable by an IKA chain (such as having a character's arms stretch out to touch an object that is out of reach).

When making another object the parent of an IKA chain, a requestor will appear with the message EFFECTOR AS CHILD? To designate the object as an effector parent, click on the message, or press ENTER. To dismiss the requestor (and therefore set up a normal parenting relationship), press ESC or move the mouse away from the requestor.

Note that effector parents only have an effect if the chain is set to IK mode.

360 Degree Joints

IKA chains in Blender are essentially two-dimensional. Though it is possible to rotate them a bit, there are usually problems when the effector target is moved out of the IKA's plane. This makes true 360 degree joints difficult to simulate.

To solve this problem, we place an extra bone at the root of the main chain with the same facing, but rolled 90 degrees. This new IKA becomes the child of the main chain's root, and becomes the limb-parent to the main chain (Fig. 3).

Both the chain and the limb-parent should use the same empty as an effector parent.

This technique works very well for shoulder and hip joints. If you are going to be rotating an IKA operating in IK mode, you can place an empty at the root of the IKA and make it the parent of the IKA.

Note that when you are building the skeleton, the joint IKAs should not be included in the calculation.

Figure 3

Rolling Controls

Sometimes you may find that the IKA solver leaves your limb in an awkward orientation. This happens most frequently with the arms. One way to solve this is to use an empty to control the roll of the limb.

Create an empty and position it at the base of the limb (you can move the cursor to the exact location of the base by selecting the IKA and pressing SHIFT+S >>CURS->SEL). Clear the empty's rotation by pressing ALT+R >>CLEAR ROTATION. Make this empty the parent of the limb you wish to control, and then make it the child of whatever the limb was attached to. Fig. 4 shows a rolling empty applied to a 360 degree joint.

When animating using a rolling control, make sure you clear the rotation before setting a new key. This will help prevent problems such as limbs that twist through impossible angles.

Figure 4

Advanced Rolling Controls

It is possible to roll a single limb in an IKA, rather than the entire chain, though it takes a bit more work to set it up. This is useful for joints such as elbows (The elbow is responsible for the rotation of the hand: try to rotate your palm while holding your wrist with the other hand).

Start by creating an IKA chain (Fig. 5). The limb highlighted in green is the limb to which we want to add the roll.

Figure 5

Now add some single-segment IKAs: one for each limb of the arm chain. Leave these new segments in FK mode

and make the appropriate limbs from the chain the limb-parents of the appropriate segments

Fig. 6 shows the placement of the new bones. The blue and the green bones are parented to the main chain (represented in grey). The pink bone is left unparented.

Figure 6

Add an empty at the base of the final segment, and make sure the Z-axis of the empty points along the bone. Make the empty the limb-child of the final limb of the chain, then make the segment the child of the empty (Fig. 7).

Figure 7

When calculating the skeleton, use the three single segments, rather than the actual arm bone.

Figure 8

To rotate the empty along its z axis, select it and press KEYPAD*. This sets the view perpendicular to the object. Rotating the empty in this view will roll

the bone along its length. To return to the previous view, simply press the appropriate button on the keypad (Fig. 8).

Root

The Root is a bone that does not refer to a specific part of the model. Rather it is used to move the entire model at once, and should be the parent of all of the control empties. If you wish to scale, move or rotate your character, or to have your character move along a path for example, you only need to operate on the Root bone.

The Root bone is placed at ground level between the character's feet and should be fairly large to easily distinguish it from the rest of the skeleton (Fig. 9).

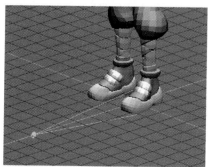

Figure 9

➡ *If you keep an un-deformed copy of the mesh on a separate layer, you can toggle the visibility of that layer to make sure that your skeleton fits the body properly.*

Spine

Depending on the design of your character, this chain may have as few as one or as many as three segments (with two segments being the typical compromise as shown in Fig. 10). More segments means more flexibility but it can make it more difficult to control the character.

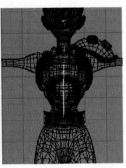

Figure 10

Neck/Head

The neck and the head are typically two separate IKAs as opposed to a two segment chain (Fig. 11). Normally, the neck doesn't move very much and most of the rotation actually occurs in the head. If you are building a character with real eyes, you should put a single IKA in each eye (with the root of the IKA at the center of the eyeball sphere).

Figure 11

The head and the neck are limb-children of the last limb in the spine. The neck should be left in FK mode, while the head may be left in either FK or IK mode depending on how you intend to animate it.

Arms/Legs

Arms and legs can be modelled with a two-segment chain, though it can be a pain to handle joint bending in such a setup.

An easier method is to use a three-segment chain (Fig. 12). This allows the skin to fold properly at the joint, without suffering

from severe "drinking straw" pinching artifacts.

Figure 12

The IKAs should be added from the top view so that the hinge allows the arms to bend forwards (Fig. 13). Try holding out your own arm in a similar position and watch how it bends. The arms should be limb-children of the last limb in the spine.

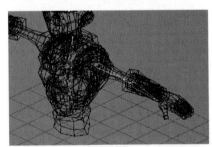

Figure 13

Legs can be modelled using a three-segment chain similar to the arm chain. The legs should be limb-children of the first limb in the spine (Fig. 14).

Figure 14

Feet

It is a good idea to use more than one bone in the feet (Fig. 15), and to make the "heel" the limb-parent of the "toe". This allows the foot to bend as the character rolls their foot forward. The last limb in the leg should be the limb-parent of the first bone in the foot.

Note that the two bones have been left in FK mode to make them easier to control.

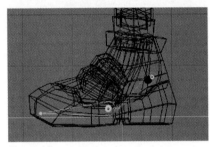

Figure 15

Control Objects

These are the empties that are being used as IK targets, as well as bones in FK mode that will be directly manipulated. Unless otherwise noted, empties used as controls should be limb-children of the ROOT bone.

> → *Control empties will be easier to locate and select if you click on the NAME TogBut in the EditMenu (F9).*

Two empties control the spine: The "Pelvis" empty is located at the base of the spine and acts as the parent to the spine chain. This is used to set the location of the spine. The effector of the spine is the limb-child of another empty, named "SpineTarget" (Fig. 16).

Figure 16

Hand and foot empties are used as effector parents to guide the arm and leg chains (Fig. 17).

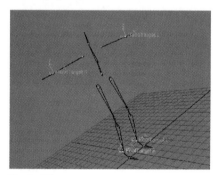

Figure 17

Deformation Objects

Deformation objects are additional IKAs or empties that have been added to the skeleton in order to modify the deformation envelope. This is necessary when you find stray vertices that do not move when the rest of the limb does (Fig. 18).

Figure 18

Deformation objects are limb-parented to IKAs in the primary frame and are left in FK mode (Fig. 19).

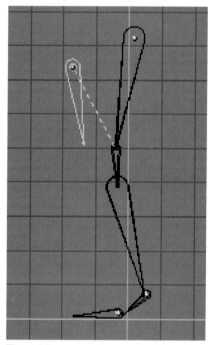

Figure 19

→ *If you manipulate an IKA in IK mode, and then press ESC to cancel the operation, you'll probably notice that the IKA chain doesn't always revert to its base position. When you are setting up the character and you are testing out the deformation, it is a good idea to save the file before moving any limbs. When you have seen the results of the move (for better or for worse), reload the file again.*
This ensures that your IKAs don't fall out of alignment and saves you having to manually reposition them in their rest post.

Working with Skeletons

Before your IKAs can smoothly deform your meshes, you must collect IKAs together and build them into a skeleton.

Press CTRL+K to calculate the skeleton. Note that the highlighted bone (the bright pink one) will be the one that contains the skeleton information (Fig 20).

IKAs can be used in multiple skeletons at the same time.

To apply a skeleton to a mesh, make the root IKA the parent of the mesh and select the USE SKELETON option when prompted.

→ *You may notice that the mesh doesn't update immediately when you make changes to the skeleton. You can force an update by changing the frame. They easiest way to do this is to press RIGHTARROW followed by LEFTARROW.*

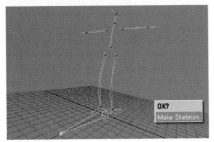

Figure 20

You can adjust the deformation radius of the skeleton elements by adjusting the Deform Max Dist and Deform Weight entries in the root bone's edit menu accessed with F9 (Fig. 21). The Max Dist is measured in grid units and refers to the diameter of the effect (rather than the radius).

Any skeleton object that has a Deform Max Dist of 0 will affect the entire mesh. This is usually not desirable, so each item in the skeleton should have a distance specified.

Avoid setting the deformation distances too high or limbs may affect vertices that they normally shouldn't be able to reach. It is better to set the distance too low and to compensate with extra deformation objects.

	Deform Max Dist	Deform Weight
Torso :	3.00	0.010
LegR (0):	1.50	3.000
LegR (1):	2.00	2.000
LegR (2):	1.50	1.000
HeelR (0):	1.50	1.000
ToeR (0):	1.50	1.000
Ika (0):	3.00	1.500
Ika.003 (0):	3.00	1.000
LegL (0):	1.50	3.000

Figure 21

The deformation zone surrounding each IKA or Empty in a skeleton is an elliptical shape (Fig. 22). This radius can be non-uniformly scaled by scaling the object, or by adjusting the Deform Max Dist settings in the skeleton's EditWindow.

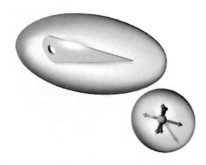

Figure 22

→ *Set the Max Dist for any empties in the skeleton to "2", and enable the "BOUNDS" TogBut in the empty's EditMenu. This makes it much easier to visualise the deformation zone of the empty. To change the size or shape of the empty's deformation, simply scale the empty and recalculate the skeleton. It is not necessary to recalculate the skeleton after making changes to the Deform Max Dist or Deform Weight entries in a skeleton although you may not see the changes until the frame changes.*

You can add bones to a skeleton by selecting all of the IKAs you wish to use (including all of the old ones), making sure that the root bone is highlighted, and pressing CTRL+K.

Before deleting a bone, or if you wish to remove one from a skeleton, you must select all of the skeleton's IKAs except for the one you wish to remove, and recalculate the skeleton. Fig. 23 shows the spinal chain being removed. If you simply delete a bone, the skeleton's deformation weight and distance settings will be lost and you will have to manually enter them again.

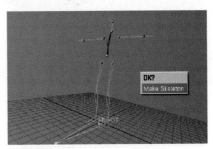

Figure 23

If you change the rest position of any of the existing bones, be sure to recalculate the skeleton. Note that when the skeleton is recalculated, any meshes that use the skeleton as a parent will reset to their rest positions. Make sure you only recalculate the skeleton when it is in its rest position, or else you will find that the skeleton and the mesh are no longer in sync with each other.

Depending on your character's design, it may make sense to calculate more than one skeleton. For example, the lower body and feet could use a different skeleton than the upper body. Since Blender normally only allows a single parent per object however, you must have designed your character so that the upper and lower body are separate objects.

Fig. 24 shows the two skeletons, represented by different colours. The ROOT bone contains the deformation information for the lower half of the body, while the spinal chain contains the information for the upper half.

The advantage to this method is that you can isolate deformations to specific parts of the body: moving the legs will not cause bending in any part of the upper body.

Figure 24

Animating

Move or rotate the entire character by manipulating the ROOT bone.

You can control most of the character's limbs by simply moving the control empties and setting LOC keys for them with IKEY >>LOC. This is easiest if you hide all layers except for the ones containing the control empties and the IKA skeleton.

Certain controls such as the Shoulder Roll empties may require ROT keys instead of LOC keys. The Pelvis and the ROOT will require both LOC and ROT keys.

Setting LOC and ROT keys for the Pelvis empty allows you to add bounce to the character's movements, as well as twisting the torso relative to the placement of the feet. The Spine Target empty controls the amount of bend in the body itself.

IKAs that have been left in FK mode (such as the head and feet) may be manipulated directly. Usually you will only need to set ROT keyframes for these limbs.

→ *Try to avoid setting keys in more IPO curves than necessary. For example, don't set ROT keys for effector targets, and don't set LOC keys for roll empties. Never set keys for any IKAs that are being controlled by the empties (which should be all of them). A good way to simplify this process is to insert LOC and/or ROT keys for all controls as appropriate on the first frame. On all subsequent frames, insert AVAIL keys. Because all objects will only receive keys in IPO curves that already exist, you will not have to decide which type of key to insert for each control. If an object doesn't have any IPO curves (such as your IKAs), they will not be affected by the INSERT command.*

Conclusion

The hierarchy can become quite complex as you add more controllers and bones. Fig. 25 shows an outline of all of the elements present in the demo file included on the CDROM.

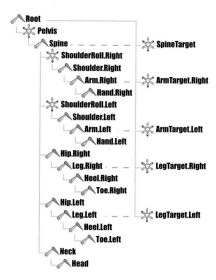

Figure 25

You can take a look at the final knight model with skeleton in the file KNIGHT_IKA.BLEND on the CDROM (fig. 26).

Figure 26

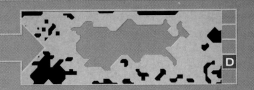

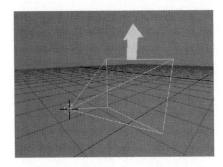

Blender always renders from the active Camera. You can have an unlimited number of Cameras, but only the Camera you activate with CTRL+NUMPAD_0 determines the display. Blender has a right-hand axis system. For a Camera display this means that the Y axis is up, the X axis runs horizontal and you look in the direction of the negative Z axis.

Each object in Blender can act as a camera (with CTRL+NUMPAD_0), but only a Camera block provides settings for the lens and clipping. The Spot Lamp is an exception to this. Now the "SpotSize" and shadow buffer limits are correctly displayed. Use this to precisely align a shadow Lamp and to adjust it. The command ALT+NUMPAD_0 always returns you to the last Camera object used.

Each 3DWindow can have its 'own' camera, apart from that of the Scene. This camera is not rendered. Use the 'lock' IconBut in the 3DHeader for this. If it is OFF, the active camera and layer data of the 3DWindow are no longer linked to the Scene. The LocalView option of a 3DWindow can also have its own - and thus temporary - camera.

Active camera's offer a number of extra options for transformations in the 3DWindow. These only work in camera view: NUMPAD_0.

Grab mode: now there is horizontal and vertical translation, from the point of view of the camera. Use the MMB toggle to zoom in and out.
Rotate mode: this allows you to align the camera with the MMB toggle.
Fly mode: (SHIFT+F). The mouse cursor jumps to the middle of the window.

The operation is as follows:
Mouse cursor movement determines the view direction
LMB click (repeated) fly faster
MMB click (repeated) fly slower
LMB+MMB: sets speed to zero.
CTRL: translation down (negative Z)
ALT: translation up (positive Z)
ESC: Camera back to the starting position; terminate Fly Mode.
SPACEKEY: Leave Camera in this position. Terminate Fly Mode. (Avoid looking straight up or down. This causes irritating turbulence.)

©2000 Oliver Saraja

The almost last step (see the next section for the last one) while working on a 3D scene is to render the stills or the animation. Depending on your needs and the media that you are producing for, you need to decide on a format for your output. For example, you may wish to make a still for printing in a high resolution and want to save it without any compression, but for a web-page you'll need to do a small JPEG-picture with high compression to cut off the loading time.

Still images

The command center for all rendering are the DisplayButtons F10. First look for the buttons defining the image size and choose here the size you need. Bear in mind, everything big costs in terms of the render time.

For quick test renderings, use the percent buttons. These will help you to render in a fraction of time!

Now render the picture by clicking the big "RENDER" button or by pressing the key F12. After the rendering process is complete you can hide the render window with F11 or ESC.

A big impact on image quality is the "OSA" option under the "RENDER" button. Activate it to produce anti-aliased pictures. It is recommended that you use this option in most cases. You can control the value of the anti-aliasing by choosing one of the number buttons below the "OSA" button. Bigger values result in higher render times but also in better image quality.

In the render window you can switch between two buffers with JKEY. This helps you compare different render options.

Now it is time to choose the output format for saving to disk. Blender offers some file types for stills that have differing capabilities.

Targa: A format that saves your picture compressed without any loss. Ideal for reusing or working in 2D paint programs. Transparency information (Alpha Channel) is preserved with this format (using the RGBA option).
Iris: Similar capabilities like Targa, but more common on SGI IRIX.
JPEG: One of the most common formats used on the internet. But be aware that JPEG format uses a 'lossy' compression! It produces very small files, but is not recommended if you're intending to process the images at a later time. The quality setting of 100% means that there are (normally) no visible compression artifacts for the naked eye.

Now hit F3 to save your image. You will get the FileWindow, where you can browse to a directory for your images and enter a filename in the lower TextButton. Now press ENTER twice to save your image. You will need to specify a filename extension if your operating system requires it.

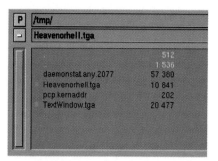

Animations

The way of saving animations is a little bit different than the way you save stills. In common with stills, it has a setting for the image size and for choosing an image format. When you choose an image format, Blender will save the animation as single numbered images to your hard disk. This is suitable for post-processing the pictures later. To create an animation in one part you can choose the AVI format, common for the Windows systems, or the SGI-Movie format. The AVI-format allows you to save JPEG compressed animation with all the advantages and disadvantages described above. The uncompressed AVI-format will generate big files not well suited for playing them or distribution, but ideal for processing in a computer-based video editing tool.

Before we press the big "ANIM" button, we need to tell Blender where to save our animation. This is done in the text input on the left of the DisplayButtons.

In the first input you can type in a valid path and the image name. You can also browse to a directory using the square button to the left of the "Pics" TextButton. Everything shown after the trailing directory seperator ("/", "\" on Windows) will be used as the image name. Blender will extend the name with the number of the actual image. You can activate the "Extensions" option to let Blender append a filename extension to your files.

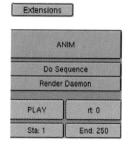

Define the range that should be rendered with "Sta:" and "End:" and hit "ANIM" to start the rendering process. After Blender is ready, use "PLAY" to view the saved animation.

Sequence editor

tutorial By B@rt Veldhuizen

Introduction

An often-underestimated function of Blender is the Sequence Editor. It is a complete video editing system that allows you to combine multiple video channels and add effects to them. Even though it has a limited number of operations, you can use these to create powerful video edits, especially when you combine it with the animation power of Blender!

This tutorial shows you how to prepare some material and create a stunning end result.

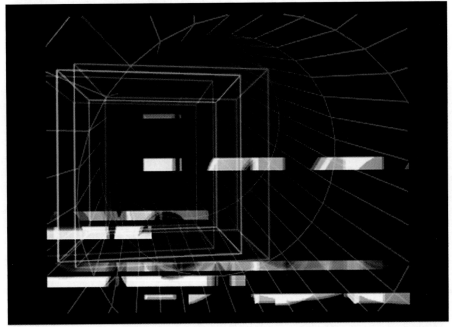

Final result

Animation 1: two cubes

Let's start with something simple and see where it leads. Start a clean Blender and remove the default plane. Split the 3DWindow and switch one of the views to the camera view with NUMPAD-0. In the top-view, add a cube and move it just outside of the dotted square that indicates the camera view.

→ *When you are planning to show your work on television, note the inner dotted square. Since not all tele-visions are the same, there is always a part of the picture that is 'cut off'. The inner square indicates which area is guaranteed to be viewable. The area between the dotted lines is referred to as the 'overscan area'.*

Moving the cube out of the camera view

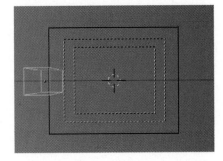

I want to create a simple animation of the cube where it moves into view, rotates once and then disappears. Set the animation end to 61 (set the 'End:' value in the Render Buttons window - F10) and insert a LocRot keyframe on frame 1 with IKEY - this will store both the location and the rotation of the cube on this frame.

Go to frame 21 (press ARROW_UP twice) and move the cube closer to the camera. Insert another keyframe. On Frame 41, keep the cube on the same location but rotate it 180 degrees and insert another keyframe.

Finally on frame 61 move the cube out of view, to the right and insert the last keyframe.

> ➡️ To check, select the cube and press KKEY to show all keyframes in the 3DWindow. If you want, you can easily make changes by selecting a keyframe with PAGEUP or PAGEDOWN (the active keyframe will be displayed as a brighter yellow colour than the other keyframes) and moving or rotating the cube. With the keys displayed, you do not need to re-insert the keyframes - they are automatically updated.

Defining keyframes for the cube

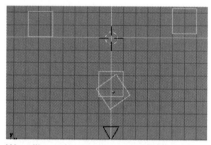

We will need two versions of the animation: one with a solid material and one with a wireframe. For the material, I have used plain white and I have added two bright lamps - a white one and a blue one with an energy value of two.

For the wireframe cube, set the material type to 'Wire' and change the colour to green.

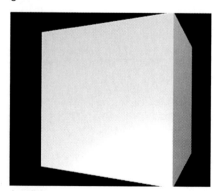

A solid ...

... and a wireframe cube

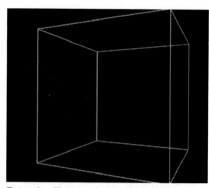

Enter the filename in the 'Pics' field of the Render Buttons window (F10).

Set the animation output filename.

Render the animations and save them to disk as AVI files - use AVI JPG if you are short on disk space. If not, use AVI RAW for higher quality. First render the animation with the white material and save it as cube_solid.avi. Then change the material to the green wireframe, render the animation again, and save the result as cube_wire.avi.

Press the ANIM button to start rendering.

Set the resolution and the number of frames and press 'Anim'

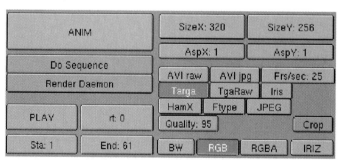

Sequence 1: delayed wireframes

The first sequence will use only two wireframe animations to create an interesting effect. I will create multiple layers of video, give them a small time offset, and then add them together. This will simulate the glowing effect that you see on radar screens.

Start a clean Blender file and change the 3DWindow to a Sequence Editor window by pressing SHIFT-F8, or by selecting the Sequence Editor icon from the window header.

Add a movie to the window by pressing SHIFT-A and selecting 'Movie'. From the FileSelectWindow, select the wireframe cube animation that you made before.

Adding a video strip

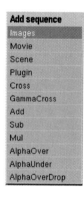

After you have selected and loaded the movie file, you will see a blue strip that represents it. After adding a strip, you are automatically in grab mode. The start and end frame are now displayed in the bar.

Take a closer look at the Sequence Editor screen. Depicted horizontally you can see the time value. Vertically, you can see the video 'channels'. Each channel can contain an image, a movie, or an effect. By layering different channels on top of each other, and applying effects, you can mix different sources together. If you select a video strip, its type, length, and filename will be printed at the bottom of the window.

Grab your video strip and let it start at frame 1. Place it in channel 1.

→ You can add lead-in and lead-out frames by selecting the triangles at the start and end of the strip (they will turn purple) and dragging them out. In the same way, you can define the length of a still image.

Placing the strip.

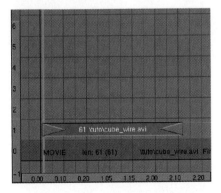

Duplicate the movie layer with SHIFT-D, place it in channel 2 and shift it one frame to the right. You now have two layers of video on top of each other, but only one will display. To mix the two layers you need to apply an effect to them.

Select both layers and press SHIFT-A. Select ADD from the requester that pops up.

Mixing two video strips

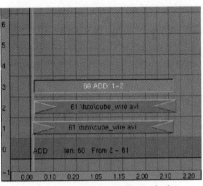

Now split the sequence editor window and select the image button in the header. This will activate the automatic preview. If you select a frame in the sequence editor window with the strips, the preview will be automatically updated (with all the effects applied!).
If you press ALT-A in the preview window, Blender will play back the animation. (Note: rendering of effects for the first time takes up a lot of processing time, so don't expect a realtime preview!).

→ If you do not like the separate render window, switch to the Render Buttons (F10) and select DispView in the bottom left.

Adding a preview window

Now it's time to add a little more mayhem to this animation! Duplicate another movie layer and add it to the ADD effect in video channel 3. Repeat this once and you will have four wireframe cubes in the preview window.

All the cubes have the same brightness, but I would like to have a falloff in brightness. This is easily arranged. Open an IpoWindow somewhere (SHIFT-F6) and select the sequence icon in the header.

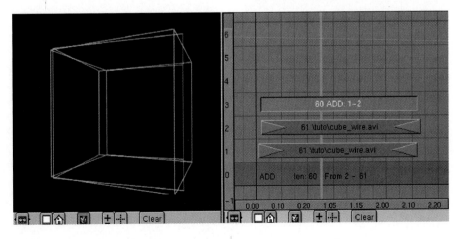

Select the first add strip (the one in channel 3), hold down CTRL and LMB click in the IpoWindow on a value of 1. This sets the brightness of this add operation to maximum. Repeat this for the other two add strips, but decrease the value a bit for each of them in turn.

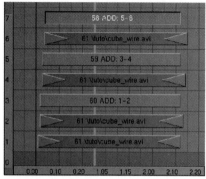

Defining the brightness of a layer with an Ipo

Depending on the ADD values that you have just set, your result should look something like this:

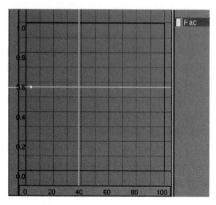

Four wireframe cubes combined.

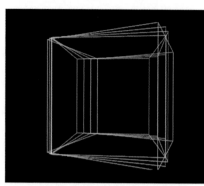

Now you already have 7 strips and we have only just begun on our animation, so you can imagine just how quickly the screen can become overcrowded! To make the project more manageable, select all strips (AKEY and BKEY work here, too), press MKEY, and press ENTER or click "Make Meta". The strips will now be combined into a meta-strip, and can be copied or moved as a whole.

With the meta-strip selected, press N and enter a name. Here I have used 'Wire/Delay'.

Named META strip

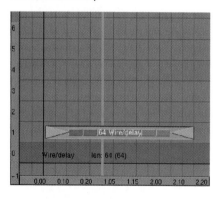

Animation 2: delayed solid cubes.

Now it is time to use some masks. I want to create two areas in which the animation plays back with a 1-frame time difference. This creates a very interesting glass-like visual effect.

Start by creating a black and white image like this one. You can use a paint pro- gram, or you can do it in Blender. The easiest way to do this in Blender is to create a white material with an emit value of 1. In this way, you do not need to set up any lamps. Save the image as mask.tga.

Animation mask

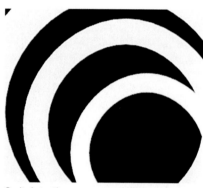

Switch to the sequence editor and move the meta-strip (that we made before) out of the way. We will reposition it later. Add the animation of the solid cube (SHIFT+A, 'Movie'). Next, add the mask image. By default, a still image will get a length of 50 frames in the sequence editor. Change it to match the length of the cube animation by dragging out the arrows on the side of the image strip with the RMB.

Now select both strips (hold down SHIFT), press SHIFT+A, and add a SUB (subtract) effect.

Subtracting the mask from the video

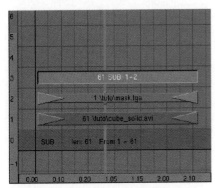

In the preview window you will now see the effect; the areas where the mask is white have been removed from the picture.

This effect is ready now; select all three strips and convert them into a META strip by pressing MKEY.

Mask subtracted

Now do the same, except that this time you won't use the SUB effect but the MUL (multiply) effect. You will only see the original image where the mask image is white. Turn the three strips of this effect into a meta-strip again.

> Add the new strips next to the one from the previous steps - this makes previewing and editing much easier. You can always move them later.

Mask multiplied

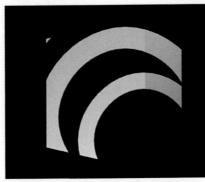

For the final step I have to combine the two effects together. Move one of the meta strips above the other one and give it a time offset of one frame. Select both strips and add an ADD effect.

Adding the two effects

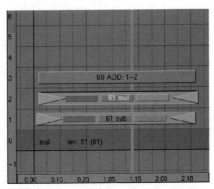

In the preview window, you can now see the result of the combination of the animation and the mask.

When you are ready, select the two meta-strips and the ADD effect and convert them into a new meta strip. (That's right! You can have meta-strips within meta-strips!)

> To edit the contents of a meta-strip, select it and press TAB. The background will turn a greenish yellow to indicate that you are working inside a meta strip. Press TAB again to return to normal editing.

Two time-shifted layers

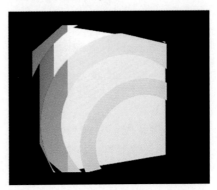

Animation 3: a tunnel

To begin with, I want to have a 3D 'tunnel' animation that I can use as a background effect. This is really simple to create. First, save your current work - you will need it later.

Start a new scene (CTRL-X) and delete the default plane. Switch to front view (NUMPAD1). Add a 20-vertex circle about 10 units under the z=0 line (the pink line in your screen).

Adding a 20-vertex circle

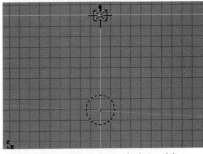

While still in editmode, switch to side view (NUMPAD3) and snap the cursor to the origin by locating it roughly at the x,y,z=0 point and pressing SHIFT-S. Select 'Curs->Grid'.

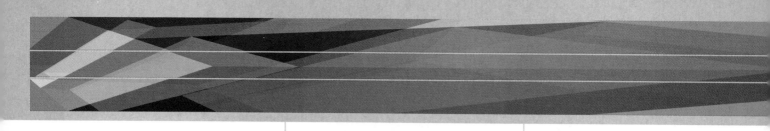

I want to turn the circle into a circular tube. For this, I will use the 'Spin' function. Go to the Edit Buttons window (F9) and enter a value of 180 in the 'Degr' field, and enter '10' in the 'Steps' field. Pressing 'Spin' will now rotate the selected vertices around the cursor at 180 degrees and in 10 steps. Leave EditMode (TAB).

Spinning the circle around the cursor

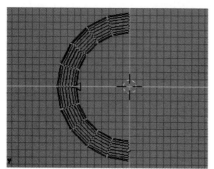

With the default settings, Blender will always rotate and scale around the object's center, displayed as a tiny dot. This dot is yellow when the object is unselected and pink when it is selected. With the cursor still in the origin, press the 'Center Cursor' button in the Edit Buttons window to move the object center to the current cursor location. Press RKEY and rotate the tube 180 degrees around the cursor.

Now it's time to move the camera into the tunnel. Open another 3DWindow and switch it to the camera view (NUMPAD+0). Position the camera in the side view window to match the screenshot- the camera view will be automatically updated.

➡ *If not all of the edges of the tunnel are showing, you can force Blender to draw them by selecting 'All Edges' in the Edit Buttons window (F9).*

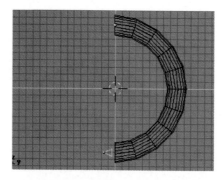

Moving the camera into the tunnel

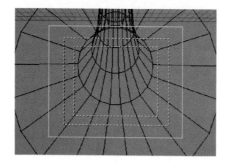

To make things a little easier, I want to render this as a looping animation. I can then add as many copies of it as I wish to the final video compilation.

There are two things to keep in mind when creating looping animations.
1 Make sure that there is no 'jump' in your animation when it loops. For this, you have to be careful when creating the keyframes and when setting the animation length. Create two keyframes: one with the current rotation of the tube on frame 1, and one with a rotation of 90 degrees (hold down CTRL while rotating!) on frame 51. In your animation, frame 51 is now the same as frame 1, so when rendering you will need to leave out frame 51 and render from 1 to 50.
2 To get a linear motion, you need to remove the ease-in and ease-out of the rotation. These can be seen in the Ipo window of the tube after inserting the rotation keyframes. Select the rotation curve, enter EditMode and select all vertices and press VKEY ('Vector') to change the curve into a linear one.

Removing the ease-in and ease-out of the animation

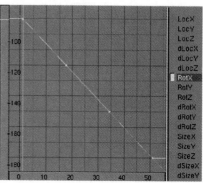

To create a more dramatic effect, select the camera while in camera view mode. The camera itself is displayed as the solid square. Press RKEY and rotate it a bit. If you now play back your animation it should loop seamlessly.

Rotate the camera to get a more dramatic effect

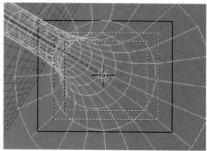

For the final touch, add a blue wireframe material to the tube and add a small lamp on the location of the camera. By tweaking the lamp's 'Dist' value (attenuation distance) you can make the end of the tube disappear in the dark without having to work with mist.

When you are satisfied with the result, render your animation and save it as 'tunnel.avi'.

A groovy tunnel:

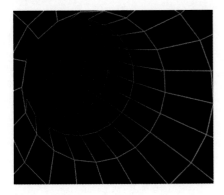

Using the tunnel as a backdrop

Reload your video compilation Blender file. The tunnel that we made in the last step will be used as a backdrop for the entire animation. To make it more interesting I will modify an ADD effect to change the tunnel into a pulsating backdrop. Prepare a completely black picture and call it 'black.tga' (try pressing F12 in an empty Blender file. Save with F3, but make sure that you have selected the TGA file format in the Render Buttons window). Add both black.tga and the tunnel animation and combine them with an ADD effect.

Setting up the backdrop effect

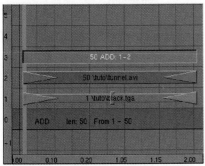

Now with the ADD effect selected, open an IpoWindow and select the Sequence Editor button in its header. From frame 1-50, draw an irregular line by using CTRL-LMB. Make sure that the values are between 0 and 1.

When you are ready, take a look at the result in a preview screen and change the animation into a meta-strip.

Save your work.

Adding randomness with a irregular Ipo

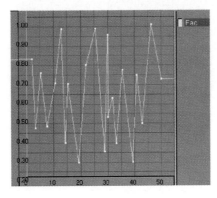

Animation 4: jumping logo

I love randomness and chaos, so let's create some more! Take a logo (I made one just by adding a text object) and let's make it jump through the screen. Again, the easiest way to do this is to add vertices directly into the IpoWindow (select a LocX, LocY or LocZ channel first), but this time you may need to be a bit more careful with the minimum and maximum values for each channel. Don't worry about the looks of this one too much - the next step will make is hardly recognizable anyway.

Save the animation as "jumpylogo.avi".

Jumping logo

Animation 5: particle bars

Our last effect will use an animated mask. By combining this with the logo of the previous step, I will achieve a streaking effect that introduces the logo to our animation. This mask is made by using a particle system.
To set one up, start a new Blender, switch to side view, add a plane to your scene and, while it is still selected, switch to the Animation Buttons window (F7). Select 'New effect' and then change the default effect (build) to 'Particles'. Change the system's settings as indicated in the figure.

Press TAB to enter EditMode, select all vertices and subdivide the plane twice by pressing WKEY and selecting 'Subdivide' from the requester.

Particle system settings

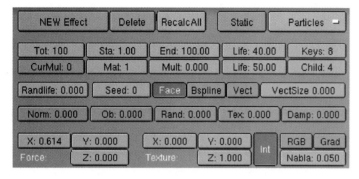

Next switch to front view and add another plane. Scale it along the X-axis to turn it into a rectangle (press SKEY and move your mouse horizontally. Then click the MMB to scale along the indicated axis only). Give the rectangle a white material with an emit value of one.

Now you'll need to change the particles into rectangles by using the dupliverts function. Select the rectangle, then the particle emitter and parent them. Select only the emiter and in the left part of the animation buttons window, select the DupliVerts button. Each particle is now replaced by a rectangle.

Dupliverted rectangles

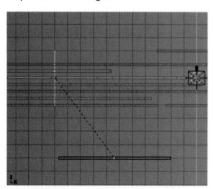

I will now add some mist as a quick 'hack' to give each of the rectangles a different shade of gray. Go to the WorldButtons window, click on the [-] button in its header and select 'Add New'. The world settings will now appear.

By default, the sky will now be rendered as a gradient between blue and black. Change the horizon colours (HoR, HoG, HoB) to black.

Setting up mist

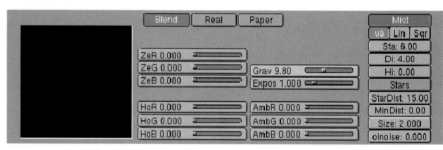

To activate rendering of mist, activate the Mist button in the middle of the screen. When using mist, you will have to indicate the distance from the camera that it will work. Select the camera, switch to the EditButtons, and enable 'ShowLimits'. Now switch to top view and return to the World Buttons window. Tweak the Sta: and Di: (Start, Distance) parameters so that the mist covers the complete width of the particle stream.

Setting the mist parameters

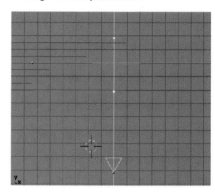

Set the animation length to 100 frames and render the animation to disk. Name the file "particles.avi".

Rendered particle rectangles

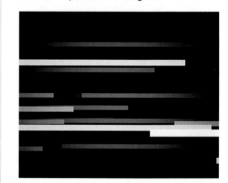

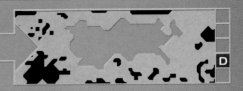

Combining the logo and the particle bars

By now you will know the drill: reload your compilation project file, switch to the Sequence Editor window and add both "particles.avi" and "logo.avi" to your project. Combine them together with a MUL effect. Since the logo animation is 50 frames and the particles animation is 100 frames, you'll need to duplicate the logo animation once and apply a second MUL effect to it.

Use the logo animation twice

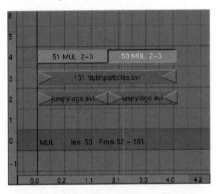

Combine these three strips into one meta-strip. If you're feeling brave you can make a few copies and give them a small time offset, just like with the wireframe cube.

The particles animation combined with the logo animation

Animation 6: zooming logo

If you choose to combine all of your animations completed so far, you'll get a really wild video compilation. But if this was to be your company's presentation, then perhaps you'd like to present the logo in a more recognisable way. The final part of our compilation will therefore concentrate on producing an animation of the logo that zooms in very slowly. Prepare this one and save it as "zoomlogo.avi". Also prepare a white picture and save it as "white.tga".

I will now use the cross effect to make a rapid transition from black to white, then from white to our logo animation. Finally, a transition to black will conclude the compilation.

Start off by placing black.tga in channel 1 and white.tga in channel 2. Make them both 20 frames long. Select them both and apply a cross effect. The cross will gradually change the resulting image from layer 1 to layer 2. In this case, the result will be a transition from black to white.

Black-white transition

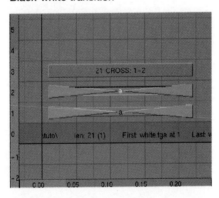

Next, add a duplicate of white.tga to layer 1 and place it directly to the right of black.tga. Make it about half as long as the original. Place the logo zoom animation in layer 2 and add a cross effect between the two. At this point, the animation looks like a white flash followed by the logo zoom animation.

White-video transition

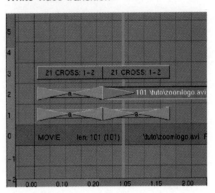

The last thing that you'll need to do is to make sure that the animation will have a nice transition to black at the very end. Add a duplicate of black.tga and apply another cross effect. When you are ready, transform everything into a meta-strip.

Video-black transition

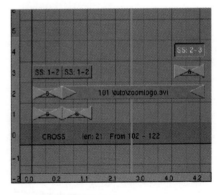

Assembling everything created so far

Now, let's add some of the compilations that we have made so far, and take a look at the work so far. The most important thing to keep in mind while you're creating your final compilation, is that when rendering your animation, the sequence editor only 'sees' the top layer of video. This means that you have to make sure that it is either a strip that is ready to be used, or it should be an effect like 'Add' that combines several underlying strips.

The foundation of the compilation will be the fluctuating tunnel. Add some duplicates of the tunnel meta-strip and place them in channel one. Combine them into one meta-strip. Do not worry about the exact length of the animation yet; you can always duplicate more tunnel strips.

On top of that, place the delayed wireframe cube in channel 2. Add channel 1 to channel two and place the add effect in channel 3.

Combining the tunnel and the wireframe cube

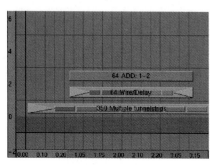

Now I'd like to add the solid cube animation. Place it in channel 4, overlapping the wireframe animation in channel 2. Add it to the tunnel animation in layer one. This is where things are starting to get a little tricky; if you choose to leave it like this, the animation in channel 5 (the solid cube together with the tube) will override the animation in channel 2

(the wireframe cube) and the wireframe cube will become invisible as soon as the solid cube shows up. To solve this, add channel 3 to channel 5.

You will often need to apply some extra add operations to fix missing parts of a video. This will most likely become apparent after you have rendered the final sequence.

Combining the tunnel, wireframe and solid cube.

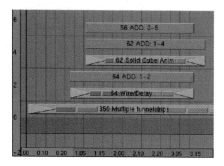

Slide the Sequence Editor window a little bit to the left and add the meta-strip with the particle/logo animation in it. Place this strip in layer 2 and place an add effect in layer 3. For some variation, duplicate the wireframe animation and combine it with the add in layer 3.

Adding the particle/logo animation

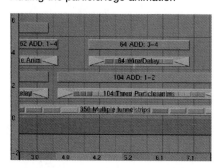

Now go to the end of the tunnel animation strip. There should be enough space to put the logo zoom animation at the end and still have some space left before it. If not, select the tunnel strip, press TAB and add a duplicate of the animation to

the end. Press TAB again to leave meta edit mode.

Adding the logo zoom animation

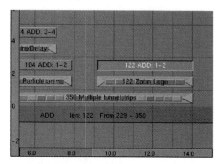

Since I still have some space left, I'll add a copy of the solid cube animation. To get it to display correctly, you'll have to apply two add channels to it: one to combine it with the particle logo animation, and one to combine it with the logo zoom animation.

Adding one last detail

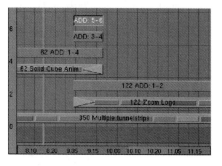

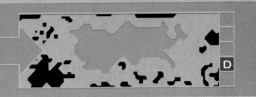

The complete sequence

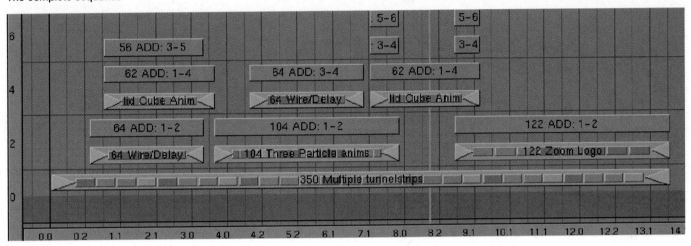

Conclusion

You are now ready to render your final video composition. To tell Blender to use the Sequence Editor information while rendering, select the 'Do Sequence' button in the Render Buttons window.

After this, rendering and saving your animation works as before.

After having persevered with this tutorial, I hope that you can now see that creating impressive video clips with Blender is a relatively easy task. It may take a bit of planning, but the tools are very flexible and fast to use.

If you want to take Blender's abilities a step further, you can explore the sequence editor plug-in possibilities. With these you can write your own filters in C and apply them to your animation. Some great stuff, like depth blur and Gaussian blur, has already been posted on our web site. Be sure to check them out.

Well that's it from me - I do hope you enjoyed your visit "Sequence Editor Land" and I wish you lots of fun with Blender.

B@rt

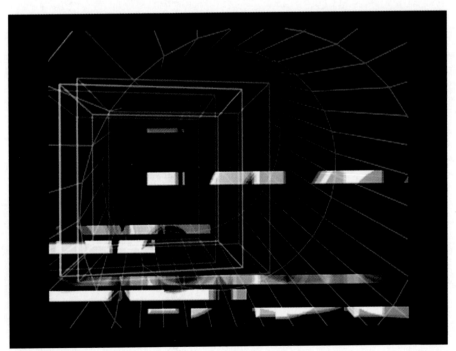

The final result

Particle effects

Chapter 10
Particle effects

The particle system of Blender is fast, flexible, and powerful. Every Mesh-object can serve as an emitter for particles. Halos (a special material) can be used as particles and with the Duplivert option, so can objects.

These dupliverted objects can be taken from every type of Blender objects, for example Mesh-objects, Curves, Meta-balls, and even Lamps. Particles can be influenced by a global force to simulate physical effects, like gravity or wind.

With these possibilities you can generate smoke, fire, explosions, fireworks, flocks of birds, or even schools of fish. With static particles you can generate fur, grass, and even plants.

1 Reset Blender to the default scene, or make a scene with a single plane added from the topview. This plane will be our particle emitter. Rotate the view so that you get a good view of the plane and the space above it.

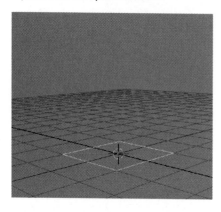

2 Switch to the AnimButtons (F7) and click the button "NEW Effect" in the middle part of the window. Change the appearing MenuButton from "Build" to "Particles". The ParticleButtons appear.

Find below the highlighted parameters which we will be using in the next steps.

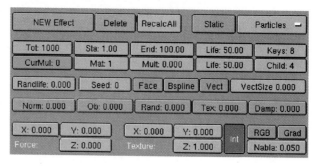

3 Increase "Norm:" to 0.100 with a click on the right part of the button or use SHIFT-LMB to enter the value by keyboard.
4 Play the animation by pressing ALT-A with the mouse over the 3DWindow. You will see a stream of particles ascending vertically.

Congratulations - you have just generated your first particle-system in a few easy steps!

To make the system a little bit more interesting, I will give you a few more hints:

1 The parameter "Tot:" controls the overall count of particles. On modern speedy CPUs you can increase the particle count without noticing a major slowdown.
2 You can change the lifetime of the particles with the "Life:" in the first row of the buttons.
3 The "Rand:" value makes the particles appear randomly. Try a value of 0.100 in your scene.
4 Use the "Force:" values to simulate wind or gravity. A "Force: Z:" value of 0.100 will make the particles fall to the ground, for example.
5 "Sta:" and "End:" control the time (in frames) in which particles are generated.

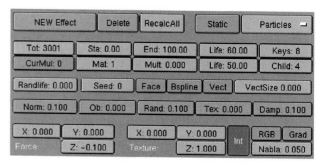

This should be enough to get you started, but don't be afraid to touch some of the other parameters while you're experimenting. We will cover them in detail in the following tutorials.

Maybe you've tried to render a picture from our example above. If the camera was aligned correctly, you would have seen a black picture with white blobby spots on it. This is the standard Halo-material that Blender assigns to a newly generated particle system.

Position the camera so that you get a good view of the particle system. If you want to add a simple environment, remember also to add some lights. The Halos are rendered without light, but other objects need lights.

Go to the MaterialButtons (F5) and add a new material for the emitter if none have been added so far. Click the Button "Halo" from the middle palette.

The MaterialButtons change to the HaloButtons. Choose "Line", and adjust "Lines:" to a value of your choosing (you can see the effect directly in the Material-Preview). Decrease "HaloSize:" to 0.30, and choose a colour for the Halo and for the lines.

You can now render a picture with F12, or a complete animation and see thousands of stars flying around.

Now select the object, then SHIFT-RMB the emitter and make it the parent of the cube using CTRL-P. Select the emitter alone and check the option "DupliVerts" in the AnimationButtons (F7). The dupliverted cubes will appear immediately in the 3DWindow.

You can also see that I have checked the option "Vect" in the particle-parameters, which causes the dupli-objects to follow the rotation of the particles, resulting in a more natural motion.

Take care to move the original object out of the cameraview, because it will be rendered also.

Objects as particles

It is very easy to use a real object as particles. Start by creating a cube, or any other object you like, in your scene. It's worth thinking about how powerful your computer is as we are going to have as many objects as "Tot:" indicates, in the scene. Scale the newly created object down so that it matches the general scene scale.

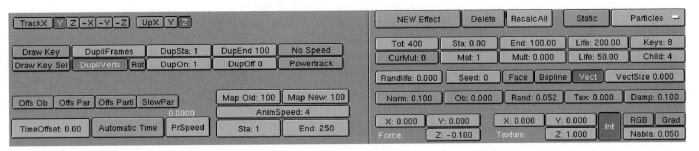

The Blender particle system is very useful for making realistic fire. This could be a candle, a campfire, or a burning house. It's useful to consider how the fire is driven by physics. The flames of a fire are hot gases.

They will rise because of their lower density when compared to the surrounding cooler air. Flames are hot and bright in the middle, and they fade and become darker towards the perimeter of their area.

Load the scene "campfire00.blend" from the CDROM. It contains a simple setup for our fire.

The particle system

Add a plane into the middle of the stone-circle. This plane will be our particle-emitter. Subdivide the plane once. You now can move the vertices to a position on the wood where the flames (particles) should originate.

Now go to the AnimationButtons F7 and add a new particle effect to the plane. The numbers given here should make for a realistic fire in the scene loaded from the CDROM. If you choose to build your own scene from scratch then some modification may be necessary.

negative (-0.008) as this will result in a fire that has a bigger volume at its basis. Use a "Force: Z:" of about 0.200. If your fire looks too slow, this is the parameter to adjust.
Make "Damp:" to 0.100 to slow down the flames after a while.
Activate the "Bspline"-button. This will use an interpolation method which gives a much more fluid movement.
To add some randomness to our particles, adjust the "Rand:"-parameter to about 0.014. Use the "Randlife:" parameter to add randomness in the lifetime of the particles; a really high value gives here a lively flame.
Use about 600-1000 particles in total for the animation ("Tot:").

In the 3DWindows, you will now get a first impression of how realistically the flames move. But the most important thing for our fire will be the material.

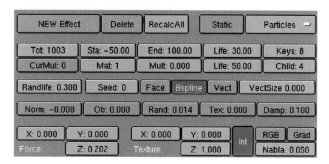

To have the fire burning from the start of the animation make "Sta:" negative. For example, try -50. The value of "End:" should reflect the desired animation length.
The "Life:" of the particles can stay at 50 for now. We will use this parameter later to adjust the height of the flames.
Make the "Norm:" parameter at bit

The fire-material

With the particle emitter selected, go to the MaterialButtons F5 and add a new material. Make the new material a halo-material by activating the "Halo"-button. Also, activate "HaloTex", located just below this button. This allows us to use a texture later.

Give the material a fully saturated red colour with the RGB-sliders. Decrease the Alpha value to 0.700; this will make the flames a little bit transparent. Increase the "Add"-slider up to 0.700, so the Halos will boost each other, giving us a bright interior to the flames, and a darker exterior.

A test rendering will now display a nice fire. But we still need to make the particles fade out at the top of the fire. We can achieve this with a material animation of the "Alpha" and the "HaloSize".

An animation for a particle material is always mapped from the first 100 frames of the animation to the lifetime of a particle. This means that when we fade out a material in frame 1 to 100, a particle with a lifetime of 50 will fade out in that time.

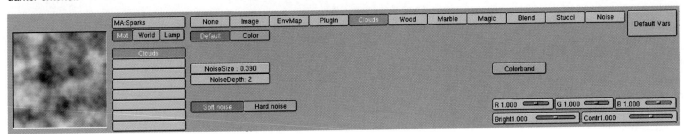

When you now do a test render, you will only see a bright red flame. To add a touch more realism, we need a texture. While the emitter is still selected, go to the TextureButtons F6. Add a new Texture and select the "Cloud"-type. Adjust the "NoiseSize:" to 0.600.

Go back to the MaterialButtons F5 and make the texture-colour a yellow colour with the RGB sliders on the right side of the material buttons. To stretch the yellow spots from the cloud texture decrease the "SizeY" value down to 0.30.

Be sure that your animation is at frame 1 (SHIFT-LEFTARROW) and move the mouse over the MaterialWindow. Now press IKEY and choose Alpha from the appearing menu. Advance the frame-slider to frame 100, set the "Alpha" to 0.0 and insert another key for the "Alpha" with IKEY. Switch one Window to an IPOWindow. Activate the MaterialIPOs by clicking on the sphere-icon in the IPOHeader. You will see one curve for the Alpha-channel of the Material.

This explosion is designed to be used as an animated texture, for composing it with the actual scene or for using it as animated texture. For a still rendering, or a slow motion of an explosion, we may need to do a little more work in order to make it look really good. But bear in mind, that our explosion will only be seen for half a second.

As the emitter for the explosion I have choosen an IcoSphere. To make the explosion not too regular, I deleted patterns of vertices with the circle select function in EditMode. For a specific scene it might be better to use an object as the emitter, which is shaped differently, for example like the actual object you want to blow up.

My explosion is composed from two particle systems, one for the cloud of hot gases and one for the sparks. I took a rotated version of the emitter for generating the sparks. Additionally, I animated the rotation of the emitters while the particles were being generated. Take a look at the scene "Explosion00.blend" for the setup.

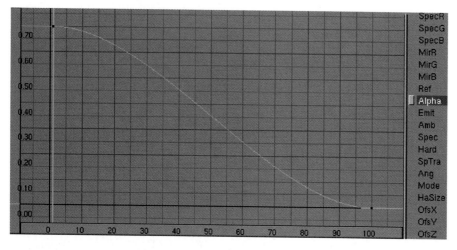

Now you can render an animation. Maybe you will have to fine-tune some parameters like the life-time of the particles. You can add a great deal of realism to the scene by animating the lights (or use shadow-spotlights) and adding a sparks particle-system to the fire. Also recommended is to animate the emiter in order to get more lively flames, or use more than one emitter.

A scene using some of these tricks can be found on the CDROM, as "campfire05.blend", and as a rendered animation.

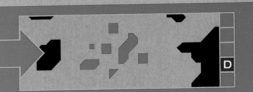

The materials

The particles for the explosion are very straightforward halo materials, with a cloud texture applied to add randomness.

Material for the explosion cloud

Material for the sparks

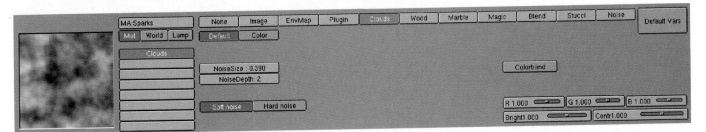

Animate the Alpha-value of the Haloparticles from 1.0 to 0.0 at the first 100 frames. This will be mapped to the life-time of the particles, as is usual. Notice the setting of "Star" in the sparks material. This shapes the sparks a little bit. We could have also used a special texture to achieve this, however, in this case setting "Star" is the easiest option.

The particle-systems

Particle system for the cloud

Particle system for the sparks

As you can see in the images, the parameters are basically the same. The difference is the "Vect" setting for the sparks, and the higher setting of "Norm:" which causes a higher speed for the sparks. I also set the "Randlife:" for the sparks to 2.000 resulting in an irregular shape.

I suggest that you start experimenting, using these parameters to begin with. The actual settings are dependent on what you want to achive. Try to add more emitters for debris, smoke, etc.

A button we have not used so far is the "CurMul:" button, located with the particle buttons. The whole third line of buttons is related to this. Load the scene "Fireworks00.blend" from the CDROM, and add a particle system to the plane.

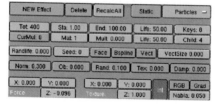

Adjust the parameters so that you get some particles flying into the sky, then increase the value of "Mult:" to 1.0. This will cause 100% of the particles to generate child particles when their life ends. Right now, every particle will generate four children. So we'll need to increase the "Child:" value to about 90. You should now see a convincing firework made from particles, when you preview the animation with ALT-A.

When you render the firework it will not look very impressive. This is because of the standard halo material that Blender assigns. Consequently, the next step is to assign a nice material.

Ensure that you have the emiter selected and go to the MaterialButtons F5. Add a new material with the MenuButton, and set the type to "Halo".

Material 1

I have used a pretty straightforward halo material; you can see the parameters in the figure "Material 1". The rendered animation will now look much better.

While the emiter is selected go to the EditButtons F9 and add a new material index by clicking on the "New" button.

Now switch back to the MaterialButtons. You will see that the material data browse in the header has changed colour to blue. The button labeled "2" indicates that this material is used by two users. Now click on the "2" button and confirm the popup. Rename the Material to "Material 2" and change to the colour of the halo and the lines.

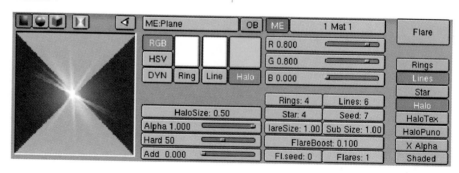

Material 2

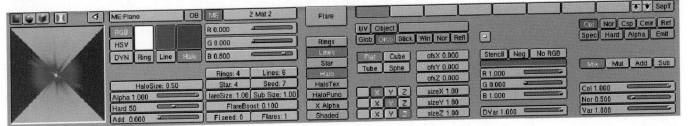

Switch to the particle parameters and change the "Mat:" button to "2". Render again and you see that the first generation of particles is now using the first material and the second generation the second material. This way you can have up to 16 (that's the maximum of material indices) materials for particles.

→ *In addition to changing materials you also can use the material IPOs to animate material settings.*

In this tutorial, we will create a particle system that emits real objects. This kind of particle system can be used to make schrapnels for explosions, or animate groups of animals. We will use the fish from the UV-Texturing tutorial, to create a shoal of fish that can be used to add some life and motion to underwater scenes.

Please load the scene "FlockOfFish00.blend" from the CDROM. It contains an underwater environment. By doing a render you will be able to view it.

The emitter

Switch to layer three (3KEY) to hide the layers with the environment, and add a plane in the sideview window at the 3DCursor location. Without leaving the EditMode, subdivide the plane two times and then leave EditMode.

Go to the AnimationButtons F7 and add a particle effect to the plane.

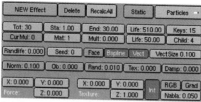

Set up your emitter as shown in the picture. I used 30 as the total number of particles, and I stopped the generation at frame 30. This is so that every second a new particle is generated. A small amount of randomness should be used. The lifetime of the particles should be long enough to make sure that the particles don't vanish in front of the camera. Activate the Bspline and Vect options; these become important later.

Now we have to load the fish from the UV-Texture tutorial. Press SHIFT-F1 to append the fish from the "UVTexFish.blend". It will appear textured in the camera view if you have set it to textured mode (ALT-Z). If it is too big, scale it down and then move it out of the camera view.

Select the fish and extend your selection to the particle emitter. Press CTRL-P to make the emitter the parent of the fish. Now select only the emitter and go to the AnimButtons (F7) and switch on Dupliverts.
Instances of the fish will appear at the position of every single particle. In case the fish is oriented incorrectly, select the base object and do a clear rotation with ALT-R. Now you can play back the animation in the camera view to see how the fish are moving. Experiment a bit with the particle setting until you get a realistic looking shoal of fish.

Using a Lattice to control the particles

Create a Lattice with the Toolbox. Scale it so that it just covers the shoal of fish. Switch to the EditButtons (F9) and set the "U:" resolution of the lattice to something approaching 10. Then select the emitter, extend your selection with the Lattice, and make it the parent of the emitter. You can now deform the Lattice and the particle system will follow. After you have changed something, leave EditMode and do a "Recalc All" for the particle system. This will update them.

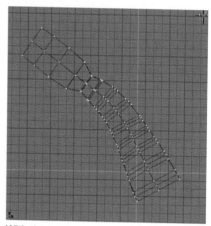

With the Lattice you can make curved paths for the fish, or make the shoal extend and join by scaling certain areas of the lattice.

Static particles are useful when making objects like fibers, grass, fur and plants.

Try making a little character, or just a ball, to test the static particles. I modelled a little guy I had sitting on my monitor a while ago. An emitter is not rendered, so duplicate the mesh (or whatever object type you used and convert (ALT-C) it into a mesh). I then did a fractal subdivide to the mesh to get some randomness into it. If you end up with a mesh that is too dense, use "Remove Doubles" with an increased limit. I also cut out parts with the circle select where I did not want to have fur.

Now, assign the particle system and, switch on the "Static" option.

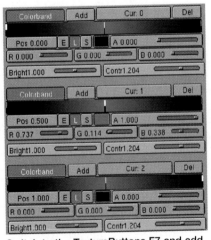

I used these parameters. With the combination of "Life" and "Norm" you can control the length of the hair. Use a force in a negative z-direction to let the hair bend. Check "Face" to generate the particles, not only on the vertices but also distributed on the faces. Also check "Vect"; this will generate fiber like particles. The step value defines how many particles per lifetime are generated. Set this to a lower value to get smoother curves for the particles, and be sure not to overlook setting the "Rand" value.

When you now render, you will get very blurred particles. The material used for static particles is very important, so add a material for the emitter in the MaterialButtons F5.

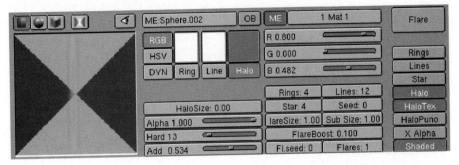

I use a very small Halosize (0.001). In the NumberButton you can't see that, so to adjust click the button with the LMB while holding SHIFT. Enable the "Shaded"-option to have the particles influenced by the lights in the scene, and then activate "HaloTex". We are going to use a texture to shape the hairs.

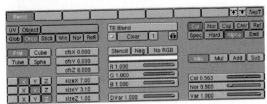

Switch to the TextureButtons F7 and add a new "Blend"-texture. Choose "Lin" as type. Activate the colourband option and adjust the colours as in the figure. You will get a nice blend, from transparent through to purple and back again to transparent.

Go back to the MaterialButtons and make sure that "Alpha" is activated in the texture mapping output on the right of the MaterialButtons. Then use "sizeX" and "sizeY" to shape the halo in the material preview to a small fiber.

If your fur is not dense enough, then increase the particle count with "Tot" or add more emitters. Also, change the particle parameters for these additional emitters a little so that you get some variation in the hairs.

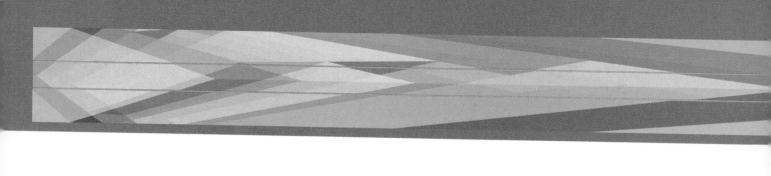

Python scripting

Chapter 11
Python scripting

The Python integration into Blender is an evolving subject. Therefore, all we can give you here is just a quick overview of the possibilities of Python in Blender.

The new API is closer to the data structure of Blender. It is strongly oriented on what you can visualise in the Oops-Window. There are classes for Scene, Object, Mesh, Curve etc., and functions to connect and create them.

Be sure to check the latest developments on our website: "www.blender.nl". General information about Python is available at "www.python.org".

Load the file "KeepOnGround.blend" from the CDROM. This scene contains a very simple script, which keeps objects above the ground plane. This script is simple enough to show the general use of Python in Blender and also quite useful.

```
001: # Keeps objects above the
     floor!
002:
003: import Blender
004:
005: if (Blender.bylink):
006: obj = Blender.link
007: if (obj.LocZ <0.0): obj.LocZ
     = 0.0
```

Line 001 is a comment, everything after the number sign "#" is ignored by the Python-interpreter. Empty lines are used to structure the source. A very important aspect in Python is that logical blocks are kept together with the same indention. It is best to use TABs for this. The first functional line is line 003: here we import the Blender module, and it provides us with the functionality to access Blender's functions.

The if clause in line 005 uses the "Blender.bylink" function to determine if the script is linked to an object. This linking is done on the *left* side of the ScriptButtons.

| Redraw | ⌐ | OnGround | 1 Scr: 1 | New | Del |

Select the desired object and click "New". Then fill in the name of the script in the textfield. With the MenuButton you now can choose between "FrameChanged" and "Redraw". "FrameChanged" will execute the script, while a frame change (when you preview the animation, switch frames manually or while rendering). "Redraw" will execute the script also when you move the object interactively. In the little scene from above, the script uses "Redraw", if you try to move the empty below the groundplane, the script will prevent this.

The code responsible for this functionality is in lines six to seven. In line 006 we get the object data from the Blender.link function and store it into the variable "obj". In line 007, we use a second if-clause to determine if the objects location on the z-axis is below zero and if that is true we set the objects z-location to zero.

Python scripting

This section describes the integration between Blender and the Python programming language. It is not intended to teach the Python language. Programmers familiar with C/C++/Java or other high-level and/or object-oriented languages should be able to pick up the language fairly quickly with the help of a reference and examples. Further information on Python can be found at www.python.org.

Basic Python

Python scripts can be edited in the internal text editor (accessed by Shift-F11), or edited externally and imported into the text editor.

Currently scripts can be executed in two ways, scripts can be executed directly by pressing Alt-P in the Text window, and can also be attached to DataBlocks to be executed automatically when certain events occur, see the ScriptLink section.

Modules

Documentation on the Blender/Python API's is split up into sections, each section has a general description of the module, as well as a description of the functions in the module, and the objects the module uses.

Blender - Main API Module

The Blender module contains all the other modules that are part of the Blender/Python API, as well as some general functions and variables.

Functions

Method: Blender.Get(request)
This is the general data access function, *request* is a string identifying the data which should be returned. Currently the Get function accepts the following requests,

'curframe' Return the current animation frame
'curtime'   Return the current animation time
'filename' Return the name of the last file

read or written
'version'   Return the running Blender version number

The curtime requests, returns a floating point value, which incorparates motion blur and field calculations, the curframe requests simply returns the integer value of the current frame.

Method: Blender.Redraw()
This function forces an immediate redraw of all 3DWindows in the current screen. It can be used to force display of updated information (for example when an IPO curve for an Object has been changed).

Variables

Boolean: Blender.bylink
Used to test if the script was executed by a scriptlink - see the ScriptLink section for more information.

Object: Blender.link
If the script was called by a scriptlink, this variable contains the object that the script was linked to. This variable only exists when scripts have been called by scriptlinks - see the ScriptLink section for more information.

String: Blender.event
If the script was called by a scriptlink this variable contains the name of the event that the script was called by. This variable only exists when scripts have been called by scriptlinks - see the ScriptLink section for more information.

Types - Blender declared types

This module holds the type objects for all of the Blender declared objects. These types can be compared with the types returned by the type(object) function.

Variables

BezTripleType
BlockType
BufferType
ButtonType
IpoCurveType

MatrixType
NMColType
NMFaceType
NMVertType
NMeshType
VectorType

NMesh - low level mesh access

The vertex editing functionality is planned for access in two ways, low and high level. Low level access is intended for programmers familiar with mesh editing and the data structures involved (and links between them) and who intend to write intensive modules to work with Blender. High level access is for people who do not want to spend the time to handle the basic data structures themselves, or only need a quick effect. Low level editing is completely independent of Blender, while high level editing uses and builds on Blender's features.

The NMesh module represents the first step towards providing vertex level access from Python.

Functions

Method: NMesh.GetRaw([name])
If *name* is specified Blender will try to return an NMesh derived from the Blender mesh with the same name, if a mesh with that name does not exist GetRaw returns None.

If *name* is not specified then a new empty NMesh object will be returned, otherwise it will attempt to return an NMesh derived from the Blender mesh with the same name, if a mesh with that name does not exist GetRaw returns None.

When the NMesh is created Blender will set the NMesh *name*, *has_col* and *has_uvco* based on the mesh read.

Method: NMesh.PutRaw(nmesh, [name, renormal])
If name is not given (or None) PutRaw will create a new Blender object and mesh, set the mesh data to match the *nmesh*, and return the created object.

If the name is given PutRaw will attempt to replace the Blender mesh of that name with the *nmesh*, and will return None (regardless of success or failure). If a mesh with the name is in Blender, but has no users the effects are as if the name was not given (i.e. an object will be created and returned.)

The renormal flag determines whether vertex normals are recalculated. It is generally only interesting to not recalculate the vertex normals if they have been specifically modified to achieve an effect.

The *nmesh.has_uvco* and *nmesh.has_col* flags are used to determine whether or not the mesh should be created with vertex colours and/or UV coordinates.

Method: NMesh.Vert ([x, y, z])
Returns a new NMVert object, created from the given *x, y, and z* coordinates. If any of the coordinates are not passed they default to 0.0.

Method: NMesh.Face()
Returns a new NMFace object.

Method: NMesh.Col ([r,g,b,a])
Return a new NMCol object created from the given *r, g, b,* and *a* colour components. If any of the components are not passed they default to 255.

Objects

NMeshType

"name"	name of the mesh this object was derived from
"verts"	list of NMVert objects
"faces"	list of NMFace objects
"mats"	list of material names
"has_col"	flag for whether mesh has mesh colours
"has_uvco"	flag for whether mesh has UV coordinates

The *name* field of the NMesh object allows scripts to determine what mesh the object originally came from when it is otherwise unknown, for example when the mesh has been obtained from an Objects.*data* field.

In order to keep mesh sizes low mesh colours and UV coordinates are only stored when needed; if a mesh has colours or UV coordinates when it is accessed by the GetRaw function it will have the *has_col* and *has_uvco* flags set accordingly. Similarly, before a mesh is put back into Blender with the PutRaw functions the *has_col* and *has_uvco* flags must be set properly.

The *mats* field contains a list of the names of the materials that are attached to the mesh indices. Note that this is not the same as the materials that are attached to objects. The PutRaw function will remake the material list, so this field can be used to switch the materials linked by the mesh.

The *verts* field should contain a list of all the vertices that are to be in the mesh. If a vertice is listed in a face, but not present in the *verts* list, it will not be present in the face.

NMFaceType

"v"	list of NMVert objects
"col"	list of NMCol objects
"mat"	material index number for face
"smooth"	flag indicating whether face is smooth

The v field is a list of NMVert objects, and not a list of vertice indices. If the face is to be part of an NMesh each of the objects should be in the *NMesh.verts* list. The vertices determine the face in clockwise ordering. Faces should have 2,3, or 4 vertices to be stored in a mesh, faces with 2 vertices form an edge, while faces with 3 or 4 vertices form a face (a triangle or quad).

The *col* field is a list of NMCols, this list always has a length of 4, with the NMCol matching up to the NMVert in the *v* list with the same index. Extra objects in the list (ie. if the face has

less than 4 vertices) are ignored. The *mat* field contains the material index for the face, if the face is part of an NMesh this value is used with the *NMesh.mats* list to determine the material for the face.

NMVertType

"index"	Vertice index
"co"	Coordinate vector
"uvco"	UV coordinate vector
"no"	Normal vector

If the vertice is from an NMesh that has been read with the GetRaw function the *index* field will be set to contain the index of the vertice within the array. This field is ignored by the PutRaw function, and exists only to allow simplification of some calculations relating to face->vertex resolution.

The *co, uvco* and *no* fields return a special object of VectorType, this object is used to interact efficiently with Blender data structures, and can generally be used as if it is a list of floating point values, except its length cannot be changed.

The *uvco* field contains the vertex UV coordinates for the mesh, these are the coordinates that are used by the Sticky mapping option. This field is a 3 member vector, but the last (Z) member is unused.

The *no* field can be used to alter the vertex normals of a mesh, to change the way some calculations are made (for example rendering). A flag must be passed to the PutRaw function in order to prevent the normals from being recalculated if they have been modified for this purpose. Note that the vertex normals will still be recalculated if the user enters editmode or performs other operations on the mesh, regardless of the flag passed to the PutRaw function.

NMColType

"r" Red colour component
"g" Green colour component
"b" Blue colour component
"a" Alpha colour component

Draw - The window interface module

The Draw module provides the basic function that lets Blender/Python scripts build interfaces that work inside Blender. The Draw module is broken into two parts, one part handles the functions and variables needed to give a script control of a window, and the second part allows scripts to use the Blender internal user interface toolkit (buttons, sliders, menus, etc.).

Blender/Python interfaces scripts (GUI scripts for short) essentially work by providing Blender with a set of callbacks to allow passage of events and drawing, and then the script takes control of the text window it was run from.

To initiate the interface the script must call the *Draw.Register* function to specify what script functions will be used to control the interface. Generally a draw and event function are passed, though either one can be left out.

Once the script has been registered, the draw callback will be executed (with no arguments) every time the window needs to be redrawn. Drawing uses the functions in the *Blender.BGL* module to allow scripts to have full control over the drawing process. Before drawing is initiated Blender sets up the OpenGL window clipping and stores its own state on the attribute stack, to prevent scripts from interfering with other parts of the Blender interface.

When the draw function is called the window matrix will be set up to be the window width/height, so the co-ordinate to pixel mapping is 1-1. Because Blender manages its windows internally, drawing should only take place inside the draw function, if an event must trigger drawing of some kind the event function should send a redraw event (see *Draw.Redraw*).

The script event function is called when the Blender window receives input events, and the script window has input focus (the mouse is in the window). The function is called with two arguments, the event and an extra value modifier, see the Events section below for more information.

Scripts can unregister themselves and return control to the Text editor by calling the Draw.Exit function. In the event that the script fails to provide a method to exit, the key combination *Ctrl-Alt-Shift-Q* will force a script to exit.

Events

The Draw module contains all the event constants that can be passed to a registered Python event callback. The following table lists the events that are currently passed, and the meaning of the extra value argument that is passed with the event.

Functions

Method: Draw()
Forces an immediate redraw of the active Python window, this function will return *after* the window has been redrawn.

Method: Exit()
Un-registers Python from controlling the windowing interface and returns the window control to the text editor.

Method: Redraw([after])
Adds a redraw event to the window event queue. If the *after* flag is not passed (or False) the window will receive the redraw event as soon as program control returns to Blender (ie. after the running function completes.) If the *after* flag is True the window will receive the event after all other input events have been processed. This allows a window to continuously redraw, while still receiving user input, and allowing the rest of the Blender program to receive input.

Event name(s)	Value meaning
____KEY (AKEY,F2KEY, etc.)	The value is 0 or 1, 0 means a key-release, 1 means a key-press.
PAD___ (PAD1, PADENTER, etc.)	The value is 0 or 1, 0 means a key-release, 1 means a key-press.
MOUSEX, MOUSEY	The value is the window coordinates of the mouse X/Y position.
LEFTMOUSE, MIDDLEMOUSE, RIGHTMOUSE	The value is 0 or 1, 0 means a button-release, 1 means a button-press.

The list of all events is quite long, and most are fairly obvious (AKEY, BKEY, CKEY,...) so they have been shortened to ____KEY and PAD___, to find the exact name of an event you can print the contents of the Draw module (or guess), print dir(Blender.Draw).

Redraw events are buffered internally, so that regardless of how many redraw events are on the queue, the window is only redrawn once per queue-flush.

Method: Register (draw, [event, button])
The Register function is the basis of the Python window interface. The function is used to pass three callbacks which to handle window events. The first function is the *draw* function, it should be a function taking no arguments, and it is used to redraw the window when necessary.

The second function is the *event* function, used to handle all of the input events. It should be a function taking two arguments, the first is the event number, and the second is the value modifier. See the Events section above for more information on what events are passed.

The third function is the *button* event function, which handles the events which are generated by the various button types.

Any of the functions can be passed as a None, and Blender will take a default action for events that are not handled by a callback. At least one function must be passed for the Register function to have any effect.

Method: Text(string)
Draws the *string* using the default bitmap font at the current GL raster position (use the glRasterPos functions to change the current raster position).

Button Functions

Method: Button (label, event, x, y, width, height, [tooltip])
Creates a new push Button. The button will be draw at the specified *x* and *y* coordinates with the specified *width* and *height*, and the *label* will be drawn on top. If a *tooltip* is specified it will be displayed when the user places his mouse over the button, assuming they have tooltips enabled.

When the button is pressed it will pass the event number specified by *event* to the Python's button event callback, assuming one was specified to the Draw.Register function.

Method: Create(value)
Returns a new Button object containing the specified *value*, the type of the Button (int, float, or string) will be determined by the type of the *value*.

Method: Menu(options, event, x, y, width, height, default, [tooltip]
Creates a new push Button. The button will be drawn at the specified *x* and *y* coordinates with the specified *width* and *height*. If a *tooltip* is specified it will be displayed when the user places his mouse over the button, assuming they have tooltips enabled.

The menu options are encoded in the *options* argument. Options are seperated by the '|' (Pipe) character, and each option consists of a name followed by a format code. Valid format codes are:
"%t" The option should be used as the title for the menu
"%xN" The option should set the integer N in the button value

The *default* argument determines what values will initially be present in the Button object, and which menu option will initially be selected.

When the menu item is changed the button value is set to the value specified in the selected menu option and the button will pass the event number specified by *event* to the Python's button event callback, assuming one was specified to the Draw.Register function.

For example, if the menu *options* argument is "Colour %t| Red %x1| Green %x2| Blue %x3", and the default is 2, then the menu will initially display "Green", and when the user selects the menu it will display 3 items ("Red", "Green", and "Blue") and the title "Colour". Selecting the "Red", "Green", or "Blue" options will cause the button

value to change to 1, 2, or 3 respectively, and the *event* will be passed to the button event callback.

Method: Number(label, event, x, y, width, height, initial, min, max, [tooltip])
Creates a new number Button. The button will be drawn at the specified *x* and *y* coordinates with the specified *width* and *height*, and the *label* will be drawn to the left of the input field. If a *tooltip* is specified it will be displayed when the user places his mouse over the button, assuming they have tooltips enabled.

The type of number button is determined by the type of the *initial* argument, if it is an int the number button will hold integers; if it is a float, the number button will hold floating point values. The value of the Button return will range between *min* and *max*, with the *initial* argument determining which value is set by default.

When the button is pressed it will pass the event number specified by *event* to the Python's button event callback, assuming one was specified to the Draw.Register function.

Method: Scrollbar (event, x, y, width, height, initial, min, max, [update, tooltip])
Creates a new scrollbar Button. The scrollbar will be drawn at the specified *x* and *y* coordinates with the specified *width* and *height*. If a *tooltip* is specified it will be displayed when the user places his mouse over the button, assuming they have tooltips enabled.

The type of scrollbar is determined by the type of the *initial* argument, if it is an int the scrollbar will hold integers, if it is a float the scrollbar will hold floating point values. The value of the Button return will range between *min* and *max*, with the *initial* argument determining which value is set by default.

When the scrollbar is repositioned it will pass the event number specified by *event* to the Python's button event callback, assuming one was specified to the

Draw.Register function. If the *update* argument is not passed (or True) then the events will be passed for every motion of the scrollbar, otherwise if the *update* argument is False the events will only be sent after the user releases the scrollbar.

Method: Slider (label, event, x, y, width, height, initial, min, max, [update, tooltip])
Creates a new slider Button. The button will be drawn at the specified *x* and *y* coordinates with the specified *width* and *height*, and the *label* will be drawn to the left of the input fields. If a *tooltip* is specified it will be displayed when the user places his mouse over the button, assuming they have tooltips enabled.

The type of slider button is determined by the type of the *initial* argument, if it is an int the slider button will hold integers, if it is a float the slider button will hold floating point values. The value of the Button return will range between *min* and *max*, with the *initial* argument determining which value is set by default.

When the slider is repositioned it will pass the event number specified by *event* to the Python's button event callback, assuming one was specified to the Draw.Register function. If the *update* argument is not passed (or True) then the events will be passed for every motion of the slider, otherwise if the *update* argument is False the events will only be sent after the user releases the slider.

Method: String(label, event, x, y, width, height, initial, length, [tooltip])
Creates a new string Button. The button will be drawn at the specified *x* and *y* coordinates with the specified *width* and *height*, and the *label* will be drawn to the left of the string input field. If a *tooltip* is specified it will be displayed when the user mouses over the button, assuming they have tooltips enabled.

The value of the Button returned will be a string, reflecting the current state of the toggle. The *initial* argument will determine which value is initially present in the

button. The *length* field specifies the maximum length string allowed to be entered in the button.

After the string has been edited it will pass the event number specified by *event* to the Python's button event callback, assuming one was specified to the Draw.Register function.

Method: Toggle(label, event, x, y, width, height, default, [tooltip])
Creates a new toggle Button. The button will be drawn at the specified *x* and *y* coordinates with the specified *width* and *height*, and the *label* will be drawn on top. If a *tooltip* is specified it will be displayed when the user places his mouse over the button, assuming they have tooltips enabled.

The value of the Button returned will be 0 or 1, reflecting the current state of the toggle. The *default* will determine which value is initially set.

When the button is pressed it will pass the event number specified by *event* to the Python's button event callback, assuming one was specified to the Draw.Register function.

Objects

ButtonType

"val" The current value of the button

Depending on the method with which the button was created the *val* field will have several different types, possible types are Int, Float, and String.

BGL - Blender OpenGL module

In order to allow scripts to draw sophisticated interfaces within Blender the BGL module has been included. It is essentially a flat wrapper around the entire OpenGL library, which allows programmers to use standard OpenGL tutorials and references for programming Blender/Python interface scripts.

The BGL module contains all the defines and functions for OpenGL with one exception. No extensions are supported, and no platform specific functions are supported. All function names remain the same as with the C OpenGL implementation, although in some cases this makes less sense, for example the ___f, ___i, ___s function variants are meaningless to Python.

The only exception to this rule is for functions that take pointer arguments. Since Python has no direct pointer access the BGL module includes a special type (Buffer) which essentially provides a wrapper around a pointer/malloc. Any OpenGL functions which take a pointer should be passed a Buffer object instead.

The BGL module is a flat wrapper, it performs no extra error checking or handling. This means that it is possible to cause crashes when using the module, namely when an OpenGL function is passed a Buffer object that is of the incorrect size.

Because Blender uses one OpenGL context, and the entire interface is drawn with OpenGL, it is important that scripts cannot inadvertently alter some critical state value. To effectively "sandbox" the scripts, during drawing Blender sets up the window to be drawn, and also pushes all OpenGL stack attributes onto the attribute stack. When the draw function returns the attributes are popped. It is important that BGL calls are only made during the draw function.

Functions

Method: Buffer (type, dimensions, [template])
This function creates a new Buffer object to be passed to OpenGL functions expecting a pointer. The *type* argument should be one of *GL_BYTE*, *GL_SHORT*, *GL_INT* or *GL_FLOAT* indicating what type of data the buffer is to store.

The *dimensions* argument should be a single integer if a one-dimensional list is to be created, or a list of dimensions if a multi-dimensional list is desired. For example, passing in [100, 100] would create a two-dimensional square buffer (with a total of 100*100=10,000 elements). Passing in [16, 16, 26] would create a three-dimensional buffer, twice as deep as it is wide or high (with a total of 16*16*32=8192 elements).

The *template* argument can be used to pass in a multi-dimensional list that will be used to initialise the values in the buffer, the *template* should have the same dimensions as the Buffer to be created. If no template is passed all values are initialised to zero.

Object

  BufferType

  "list" Returns the contents of the
        Buffer as a multi-dimensional list

The Buffer object can be indexed, assigned, sliced, etc. just like Python multi-dimensional list (list of lists) with the exception that its size cannot be changed.

Object - Object object access

The Object access module.

Functions

Method: Get([name])
If *name* is specified returns the Blender-object with the same name (or None if a match is not found).

If *name* is not specified returns a list of all the Object objects in the current scene.

Method: GetSelected()
Returns a list of all selected objects in the current scene. The active object is the first object in the list.

Method: Update(name)
Updates the object with the specified *name* during user-transformation. This is an experimental function for combating lag, mainly with regard to IKA being recalculated properly.

Objects

  BlockType

"name"	name of the blender object this object references
"block_type"	"Object"
"properties"	list of extra data properties
"parent"	link to the Objects' parent
"track"	link to the Object this object is tracking
"ipo"	link to the Ipo for the Object
"data"	link to the data for the Object
"math"	the object matrix
"loc"	the location coordinate vector
"dloc"	the delta location coordinate vector
"rot"	the rotation vector (angles are in radians)
"drot"	the delta rotation vector (angles are in radians)
"size"	the size vector
"dsize"	the delta size vector
"LocX"	X location coordinate
"LocY"	Y location coordinate
"LocZ"	Z location coordinate
"dLocX"	X delta location coordinate
"dLocY"	delta location coordinate
"dLocZ"	Z delta location coordinate
"RotX"	X rotation angle (in radians)
"RotY"	Y rotation angle (in radians)
"RotZ"	Z rotation angle (in radians)
"dRotX"	X delta rotation angle (in radians)
"dRotY"	Y delta rotation angle (in radians)
"dRotZ"	Z delta rotation angle (in radians)
"SizeX"	X size
"SizeY"	Y size
"SizeZ"	Z size
"dSizeX"	X delta size
"dSizeY"	Y delta size
"dSizeZ"	Z delta size
"EffX"	X effector coordinate
"EffY"	Y effector coordinate
"EffZ"	Z effector coordinate
"Layer"	object layer (as a bitmask)

The name, block_type, and properties fields are common to all BlockType objects.

The *loc*, *dloc*, *rot*, *drot*, *size*, and *dsize* fields all return a Vector object, which is used to interact efficiently with Blender data structures. It can generally be used as if it was a list of floating point values, but its length cannot be changed.

For the *parent*, *track*, *ipo*, and *data* fields if the object does not have one the data, or the data is not accessible to Python, the field returns None.

Lamp - Lamp object access
The Lamp access module.

Functions

Method: Get([name])
If *name* is specified returns the Lamp object with the same name (or None if a match is not found).

If *name* is not specified returns a list of all the Lamp objects in the current scene.

Objects

BlockType

"name"	name of the lamp this object references
"block_type"	"Lamp"
"properties"	list of extra data properties
"ipo"	link to the Ipo for the lamp
"R"	red light component
"G"	green light component
"B"	blue light component
"Energ"	lamp energy value
"Dist"	lamp distance value
"SpoSi"	lamp spot size
"SpoBl"	lamp spot blend
"HaInt"	lamp halo intensity
"Quad1"	lamp quad1 value
"Quad2"	lamp quad2 value

The name, block_type, and properties fields are common to all BlockType objects.

If the lamp does not have an Ipo the *Lamp.ipo* field returns None.

Camera - Camera object access

The Camera access module.

Functions

Method: Get([name])
If name is specified returns the Camera object with the same name (or None if a match is not found).

If name is not specified returns a list of all the Camera objects in the current scene.

Objects

BlockType

"name"	name of the camera this object references
"block_type"	"Camera"
"properties"	list of extra data properties
"ipo"	link to the Ipo for the camera
"Lens"	lens value for the camera
"ClSta"	clip start value
"ClEnd"	clip end value

The name, block_type, and properties fields are common to all BlockType objects.

If the camera does not have an Ipo the *Camera.ipo* field returns None.

Material - Material object access

The Material access module.

Functions

Method: Get([name])
If *name* is specified returns the Material object with the same name (or None if a match is not found).

If *name* is not specified returns a list of all the Material objects in the current scene.

Objects

BlockType

"name"	name of the material this object references
"block_type"	"Material"
"properties"	list of extra data properties
"ipo"	link to the Ipo for the material
"R"	red material colour component
"G"	green material colour component
"B"	blue material colour component
"SpecR"	red material specular component
"SpecG"	green material specular component
"SpecB"	blue material specular component
"MirR"	red material mirror component
"MirG"	green material mirror component
"MirB"	blue material mirror component
"Ref"	material reflectivity
"Alpha"	material transparency
"Emit"	material emittance value
"Amb"	material ambient value
"Spec"	material specular value
"SpTra"	material specular transparency
"HaSize"	material halo size
"Mode"	material mode settings
"Hard"	material hardness

The name, block_type, and properties fields are common to all BlockType objects.

If the material does not have an Ipo the *Material.ipo* field returns None.

World - World object access

The World access module.

Functions

Method: Get ([name])
If name is specified returns the World object with the same name (or None if a match is not found).

If name is not specified returns a list of all the World objects in the current scene.

Method: GetActive()
Returns the active world (or None if there isn't one)

Objects

BlockType

"name"	name of the world this object references
"block_type"	"World"
"properties"	list of extra data properties

"ipo"	link to the Ipo for the world
"HorR"	the red horizon colour component
"HorG"	the green horizon colour component
"HorB"	the blue horizon colour component
"ZenR"	the red zenith colour component
"ZenG"	the green zenith colour component
"ZenB"	the blue zenith colour component
"Expos"	the world exposure value
"MisSta"	the mist start value
"MisDi"	the mist distance value
"MisHi"	the mist height value
"StarDi"	the star distance value
"StarSi"	the star size value

The name, block_type, and properties fields are common to all BlockType objects.

If the world does not have an Ipo the *World.ipo* field returns None.

Ipo - Ipo object access

The Ipo access module.

Functions

Method: Get ([name])
If *name* is specified returns the Ipo object with the same name (or None if a match is not found).

If *name* is not specified returns a list of all the Ipo objects in the current scene.

Method: BezTriple()
Returns a new BezTriple object

Method: Eval (curve, [time])
Returns the value of the curve at the given *time*. If the *time* is not passed the current time is used.

Method: Recalc(ipo)

Recalculates the values of the curves in the given *ipo*, and updates all objects in the scene which reference the ipo with the new values.

Objects

BlockType

"name"	name of the Ipo this object references
"block_type"	"Ipo"
"properties"	list of extra data properties

"curves" list of IpoCurve objects making up this Ipo block

The name, block_type, and properties fields are common to all BlockType objects.

IpoCurveType

"name"	name of this ipo curve
"type"	the type of interpolation for this curve
"extend"	the type of extension for this curve
"points"	list of BezTriple's comprising this curve

In order to be able to easily and quickly edit ipo curves, there needs to be a mechanism to allow Blender to be able to recalculate curve specific data, without the data being recalculated during every script operation.

To handle this, the *points* field returns a list of the BezTriples that make up the curve.
This list can be edited without any intervention by Blender. To update the curve, the list must be reassigned to the *points* field.

One unfortunate side effect of this is that single points cannot simply be edited, editing *IpoCurve.points[0]* in place will not update the curve.

The *type* field returns one of the following values,

'Constant'	Curve remains constant between points
'Linear'	Curve uses linear interpolation of points
'Bezier'	Curve uses bezier interpolation of points

The *extend* field returns one of the following values,

'Constant'	Curve remains constant after endpoints
'Extrapolate'	Curve is extrapolated after endpoints
'Cyclic'	Curve repeats cyclically
'CyclicX'	Curve repeats cyclically-extrapolated

BezTripleType

"h1"	the first (leftmost) handle coordinate vector
"pt"	the point coordinate vector
"h2"	the second (rightmost) handle coordinate vector
"f1"	flag for h1 selection (True==selected)
"f2"	flag for pt selection (True==selected)
"f3"	flag for h2 selection (True==selected)
"h1t"	the first (leftmost) handle type
"h2t"	the second (rightmost) handle type

The *h1*, *pt*, and *h2* fields all return a Vector object, which is used to interact efficiently with Blender data structures. It can generally be used as if it were a list of floating point values, but its length cannot be changed.

The *h1t* and *h2t* fields determine the handle types, they return and can be set to the following values,

'Free'	Handle is free (unconstrained)
'Auto'	Handle is automatically calculated
'Vect'	Handle points towards adjoining point on curve
'Align'	Handle is aligned with the other handle

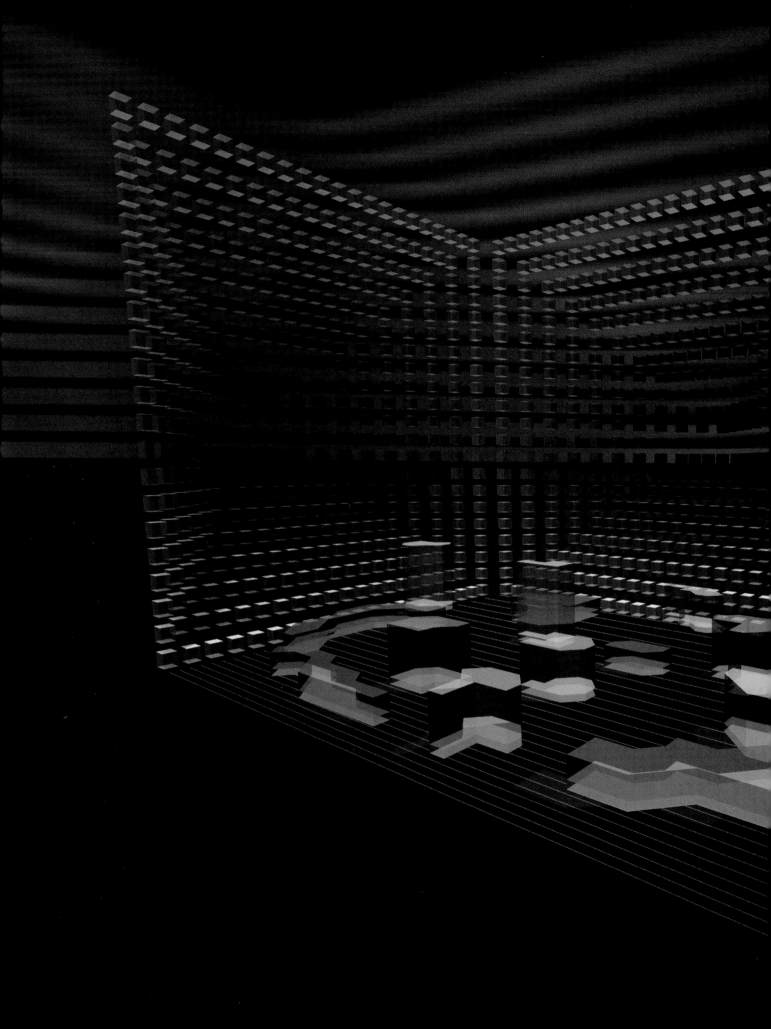

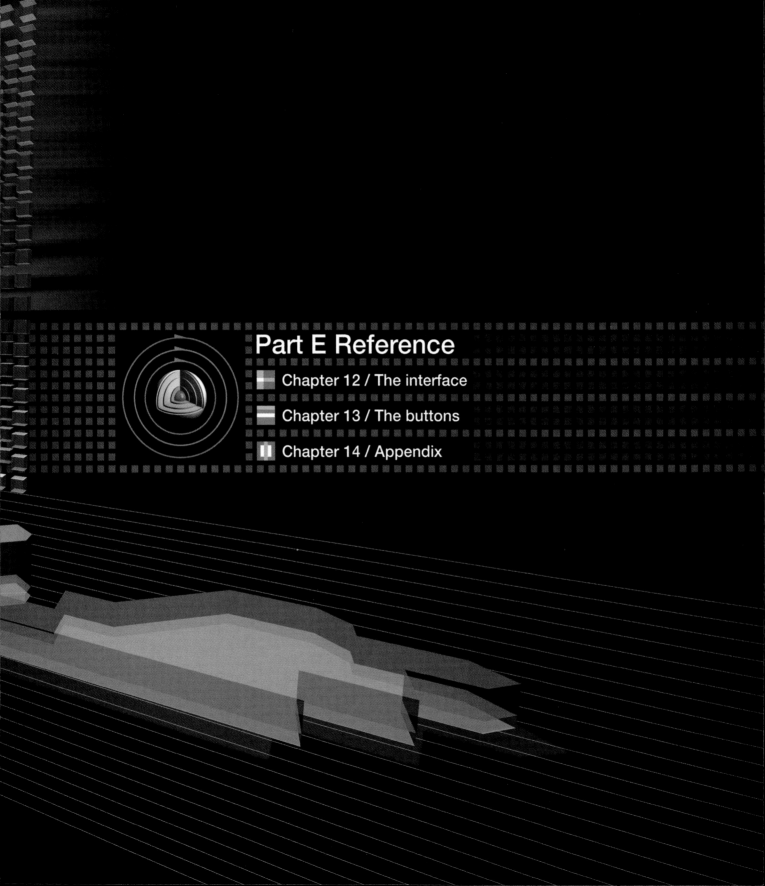

Part E Reference

Chapter 12
The interface

This section describes the general functions of the mouse and keyboard, both of which work uniformly throughout the Blender interface. Each Blender window also offers a number of specific options. These options are described in the following sections.

The Mouse

Each time you place the mouse cursor over the edge of a Blender window, the mouse cursor changes shape. When this happens, the following mouse keys are activated:

(hold-move)
Drag the window edge horizontally or vertically. The window edge always moves in increments of 4 pixels, making it relatively easy to move two window edges so that they are precisely adjacent to each other, thus joining them.

or
A PopupMenu prompts for "Split Area" or "Join Areas".

Choosing "Split Area", Blender allows you to indicate the exact split point or to cancel "split" by pressing ESC. "Split" divides the window into two windows, creating an exact copy of the original window.

Choosing "Join Areas", Windows with a shared edge are joined if possible. The active Window remains.

If there is no Header in the Window, the PopupMenu contains also the item "Add Header".

The Window Header

Blender window headers offer the following extra options in combination with mouse keys:

on the header
The entire Blender window pops to the foreground.

CTRL + on the header
The entire Blender window pops to the background.

(hold-move) on the header
If the Blender window is not wide enough to display the entire header, the MiddleMouse key can be used to horizontally shift the header.

on the header
A PopupMenu appears asking for "Top", "Bottom" or "No Header". That way the header can be moved to the top or the bottom of the Blender window or can be hidden.

Header
Top
Bottom
No Header

You can add a header to a Window by pressing the middle Mouse over an edge of a headerless Window.

Window HotKeys

Certain window managers also use the following hotkeys. So ALT-CTRL can be substituted for CTRL to perform the functions described below.

CTRL + ←
Go to the previous Screen.

CTRL + →
Go to the next Screen.

CTRL + ↑ or CTRL + ↓
Maximise the window or return to the previous window display size.

SHIFT + F4
Change the window to a DataView.

SHIFT + F5
Change the window to a 3DWindow.

SHIFT + F6
Change the window to an IpoWindow.

SHIFT + F7
Change the window to a ButtonsWindow.

SHIFT + F7
Change the window to a Sequence-Window.

SHIFT + F9
Change the window to an OopsWindow.

SHIFT + F10
Change the window to an ImageWindow.

SHIFT + F11
Change the window to a TextWindow.

SHIFT + F12
Change the window to a SoundWindow.

Universal HotKeys

The following HotKeys work uniformly in all Blender windows:

ESC
This key always cancels Blender functions without changes.
or: FileWindow, DataView and Image-Select: back to the previous window type.
or: the RenderWindow is pushed to the background (or closed, that depends on the operating system).

SPACE
Open the main menu of Blender, the Toolbox.

TAB
Start or quit EditMode.

F1
Loads a Blender file. Changes the window to a FileWindow.

SHIFT + F1
Appends parts from other files, or loads as Library-data. Changes the window to a FileWindow, making Blender files accessible as a directory.

F2
Writes a Blender file. Change the window to a FileWindow.

SHIFT + F2
Exports the scene as a DXF file.

CTRL + F2
Exports the scene as a VRML1 file.

F3
Writes a picture (if a picture has been rendered). The fileformat is as indicated in the DisplayButtons. The window becomes a FileWindow.

CTRL + F3
Saves a screendump of the active window. The fileformat is as indicated in the DisplayButtons. The window becomes a FileWindow.

SHIFT + CTRL + F3
Saves a screendump of the whole Blender screen. The fileformat is as indicated in the DisplayButtons. The window becomes a FileWindow.

F4
Displays the LampButtons (if a Buttons-Window is available).

F5
Displays the MaterialButtons (if a ButtonsWindow is available).

F6
Displays the TextureButtons (if a Buttons-Window is available).

F7
Displays the AnimButtons (if a Buttons-Window is available).

F8
Displays the RealtimeButtons (if a ButtonsWindow is available).

F9
Displays the EditButtons (if a Buttons-Window is available).

F10
Displays the DisplayButtons (if a Buttons-Window is available).

F11
Hides or shows the render window.

F12
Starts the rendering of the active camera.

←
Go to the previous frame.

SHIFT + →
Go to the first frame.

→
Go to the next frame.

SHIFT + ←
Go to the last frame.

↑
Go forward 10 frames.

↓
Go back 10 frames.

ALT + A
Change the current Blender window to Animation Playback mode. The cursor changes to a counter.

ALT + SHIFT + A
The current window, plus all 3DWindows go into Animation Playback mode.

ALT + E
Start or leave EditMode.

I
Insert Key menu. This menu differs from window to window.

J
Toggle the render buffers. Blender allows you to retain two different rendered pictures in memory.

N
Number buttons. These buttons differ depending on the type of Blender window. Numeric information for the active selection can be visualised and specified using these buttons.

CTRL + O
Opens the last saved file.

Q
"OK? Quit Blender". This key closes Blender. "Blender quit" is displayed in the console if Blender is properly closed.

ALT + CTRL + T
TimerMenu. This menu offers access to information about drawing speed. The results are displayed in the console.

CTRL + U
"OK Save User defaults". The current project (windows, objects, etc.), including UserMenu settings are written to the default file that will be loaded every time you start Blender or set it to defaults by pressing CTRL-X.

CTRL + W
Write file. This key combination allows you to write the Blender file without opening a FileWindow.

ALT + W
Write Videoscape file. Changes the window to a FileWindow.

CTRL + X
Erase All. Everything (except the render buffer) is erased and released. The default scene is reloaded.

EditMode HotKeys - General

TAB / ALT + E

This button starts and stops EditMode.

A

Select/deselect all vertices.

SHIFT + A

"Add Menu". In EditMode, this menu can only be used to add primitives of the same type like the Object that is in "Edit-Mode". If a different Object type is added Blender automatically leaves EditMode.

B

Border Select. In EditMode, this function only works on the vertices. It works as described in the previous section.

B - B

Circle Select. If you press BKEY a second time after starting Border Select, Circle Select is invoked. This mode selects vertices with LeftMouse and deselects vertices with MiddleMouse. Use PAD_PLUS or PAD_MINUS to adjust the circle size. Leave Circle Select with RMB or ESC.

N

NumberMenu. In EditMode Mesh, Curve, Surface: The location of the active vertex is displayed.

P

seParate. All selected vertices, edges, faces and curves are removed from the EditMode and placed in a new Object. This operation is the opposite of Join (CTRL + J).

CTRL + P

"Make Vertex Parent". Select 1 or 3 vertices from a Mesh, Curve or Surface. Now this Object becomes the Vertex Parent of the selected Objects. If only 1 vertex is selected, only the location of this vertex determines the Parent transformation; the rotation and dimensions of the Parent do not play a role here. If three vertices are selected, it is a 'normal' Parent relationship in which the 3 vertices determine the rotation

and location of the Child together. This method produces interesting effects with Vertex Keys. In EditMode, other Objects can be selected with CTRL+RMB.

CTRL + S

Shear. In EditMode this operation enables you to make selected forms 'slant'. This always works via the horizontal screen axis.

U

(For Font Objects: ALT + U) Reload Original Data. When starting EditMode, the original ObData block is saved. This option enables you to restore the previous situation. By continually leaving EditMode while working (TAB-TAB) you can refresh this 'undo buffer'.

W

Specials PopupMenu. A number of tools are included in this PopupMenu as an alternative to the EditButtons. This makes the buttons accessible as shortcuts, e.g. EditButtons->Subdivide is also 'WKEY, 1KEY'.

SHIFT + D

Add Duplicate. The selected vertices (faces, curves, etc.) are copied. Grab mode starts immediately thereafter.

SHIFT + W

Warp. Selected vertices can be bent into curves with this option. It can be used to convert a plane into a tube or even a sphere. The centre of the circle is the 3DCursor. The mid - line of the circle is determined by the horizontal dimensions of the selected vertices. When you start, everything is already bent 90 degrees. Moving the mouse up or down increases or decreases the extent to which warping is done. By zooming in/out of the 3D-window, you can specify the maximum degree of warping. The CTRL limitor increments warping in steps of 5 degrees.

EditMode Mesh Hotkeys

E

Extrude Selected. "Extrude" in EditMode transforms all the selected edges to

faces. If possible, the selected faces are also duplicated. Grab mode is started directly after this command is executed.

F

Make Edge/Face. If 2 vertices are selected, an edge is created. If 3 or 4 vertices are selected, a face is created.

SHIFT + F

Fill selected. All selected vertices that are bound by edges and form a closed polygon are filled with triangular faces. Holes are automatically taken into account. This operation is 2D; various layers of polygons must be filled in succession.

ALT + F

Beauty Fill. The edges of all the selected triangular faces are switched in such a way that equally sized faces are formed. This operation is 2D; various layers of polygons must be filled in succession. The Beauty Fill can be performed immediately after a Fill.

H

Hide Selected. All selected vertices and faces are temporarily hidden.

SHIFT + H

Hide Not Selected: All non - selected vertices and faces are temporarily hidden.

ALT + H

Reveal. All temporarily hidden vertices and faces are drawn again.

L

Select Linked. If you start with an un-selected vertex near the mouse cursor, this vertex is selected, together with all vertices that share an edge with it.

SHIFT + L

Deselect Linked. If you start with a selected vertex, this vertex is deselected, together with all vertices that share an edge with it.

CTRL + L

Select Linked Selected. Starting with all selected vertices, all vertices connected to them are selected too.

CTRL + N

Calculate Normals Outside. All normals from selected faces are recalcultated and consistently set in the same direction. An attempt is made to direct all normals 'outward'.

SHIFT + CTRL + N

Calculate Normals Inside. All normals from selected faces are recalculated and consistently set in the same direction. An attempt is made to direct all normals 'inward'.

CTRL + T

Make Triangles. All selected faces are converted to triangles.

X

Erase Selected. A PopupMenu offers the following options:

"Vertices": all vertices are deleted. This includes the edges and faces they form.
"Edges": all edges with both vertices selected are deleted. If this 'releases' certain vertices, they are deleted as well. Faces that can no longer exist as a result of this action are also deleted.
"Faces": all faces with all their vertices selected are deleted. If any vertices are 'released' as a result of this action, they are deleted.
"All": everything is deleted.
"Edges and Faces": all selected edges and faces are deleted, but the vertices remain.
"Only Faces": all selected faces are deleted, but the edges and vertices remain.

Y

Split. This command 'splits' the selected part of a Mesh without deleting faces. The split parts are no longer bound by edges. Use this command to control smoothing. Since the split parts have vertices at the same position, selection with LKEY is recommended.

EditMode Curve Hotkeys

C

Set the selected curves to cyclic or turn cyclic off. An individual curve is selected if at least one of the vertices is selected.

E

Extrude Curve. A vertex is added to the selected end of the curves. Grab mode is started immediately after this command is executed.

F

Add segment. A segment is added between two selected vertices at the end of two curves. These two curves are combined into 1 curve.

H

Toggle Handle align/free. Toggles the selected Bezier handles between free or aligned.

SHIFT + H

Set Handle auto. The selected Bezier handles are converted to auto type.

CTRL + H

Calculate Handles. The selected Bezier curves are calculated and all handles are assigned a type.

L

Select Linked. If you start with an non-selected vertex near the mouse cursor, this vertex is selected together with all the vertices of the same curve.

SHIFT + L

Deselect Linked. If you start with a selected vertex, it is deselected together with all the vertices of the same curve.

T

Tilt mode. Specify an extra axis rotation, i.e. the tilt, for each vertex in a 3D curve.

ALT + T

Clear Tilt. Set all axis rotations of the selected vertices to zero.

V

Vector Handle. The selected Bezier handles are converted to vector type.

W

The special menu for curves appears:

Subdivide. Subdivide the selected vertices. Switch direction. The direction of the selected curves is reversed. This is mainly for Curves that are used as paths!

X

Erase Selected. A PopupMenu offers the following options:
"Selected": all selected vertices are deleted.
"Segment": a curve segment is deleted. This only works for single segments. Curves can be split in two using this option. Or use this option to specify the cyclic position within a cyclic curve.
"All": delete everything.

EditMode Font Hotkeys

A complete list of all key combinations for special characters can be found in the text section of Curves and Surfaces (chapter 5.3).

SHIFT + TAB
The ASCII code for TAB.

→

Move text cursor 1 position forward.

SHIFT + →

Move text cursor to the end of the line.

←

Move text cursor 1 position backwards.

SHIFT + ←

Move text cursor to the start of the line.

↓

Move text cursor 1 line forward.

SHIFT + ↓

Move text cursor to the end of the text.

↑

Move text cursor 1 line back.

SHIFT + ↑

Move text cursor to the beginning of the text.

ALT + U

"Reload Original Data" (undo). When EditMode is started, the original text is saved. You can restore this original text with this option.

ALT + V

Paste text. The text file "/tmp/.cutbuffer" is inserted at the cursor location.

EditMode Surface Hotkeys

C

Toggle Cyclic menu. A PopupMenu asks if selected surfaces in the 'U' or the 'V' direction must be cyclic. If they were already cyclic, this mode is turned off.

E

Extrude Selected. This makes surfaces of all the selected curves, if possible. Only the edges of surfaces or loose curves are candidates for this operation. Grab mode is started immediately after this command is completed.

F

Add segment. A segment is added between two selected vertices at the ends of two curves. These two curves are combined into 1 curve.

L

Select Linked. If you start with an non-selected vertex near the mouse cursor, this vertex is selected together with all the vertices of the same curve or surface.

SHIFT + L

Deselect Linked. If you start with a selected vertex, this vertex is deselected together with all vertices of the same curve or surface.

SHIFT + R

Select Row. Starting with the last selected vertex, a complete row of vertices is selected in the 'U' or 'V' direction. Selecting "Select Row" a second time with the same vertex switches the 'U' or 'V' selection.

W

The special menu for curves appears:

Specials
Subdivide
Switch Direction

Subdivide. Subdivide the selected vertices. Switch direction. This will switch the normals of the selected parts.

X

Erase Selected. A PopupMenu offers the following choices:

"Selected": all selected vertices are deleted.
"All": delete everything.

Ika Hotkeys

TAB

Turns the calculation of 'Inverse Kinematics' on or off.

E

Extrude Ika. An extra Limb is added to the selected Ikas. Grab mode is started immediately thereafter.

CTRL + K

Make sKeleton. A Skeleton is created (anew) in the active Ika Object. All selected Ikas and Empty Objects become part of the Skeleton. To indicate that an Ika has a Skeleton, the 'end - effector' is now drawn in blue (instead of yellow).

CTRL + P

Make Parent. If the Parent is an Ika, a PopupMenu offers three options:

"Use vertex": one of the vertices from the Ika chain becomes the Parent. Only the location transformation is passed on to the Child Objects. Indicate which vertex with the NumberButton that pops up.
"Use limb": one of the limbs of the Ika becomes the Parent. Indicate which Limb with the NumberButton that pops up.
"Use skeleton": all Ikas and Emptys that make up the skeleton, become the Parent and can distort the Child Objects. Distortion only works on Objects that are directly parented to the Skeleton.

VertexPaint Hotkeys

SHIFT + K

All vertex colours are erased; they are changed to the current drawing colour.

U

Undo. This undo is 'real'. Pressing Undo twice returns you to the previous situation.

W

"Shared Vertexcol": The colours of all faces that share vertices are blended.

FaceSelect Hotkeys

TAB

Switches to EditMode, selections made here will show up when switching back to FaceSelectMode with TAB.

A

Selects all faces.

B

Border select.

R

Calls a menu allowing to rotate the UV coordinates or the VertexCol.

U

Calls the "UV Calculation" menu. The following modes can the applied to the selected faces:

"Cube": Cubical mapping, a number button asks for the cubemap size
"Cylinder": Cylindrical mapping, calculated from the center of the selected faces.
"Sphere": Spherical mapping, calculated from the center of the selected faces.
"Bounds to x": UV coordinates are calculated from the actual view, then scaled to a boundbox of 64 or 128 pixels in square.
"Standard" x: Each face gets default square UV coordinates.
"From Window": The UV coordinates are calculated using the projection as displayed in the 3Dwindow.

 File Edit View Tools — SCR:screen.001 [X] — SCE:1 [X] www.blender.nl 203 Ve:4 Fa:1 Ob:4-1 La:2 Mem:1.56M Plane

InfoHeader

WindowType (IconMenu)

As in all Blender window headers, the first button allows you to configure the window type.

Menus

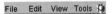 File Edit View Tools

With the menus you can easily access common commands, like saving and loading.

The menu entries are very common and doing the things they are labeled. A special thing is the Tools menu:

> Pack Data
> Unpack Data to current dir
> Advanced Unpack

With Pack Data you can pack Images, Fonts and Sounds into the Blend-file, allowing to distribute easily your files as a single file. As a sign that your file is packed, a little icon of a parcel appears in the menu-bar.

Unpack Data into current dir unpacks into the current directory on your harddisk. It creates directories for textures, sounds and fonts there.

> **Unpack 2 files**
> Use files in current directory (create when necessary)
> Write files to current directory (overwrite existing files)
>
> Use files in original location (create when necessary)
> Write files to original location (overwrite existing files)
>
> Disable AutoPack, keep all packed files
> Ask for each file

The Advanced Unpack menu gives you more control to unpack files. The entries are self-explaining.

> — SCR:screen.001 [X]

Screen Browse (MenuBut)

Allows you to select a different Screen from a list. The option "Add New" creates an exact copy of the current Screen. The copy is 'invisible': only the name on the adjacent button changes. HotKey for next or previous Screen:
CTRL+ARROWLEFT or
CTRL+ARROWRIGHT

SCR: (TextBut)

Assign a new and unique name to the current Screen and then adds the new name to the list in alphabetical order.

Delete Screen (But)

"Delete Current Screen?" The current Screen is deleted and released.

> — SCE:1 [X]

Scene Browse (MenuBut)

Select a different scene from a list. This button is blocked in EditMode.

"Add New" displays a PopupMenu with four options:

"Empty": create a completely empty scene.
"Link Objects": all Objects are linked to the new scene. The layer and selection flags of the Objects can be configured differently for each Scene.
"Link ObData": duplicates Objects only. ObData linked to the Objects, e.g. Mesh and Curve, are not duplicated.
"Full Copy": everything is duplicated.

SCE: (TextBut)

Assigns a new and unique name to the current Scene and places the new name in the list in alphabetical order.

Delete Scene (But)

"OK? Delete Current Scene". This button deletes and releases the current Scene

without deleting Objects. Objects without users are not written to a file.

The information text

www.blender.nl 203 Ve:4 Fa:1 Ob:4-1 La:2 Mem:1.56M Plane

The standard text is:

- www.blender.nl: the location at which the software can be obtained.
- V 2.03: the version of Blender. This manual is applicable to the V2.x series only.
- Ve: 4 Fa: 1: the number of vertices and faces in the current 3DWindow. If in doubt, use NUMPAD-9 to count the vertices and faces again.
- Ob: 0-1: the number of selected Objects and the total number of Objects in the current 3DWindow.
- La: 1: the number of lamps in the current 3Dwindow.
- Mem: 1.9M: the amount of memory in use in Megabytes, not including fragmented memory.
- Time: 00.01.56 (00:44): the pure rendering time for the last picture rendered in minutes/seconds/hundredths of a second and the actual extra rendering time in seconds/hundredths of a second. Excessive swap time or poor file accessibility can cause high 'extra rendering time'.
- Plane (or similar): the name of the active Object.

Changes in EditMode:
Ve: 0 - 4 Fa: 0 - 1: The first numeric value is the number of selected vertices, the second is the total number of vertices. The numeric values for the second variable apply to faces and have the same significance. During and after rendering: The values for the totals are changed to reflect the rendered picture. These values may be different from the totals displayed in the 3DWindow.

The Toolbox - icon
Clicking the Toolbox - icon will pop up the Toolbox, similar to SPACE.

UserMenu

The UserMenu allows you to configure personal settings. These settings are automatically loaded from the file $HOME/.B.blend each time Blender is started.
Personal settings cannot be written to a file other than.B.blend. The HotKey CTRL-U can be used to overwrite the file.B.blend.

Font: (TextBut)

The directory from which Blender retrieves vector fonts for Font Objects.

Render: (TextBut)

The directory to which Blender renders by default.

Textures: (TextBut)

The directory from which Blender retrieves pictures for textures and texture plugins.

TexPlugin: (TextBut)

The directory from which Blender retrieves Texture plugins.

SeqPlugin: (TextBut)

The directory from which Blender retrieves Sequence plugins.

Sounds (TextBut)

The directory from which Blender retrieves soundfiles by default.

Auto Temp Save (TogBut)

Blender can save 'temp' files at regular intervals as a temporary backup or as extra protection against disasters. The files are identical to Blender files saved in the normal manner. If Blender is in EditMode when this function is used, only the original Data are saved, without saving the Data with which you are working. Blender saves 'temp' files in the specified 'temp' directory with the name "<process-id>.blend". This results in unique names for all 'temp' files, allowing multiple Blenders to simultaneously write 'temp' files on the same computer. When Blender is closed down, the file is renamed "quit.blend", making it easy to retrieve work in progress if the user inadvertently quits Blender. Blender writes files very quickly, which means that waiting time is kept to a minimum, allowing the user to continue working within a split second after saving files of 1-2 Mb.

Time: (NumBut)
The time interval in minutes required to write 'temp' files.

Dir: (TextBut)
The directory to which 'temp' files are written. Do not use network drives if possible. Instead, use a local directory on your own workstation.

Load Temp (But)
This button, the Blender 'disaster' button, loads the most recently saved 'temp' file.

Versions (NumBut)
This option also allows you to work with Blender more safely. When this option is activated, files that are overwritten by Blender are assigned a new file name with a version number. For example: If 'Versions' has a value of '2' and the file 'rt.blend' is being written:

rt.blend2 is deleted
rt.blend1 is renamed to rt.blend2
rt.blend is renamed to rt.blend1
rt.blend is rewritten.

Scene Global (TogBut)
Each Screen can display a different Scene. In cases involving numerous active Screens, this can be somewhat confusing. This option can be used to display the current Scene in all Screens.

NoCapsLock (TogBut)
This button can be used to deactivate the CapsLock key. This button only applies to the TextButton.

ViewMove (TogBut)
By default, MiddleMouse causes a rotation in the 3Dwindow and SHIFT + MiddleMouse causes a translation. The option "ViewMove" toggles the key code.

TrackBall (TogBut)
There are two methods to rotate a 3DView with MiddleMouse. The TrackBall method offers more freedom than the other option, the turn table method.

2 - Mouse (TogBut)
With this option activated, the third mouse button is emulated by pressing ALT + LeftMouse.

Mat on Obj (TogBut)
By default, Blender assumes that Materials are linked to the ObData when new Objects are created. This option toggles between the default and the alternative, which links Materials directly to the Object.

ToolTips (TogBut)
With this option activated, tooltips are shown when you stop with the mousepointer over a button. The tooltip will briefly describe the function.

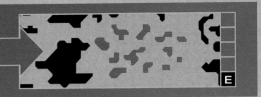

Grid options

By default, the following limitors apply to grabbing rotating and scaling (press the keys after click and hold with the mouse):

(no key): fluid change
SHIFT: finer control
CTRL: large grid steps
SHIFT-CTRL: small grid steps

The following alternatives can also be used (when the Viewmove option is set):

(no key): large grid steps
SHIFT: small grid steps
CTRL: fluid change
SHIFT - CTRL: finer control

Grab Grid (TogBut)
Toggle to the alternative limitors for translations.

Size Grid (TogBut)
Toggle to the alternative limitors for scaling.

Rot Grid (TogBut)
Toggle to the alternative limitors for rotation.

Duplication / Linking presets

One of Blender's most advanced features is its use of object-oriented functions. Blender allows you to reuse (i.e. link) data blocks to construct compact and efficient structures.

When one of these buttons is pressed, the indicated DataBlock is duplicated instead of linked when using SHIFT-D. The ALT-D command always makes a copy of the selected Objects with all other data linked.

The most common use of links is when activating the Duplicate commands:

ALT + D
Create a copy of the selected Objects, reusing (i.e. linking to) all other data, including Meshes and Materials.

SHIFT + D
Create a copy of the selected Objects, using these button settings to determine whether links to other data are created or duplicates of other data are created.

©2000 Rob Debrichy

 LOAD FILE Free: 62.809 Mb   Files: (0) 33   (0.000) 5.442 Mb

FileHeader

WindowType (IconMenu)
As with every window header, the first button enables you to set the window type.

Full Window (IconTog)
Expands the window to full screen or returns to the previous window display size; returns to the original screen setting. HotKey: CTRL + UPARROW

Sort Alpha (IconRow)
Files are sorted alphabetically. Directories are always sorted first.

Sort Time (IconRow)
Files are sorted by creation date.

Sort Size (IconRow)
Files are sorted by size.

LOAD FILE

File type
Indicates what type of FileWindow this is. It is extremely important to continually verify that the correct LOAD or SAVE option is selected.

Short Text (IconTog)
Indicates whether the file names are displayed in long or short format.

Hide dot - files (IconTog)
The ghost button hides dot-files (filenames with a leading dot).

Free: 62.809 Mb   Files: (0) 33   (0.000) 5.442 Mb

Info Text
The header provides extra information about the status of the selected directory.

- Free: 81.106 Mb: the free disk space available
- Files: (0) 72: the number of selected files between parentheses, followed by the total number of files.

- (0.000) 8.600 Mb: the total number of bytes in the selected files between parentheses, followed by the total for the entire directory.

/usr/people/cw/work/grafik/Blender/Space/

Space39.blend

	512	rwx	r-x	r-x	cw	13:55	14-Sep-00
..	13 312	rwx	r-x	r-x	cw	14:50	12-Sep-00
sounds	70	rwx	r-x	r-x	cw	22:47	07-Sep-00
3DTrackTest.blend		rw-	r--	r--	cw	22:47	07-Sep-00
ngc_2024.jpg		rw-	r--	r--	cw	22:47	07-Sep-00
Pferdekopf1.jpg		rw-	r--	r--	cw	22:47	07-Sep-00
Rocket.blend	61 596	rw-	r--	r--	cw	19:07	10-Sep-00
Rocket.blend1	60 708	rw-	r--	r--	cw	19:03	10-Sep-00
Space10.blend	720 896	rw-	r--	r--	cw	22:47	07-Sep-00
Space10.blend1		rw-	r--	r--	cw	22:49	07-Sep-00
Space38.blend	5 902 332	rw-	---	---	cw	22:52	07-Sep-00
Space38_Rocket.blend	5 669 716	rw-	r--	r--	cw	19:15	10-Sep-00
Space39.blend	5 646 512	rw-	r--	r--	cw	13:55	14-Sep-00
Space39.blend1	5 646 512	rw-	r--	r--	cw	23:28	13-Sep-00

FileWindow

The FileWindow is generally called up to read and write files. However, you can also use it to manage the entire file system. It also provides a handy overview of the internal Blender structure.

There are 4 'modes' for the FileWindow

- FileManager: the standard mode.
- FileSelect: the FileHeader shows the action to be performed (Load, Save, etc.).
- DataSelect: display the Blender data system as files.
- DataBrowse: like DataSelect, but now as an alternative to a PopupMenu.

The FileWindow is optimised for reuse. The second and subsequent times the same directory is called up, the file system is not re-read. This saves considerable time, but can sometimes cause confusion if other processes have written files to the directory (the directory is always read again after Blender writes to it).

If you have any doubts about the validity of the current display, press DOTKEY.

P (But)
Displays the parent directory. You can also use: PKEY.

DirName: (TextBut)
This button displays the current directory. You can also create a new directory. When you leave the button (with Left-Mouse or ENTER), you will be asked: "OK? Make dir".

Preset Directories (MenuBut)
The file $HOME/.Bfs contains a number of presets that are displayed in this menu. If a file is read or written, the directory involved is temporarily added to the menu.

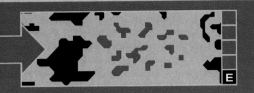

FileName: (TextBut)
The file name can be entered here. This button can also be used to select files using wildcards. Example: enter '*.tga', then press ENTER. All files with the extension '.tga' are selected.

FileSelect

Blender commands such as F1 (read file) and F2 (write file) invoke a FileWindow in FileSelect mode. This mode is used to indicate a single file, i.e. the file in the FileName button. Press ENTER to initiate the action, e.g. read a Blender file. Use ESC to cancel the action.

The FileManager functions also work in FileSelect mode. These only work on selected files. Standard functions in this window:

Indicates the active file. Its name is placed in the FileName button.

Indicates the active file and closes the FileWindow with the message OK.

Select files. For functional reasons, a RightMouse Select here does not indicate the active file!

ENTER / PAD ENTER
Closes the FileWindow, returns with an OK message.

ESC
Closes the FileWindow with no further action.

PAGE DOWN
Scrolls down one page.

PAGE UP
Scrolls up one page.

HOME
Scrolls to the first file.

END
Scrolls to the last file.

PAD + / =
Automatic file-number increase. If there is a number in the active file name (such as rt01.tga), this number is incremented by one. This is quite handy when reading or writing sequential files.

PAD - / -
Automatic file number decrease (see previous description).

/
Make the current directory the root directory: "/"

.
Re-read the current directory.

E
For the active file: start the Unix command: $WINEDITOR. For viewing text files.

I
For the active file: start the Unix command: $IMAGEEDITOR. For viewing or Editing images.

LOAD FILE   Free: 62.809 Mb   Files: (0) 33   (0.000) 5.442 Mb

Read Libraries

Blender allows you to read in, append, or link (parts of) other files. If 'Load Library' is selected - SHIFT+F1 - the FileSelect appears in a special mode. Blender files are now highlighted as directories. They are accessible as a directory as well; they then display a situation in much the same way as DataView displays the internal Blender structure.

Now you can select any number of blocks you wish using RightMouse and append them to the current structure with a simple ENTER. The complete 'underlying' structure is included: thus, if an Object is selected, the associated Ipo, ObData, Materials and Textures are included as well. If a Scene is selected, the entire Scene is appended to the current structure, Objects and all. You can specify how you want this to be appended in the FileSelect Header:

Append (RowBut)

External blocks become a normal part of the current structure, and thus of the file as well, if the file is saved. Appending a second time causes the entire selection to be added again in its entirety. Since block names must be unique, the name of the appended blocks will differ slightly from the existing name (only the number in the name).

Link (RowBut)

This is the 'normal' use of Libraries. The specified blocks are added to the current structure here as well, but Blender remembers the fact that they are Library blocks. When the file is saved, only the name of the Library block and the name of the file from which the blocks were copied are saved, thus keeping the original file compact. When you read the file again, Blender reads the original file and then reads all the Library blocks from the other file(s). The names of the files and the blocks must not be changed, however.

Blender keeps track of what Library blocks have already been read. Appending the same blocks twice has no consequences.

This enables more animators working on a project. Therefore a linked Object cannot be changed from the scene it is imported in.

FileManager

The FileManager function only works with selected files. The active file does not play a role here. Most of these commands do expect two FileWindows to be open. Commands such as RKEY (remove) and TKEY (touch) also work with a single Window. Note: when we say files here, we also mean directories.

A

Select/deselect all files.

B

Backup files to the other FileWindow. This allows files to be copied without changing the file date.

C

Copy files to the other FileWindow. (Unix: cp -r) read.

L

Link files to the other FileWindow. (Unix: ln)

M

Move files to the other FileWindow. (Unix: mv)

R

Remove files. For safety's sake: only empty directories. (Unix rm -f)

SHIFT + **R**

Remove files recursively. This deletes the entire contents of directories. (Unix: rm -rf)

T

Update modification times of files. (Unix: touch)

P	Object/			
-	Sparks			

Plane.030	1	ShuttleTrack.001	1
Plane.033	1	Sparks	1
Plane.034	1	Sphere	1
Plane.039	1	Cube	1
Plane.041	1	Sphere.001	1
Plane.045	1	Plane	1
Plane.046	1	Empty	1
Plane.048	1	Sphere.002	1
Plane.049	1	Lamp	1
Plane.050	1	Sphere.003	1
Plane.085	1	Sphere.004	1
Plane.086	1	Circle	1
Plane.087	1	Sphere.006	1
Plane.088	1	Sphere.008	1
Plane.089	1	Sphere.009	1
Plane.091	1	Sphere.010	1
Plane.092	1	Sphere.011	1
Plane.093	1	Star	1
Plane.094	1	Track	1
Plane.096	1	Camera	1
Pointer.001	1		1
Shield	1	Tube	1
Shuttle	1	Tube.001	1
ShuttleTrack	1		

DataView and DataBrowse

The DataView window can be invoked with SHIFT+F4. It allows you to view the entire internal Blender structure as a file system. Each DataBlock is listed as a file name. They are sorted by type in directories.

Currently, the functions are limited to:

Select Objects by name. Click Right-Mouse on the file name. A LeftMouse click on a name makes the Object active. Note that an activated Object can also reside in a hidden layer.
Setting and deleting Fake Users. (Press FKEY). A Fake User ensures that a Data-Block is always saved in a file, even if it has no users.
Link Materials (CTRL+L). The links to selected Materials are all replaced by a link to the active Material (LeftMouse, in the FileName button). This link option will be expanded to other DataBlock types.

PopupMenus that contain more than 24 items and are thus unmanageably large, are replaced by the DataBrowse windows.

Standard functions in this window:

Display the active DataBlock. This is placed in the FileName button.

Display the active DataBlock and close the DataBrowse with an OK message.

ENTER / PAD **ENTER**

Close the DataBrowse, return with an OK message.

ESC

Close the DataBrowse with no further action.

PAGE DOWN

Scroll down one page.

PAGE UP

Scroll up one page.

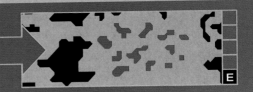

 [header toolbar icons]

3DHeader

WindowType (IconMenu)

As with every window header, the first button allows you to set the window type.

FullWindow (IconTog)

Maximise the window, or return it to its original size; return to the old screen setting. Hotkey: CTRL+UPARROW

Home (IconBut)

All Objects in the visible layers are displayed completely, centered in the window. Hotkey: HOMEKEY.

Layers (TogBut)

These 20 buttons show the available layers. In fact, a layer is nothing more than a visibility flag. This is an extremely efficient method for testing Object visibility. This allows the user to divide the work functionally.

For example: Cameras in layer 1, temporary Objects in layer 20, lamps in layers 1, 2, 3, 4 and 5, etc. All hotkey commands and tools in Blender take the layers into account. Objects in 'hidden' layers are treated as unselected.

Use LeftMouse for the buttons, SHIFT+LeftMouse for extend select layers.

Hotkeys: 1KEY, 2KEY, etc. 0KEY, MINUSKEY, EQUALKEY for layers 1,2,3,4, etc. Use ALT +(1KEY, 2KEY, ... OKEY) for layers 11, 12, ... 20. Here, as well, use SHIFT +Hotkey for extend select.

Lock (TogBut)

Every 3DWindow has its own layer setting and active Camera. This is also true for a Scene: here it determines what layers - and what camera - are used to render a picture. The lock option links the layers and Camera of the 3DWindow to the Scene and vice versa: the layers and Camera of the Scene are linked to the 3DWindow. This method passes a layer change directly to the Scene and to all other 3DWindows with the "Lock" option ON. Turn the "Lock" OFF to set a layer or Camera exclusively for the current 3DWindow. All settings are immediately restored by turning the button back ON.

LocalView (IconTog)

 LocalView allows the user to continue working with complex Scenes. The currently selected Objects are taken separately, centered and displayed completely. The use of 3DWindow layers is temporarily disabled. Reactivating this option restores the display of the 3D-Window in its original form. If a picture is rendered from a LocalView, only the Objects present are rendered plus the visible lamps, according to the layers that have been set. Activating a new Camera in LocalView does not change the Camera used by the Scene. Normally, LocalView is activated with the hotkey PAD_SLASH.

ViewMode (IconMenu)

 A 3DWindow offers 3 methods for 3D display:

- Orthonormal. Blender offers this method from every view, not just from the X, Y or Z axes.
- Perspective. You can toggle between orthonormal and perspective with the hotkey PAD_5.
- Camera. This is the view as rendered. Hotkey: PAD_0.

ViewDirection (IconMenu)

 These presets can be used with either ortho or perspective. Respectively, these are the:

Top View, hotkey PAD_7
Front View, hotkey PAD_1
Right View, hotkey PAD_3

The hotkeys combined with SHIFT give the opposite view direction. (Down View, Back View, Left View)

DrawMode (IconMenu)

 Set the drawing method. Respectively:

- BoundBox. The quickest method, for animation previews, for example.
- WireFrame.
- Solid. Zbuffered with the standard OpenGL lighting. Hotkey: ZKEY, this toggles between WireFrame and Solid.
- Shaded. This is as good an approach as is possible to the manner in which Blender renders - with Gouraud shading. It displays the situation from a single frame of the Camera. Hotkey: SHIFT+Z. Use CTRL+Z to force a recalculation.
- Textured.

Objects have their own Draw Type, independent of the window setting (see EditButtons->DrawType). The rule is that the minimum DrawMode is displayed.

ViewMove (IconBut, click - hold)

 Move the mouse for a view translation. This is an alternative for SHIFT+MiddleMouse.

ViewZoom (IconBut, click - hold)

Move the mouse vertically to zoom in and out of the 3DWindow. This is an alternative for CTRL+MiddleMouse.

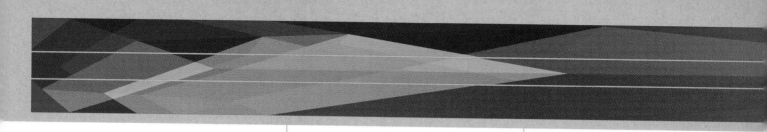

These buttons determine the manner in which the Objects (or vertices) are rotated or scaled.

AroundCenter (IconRow)

The midpoint of the boundbox is the center of rotation or scaling. Hotkey: COMMAKEY

AroundMedian (IconRow)

The median of all Objects or vertices is the center of rotation or scaling.

AroundCursor (IconRow)

The 3DCursor is the midpoint of rotation or scaling. Hotkey: DOTKEY.

Around Individual Centers (IconRow)

All Objects rotate or scale around their own midpoints. In EditMode: all vertices rotate or scale around the Object midpoint.

EditMode (IconTog)

This button starts or terminates EditMode. Hotkey: TAB of ALT+E.

VertexPaint (IconTog)

This button starts or terminates VertexPaintMode. Hotkey: VKEY.

FaceSelect (IconTog)

This button starts or the FaceSelect mode. Hotkey: FKEY.

Proportional Vertex Editing Tool (IconTog)

The Proportional Editing tool can be activated with the Icon in 3DWindow header, or OKEY.

The Proportional Editing tool is then Available in Editmode for all Object types. This tool works like a 'magnet', you select a few vertices and while editing

(grab, rotate, scale) the surrounding vertices move proportionality with it. Use the NumPad-plus and NumPad-minus keys to adjust the area of influence, this can be done "live" while editing.

You can choose between a sharp falloff and a smooth falloff.

OpenGL Renderer (IconTog)

A LeftMouse Click renders the actual view in OpenGL. CTRL-LeftMouse renders an animation in OpenGL. The rendered pictures are saved as indicated in the DisplayButtons .

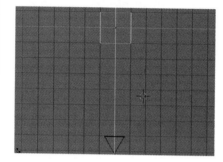

3DWindow

The standard 3DWindow has:

- A grid. The dimensions (distance between the gridlines) and resolution (number of lines) can be set with the ViewButtons. This grid is drawn as infinite in the presets of ortho ViewMode (Top, Front, Right view). In the other views, there is an finite 'floor'. Many Blender commands are adjusted to the dimension of the grid, to function as a standard unit. Blender works best if the total 'world' in which the user operates continually falls more or less within the total grid floor (whether it is a space war or a logo animation).
- Axes in colour codes. The reddish line is the X axis, the green line is the Y axis, the blue line is the Z axis. In the Blender universe, the 'floor' is normally formed by the X and Y axes. The height and 'depth' run along the Z axis.

- A 3Dcursor. This is drawn as a black cross with a red/white striped circle. A LeftMouse click moves the 3DCursor. Use the SnapMenu (SHIFT+S) to give the 3Dcursor a specific location. New Objects are placed at the 3Dcursor location.
- Layers (visible in the header buttons). Objects in 'hidden' layers are not displayed. All hotkey commands and tools in Blender take the layers into account: Objects in the 'hidden' layers are treated as not selected. See the following paragraph as well.
- ViewButtons. Separate variables can be set for each 3Dwindow, e.g for the grid or the lens. Use the SHIFT+F7 hotkey or the WindowType button in the 3DHeader. The ViewButtons are explained in detail in section 13.2.

The Mouse

The mouse provides the most direct access to the 3DWindow. Below is a complete overview:

Position the 3DCursor.

CTRL +

In EditMode: create a new vertex.

(click - hold - draw)
These are the Gestures. Blender's gesture recognition works in three ways:

Draw a straight line: start translation mode (Grabber).
Draw a curved line: start rotation mode.
Draw a V-shaped line: start scaling mode.

(click - hold)
Rotate the direction of view of the 3DWindow. This can be done in two ways (can be set in the UserMenu):
The trackball method. In this case, where in the window you start the mouse movement is important. The rotation can be compared to rotating a ball, as if the mouse grasps and moves a tiny miniscule point on a ball and moves it. If the movement starts in the middle of the window, the view rotates along the horizontal

and vertical window axes. If the movement begins at the edge of the window, the view rotates along the axis perpendicular to the window.
The turntable method. A horizontal mouse movement always results in a rotation around the global Z axis. Vertical mouse movements are corrected for the view direction, and result in a combination of (global) X and Y axis rotations.

SHIFT + 🖱 (click - hold)
Translate the 3DWindow. Mouse movements are always corrected for the view direction.

CTRL + 🖱 (click - hold)
Zoom in/out on the 3DWindow.

Select Objects or (in EditMode) vertices. The last one selected is also the active one. This method guarantees that a maximum of 1 Object and 1 vertex are always selected. This selection is based on graphics (the wireframe).

SHIFT + 🖱
Extend select Objects or (in EditMode) vertices. The last one selected is also the active one. Multiple Objects or vertices may also be selected. This selection is based on graphics too (the wireframe).

CTRL + 🖱
Select Objects on the Object-centers. Here the wireframe drawing is not taken into account. Use this method to select a number of identical Objects in succession, or to make them active.

SHIFT - CTRL + 🖱
Extend select Objects. The last Object selected is also the active one. Multiple Objects can be selected.

🖱 (click - hold - move)
Select and start translation mode, the Grabber. This works with all the selection methods mentioned.

NumPad

The numeric keypad on the keyboard is reserved for view related hotkeys. Below is a description of all the keys with a brief explanation:

PAD - /
LocalView. The Objects selected when this command is invoked are taken separately and displayed completely, centered in the window. See the description of 3DHeader->LocalView.

PAD - *
Copy the rotation of the active Object to the current 3DWindow. Works as if this Object is the camera, without including the translation.

PAD - -, PAD - +
Zoom in, zoom out. This also works for Camera ViewMode.

PAD - .
Center and zoom in on the selected Objects. The view is changed in a way that can be compared to the LocalView option.

PAD - 5
Toggle between perspective and orthonormal mode.

PAD - 9
Force a complete recalculation (of the animation systems) and draw again.

PAD - 0
View from the current camera, or from the Object that is functioning as the camera.

CTRL + PAD - 0
Make the active Object the camera. Any Object can be used as the camera. Generally, a Camera Object is used. It can also be handy to let a spotlight function temporarily as a camera when directing and adjusting it. ALT+PAD_0 Revert to the previous camera. Only Camera Objects are candidates for 'previous camera'.

PAD - 7
Top View. (along the negative Z axis, Y up)

PAD - 1
Front View. (along the positive Y axis, Z up)

PAD - 3
Right View. (along the negative X axis, Z up)

PAD - 2,
Rotate using the turntable method. Depending on the view, this is a rotation around the X and Y axis.

PAD - 4
Rotate using the turntable method. This is a rotation around the Z axis.

Hotkeys

This list contains all the hotkeys that can be used in a 3Dwindow. EditMode hotkeys are described in the following paragraph.

HOME
All Objects in the visible layer are displayed completely, centered in the window.

PAGE UP
Select the next Object Key. If more than one Object Key is selected, the selection is shifted up cyclically. Only works if the AnimButtons->DrawKey is ON for the Object.

SHIFT + PAGE UP
Extend select the next Object Key.

PAGE DOWN
Select the previous Object Key. If more than one Object Key is selected, the selection is shifted up cyclically. Only works if the AnimButtons->DrawKey is ON for the Object.

SHIFT + PAGE DOWN
Extend select the previous Object Key.

ACCENT
(To the left of the 1KEY) Select all layers.

SHIFT + ACCENT
Revert to the previous layer setting.

A
Select All / deselect All. If any Object or vertex is selected, everthing is always deselected first.

SHIFT + A
This is the AddMenu. In fact, it is the ToolBox that starts with the 'ADD' option. When Objects are added, Blender starts EditMode immediately if possible.

CTRL + A
"Apply size/rot". The rotation and dimensions of the Object are assigned to the ObData (Mesh, Curve, etc.). At first glance, it appears as if nothing has changed, but this can have considerable consequences for animations or texture mapping. This is best illustrated by also having the axis of a Mesh Object being drawn (EditButtons->Axis). Rotate the Object and activate Apply. The rotation and dimensions of the Object are 'erased'.

CTRL - SHIFT + A
If the active Object is automatically duplicated (see AnimButtons->DupliFrames or AnimButtons->Dupliverts), a menu asks "Make dupli's real?". This option actually creates the Objects.

If the active Mesh Object is deformed by a Lattice, a menu asks "Apply Lattice deform?". Now the deformation of the Lattice is assigned to the vertices of the Mesh.

B
Border Select. Draw a rectangle with the LeftMouse; all Objects within this area are selected, but not made active. Draw a rectangle with the RightMouse to deselect Objects. In orthonormal View-Mode, the dimensions of the rectangle are displayed, expressed as global coordinates, as an extra feature in the lower left corner. In Camera ViewMode,

the dimensions that are to be rendered according to the DisplayButtons are displayed in pixel units.

SHIFT + B
Render Border. This only works in Camera ViewMode. Draw a rectangle to render a smaller cut-out of the standard window frame. If the option DisplayButtons->Border is ON, a box is drawn with red and black lines.

C
Centre View. The position of the 3DCursor becomes the new centre of the 3DWindow.

SHIFT + C
CentreZero View. The 3DCursor is set to zero (0,0,0) and the view is changed so that all Objects, including the 3DCursor, can be displayed. This is an alternative for HOMEKEY.

ALT + C
Convert Menu. Depending on the active Object, a PopupMenu is displayed. This enables you to convert certain types of ObData. It only converts in one direction, everything ultimately degrades to a Mesh!

The options are:

"Font -> Curve"
"MetaBall -> Mesh" The original MetaBall remains unchanged.
"Curve -> Mesh"
"Surface -> Mesh"

CTRL + C
Copy Menu. This menu copies information from the active Object to (other) selected Objects.

Fixed components are:
"Copy Loc": the X,Y,Z location of the Object. If a Child is involved, this location is the relative position in relation to the Parent.
"Copy Rot": the X,Y,Z rotation of the Object.
"Copy Size": the X,Y,Z dimension of the Object.
"DrawType": see EditButtons->DrawType.

"TimeOffs": see AnimButtons->TimeOffs.
"Dupli": all Duplicator data from the AnimButtons
If applicable:
"Copy TexSpace": The texture space.
"Copy Particle Settings": the complete particle system from the AnimButtons.
For Curve Objects:
"Copy Bevel Settings": all beveling data from the EditButtons.
Font Objects:
"Copy Font Settings": font type, dimensions, spacing.
"Copy Bevel Settings": all beveling data from the EditButtons.
Camera Objects:
"Copy Lens": the lens value.

SHIFT + D
"Add Duplicate". The selected Objects are copied. The settings in the UserMenu (Duplication/Linking presets) determine what DataBlocks are also copied or are linked. Blender then automatically starts Grab Mode (see GKEY).

ALT + D
"Add Linked Duplicate". The selected Objects are copied. The DataBlocks linked to Objects remain linked. Blender then automatically starts Grab Mode (see GKEY).

CTRL + D
Draw the (texture) Image as wire. This option has a limited function. It can only be used for 2D compositing.

ALT + E
Start / stop EditMode. Alternative hotkey: TAB.

SHIFT + F
Fly Mode. Only from Camera ViewMode. The mouse cursor jumps to the middle of the window. It works as follows:

• Mouse cursor movement indicates the view direction.
• LeftMouse click (repeated): Fly faster.
• MiddleMouse click (repeated): Fly slower.
• LeftMouse+MiddleMouse: Set speed to zero.

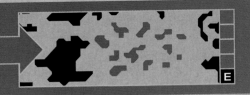

- CTRL: translation downwards
  (negative Z).
- ALT: translation upwards (positive Z).
- ESC: Camera back to its starting
  position, terminate Fly Mode.
- SPACEKEY: Leave the Camera in current
  position, terminate Fly Mode.

(Be careful when looking straight up or
down. This causes confusing turbulence.)

CTRL + F

Sort Faces. The faces of the active Mesh
Object are sorted, based on the current
view in the 3DWindow. The leftmost face
first, the rightmost last. The sequence of
faces is important for the Build Effect
(AnimButtons).

G

Grab Mode. Or: the translation mode.
This works on selected Objects and
vertices. Blender calculates the quantity
and direction of the translation, so that
they correspond exactly with the mouse
movements, regardless of the ViewMode
or view direction of the 3DWindow.

Alternatives for starting this mode:

RightMouse (click-hold-move)
LeftMouse (click-hold-draw) to draw
a straight line.

The following options are available in
translation mode:

- Limitors:
  CTRL: in increments of 1 grid unit.
  SHIFT+CTRL: in increments of
  0.1 grid unit.
- MiddleMouse toggle: A short click
  restricts the current translation to the
  X,Y or Z axis. Blender calculates which
  axis to use, depending on the already
  initiated mouse movement. Click
  MiddleMouse again to return to
  unlimited translation.
- ARROWKEYS: These keys can be used
  to move the mouse cursor exactly 1
  pixel.
- Grabber can be terminated with:
  LeftMouse, SPACEBAR or ENTER: move

to a new position.
RightMouse or ESC: everything goes
back to the old position.
- Switching mode:
  GKEY: starts Grab mode again.
  SKEY: switches to Size mode.
  RKEY: switches to Rotate mode.

ALT + G

Clear location. The X,Y,Z locations of
selected Objects are set to zero.

I

Insert Object Key. A key position is
inserted in the current frame of all
selected Objects. A PopupMenu asks
what key position(s) must be added to
the IpoCurves.

"Loc": The XYZ location of the Object.
"Rot": The XYZ rotation of the Object.
"Size": The XYZ dimensions of the Object
"LocRot": The XYZ location and XYZ
rotation of the Object.
"LocRotSize": The XYZ location, XYZ
rotation and XYZ dimensions of the
Object.
"Layer": The layer of the Object.
"Avail": A position is only added to all the
current IpoCurves.
"Effector": (only for Ika Objects) the
end-effector position is added.
"Mesh", "Lattice", "Curve" or "Surface":
depending on the type of Object,
a VertexKey can be added.

CTRL + J

Join Objects. All selected Objects of the
same type are added to the active
Object. What actually happens here is
that the ObData blocks are combined and
all the selected Objects (except for the
active one) are deleted. This is a rather
complex operation, which can lead to
confusing results, particularly when
working with a lot of linked data,
animation curves and hierarchies.

K

Show (as) Keys. The DrawKey option
is turned ON for all selected Objects.
If all of them were already ON, they are
all turned OFF.

SHIFT + K

A PopupMenu asks: "OK? Show and
select all keys". The DrawKey option is
turned ON for all selected Objects, and
all Object-keys are selected. This function
is used to enable transformation of the
entire animation system.

L

Local Menu. Makes library linked objects
local for the current scene.

SHIFT + L

Select Links menu. This menu enables
you to select Objects that share links to
DataBlock with the active Object. Use
this function to obtain an overview of the
sometimes quite complicated linked
structures Blender can create.

"Object Ipo": all Objects with the same
Object Ipo are selected.
"Object Data": all Objects with the same
ObData (Mesh, Curve, etc.) are selected.
"Current Material": all Objects with the
same active Material are selected (this
is the Material in MaterialButtons).
"Current texture": all Objects with the
same active Texture are selected (this
is the Texture in MaterialButtons).

CTRL + L

Make Links menu. This menu is used to
copy links between the active Object
and selected Objects. Only the links (the
references) are copied; the contents of
the DataBlocks involved are not changed.
The result of this operation is easy to see
in the OopsWindow.

"To Scene": the selected Objects are
also linked to another Scene. A second
PopupMenu asks the user to specify a
Scene. Objects that appear in more than
one Scene are displayed with a blue
null point.
"Object Ipo": all selected Objects are
given a link to the Object Ipo of the active
Object.

"Mesh data", "Curve data", "Font data", etc.: all selected Objects are given a link to the ObData of the active Object. Objects must be the same type! "Materials": all selected Objects are given links that are identical to the Material(s) of the active Object. The entire Material situation is copied. If the active Object does not have any Materials, all Material links for the selected Objects are erased.

M

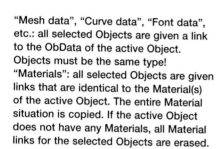

Move to Layer. This hotkey calls up a menu that can be used to view or change the layer settings of all the selected Objects. If the selected Objects have different layers, this is 'OR'ed in the menu display. Use ESC to exit the menu. Press the "OK" button or ENTER to change the layer seting. The hotkeys (ALT+)(1KEY, 2KEY, ... - 0KEY) work here as well (see 3DHeader).

N

Active Object: Plane
Rotations in degrees!
LocX: 1.00
LocY: -1.00
LocZ: 4.00
RotX: 1.00
RotY: 240.00
RotZ: 5.00
SizeX: 2.00
SizeY: 2.00
SizeZ: 0.40

These buttons allow the user to enter numbers for the position, rotation and dimensions of the active Object. Use ESC to exit the menu without changing the Object. Press the "OK" button or ENTER to assign the changes to the Object.

ALT + O

Clear Origin. The 'Origin' is erased for all Child Objects, which causes the Child Objects to move to the exact location of the Parent Objects.

CTRL + P

Make Parent. The active Object becomes the Parent of the selected Objects.

All transformations of the Parent are now passed on to the Children. This allows you to create complex hierarchies. As part of the 'Make Parent' operation, an inverse of the Parent transformation is calculated and stored in the Child Object. This inverse may make it seem as if all transformations remained unchanged after Make Parent was executed. Depending on the type of Object, special Parent relationships can be selected.

ALT + P

Clear Parent. All selected Child Objects are unlinked from the Parents. A Popup-Menu asks you to make a selection:

"Clear Parent": the selected Child Objects are unlinked from the Parent. Since the transformation of the Parent disappears, this can appear as if the former Children themselves are transformed.
"... and keep transform": the Child Objects are unlinked from the Parent, and an attempt is made to assign the current transformation, which was determined in part by the Parent, to the (former Child) Objects.
"Clear Parent inverse": The inverse matrix of the Parent of the selected Objects is erased. The Child Objects remain linked to the Objects. This gives the user complete control over the hierarchy.

R

Rotate mode. Works on selected Objects and vertices. In Blender, a rotation is by default a rotation perpendicular to the screen, regardless of the view direction or ViewMode. The degree of rotation is exactly linked to the mouse movement. Try moving around the rotation midpoint with the mouse. The rotation midpoint is determined by the state of the 3DHeader->Around buttons.

X, Y and Z

While in rotation mode, these keys switch to a global axis rotation around the corresponding axis.

Alternatives for starting rotation mode:

- LeftMouse (click-hold-draw): draw a C-shaped curve. The following options are available in rotation mode:
- Limitors:
  CTRL: in increments of 5 degrees.
  SHIFT: finer control.
  SHIFT+CTRL: finer control with increments of 1 degree.
- MiddleMouse toggle: A short click switches the current rotation axis, which is perpendicular to the screen, with the two other axes, which are vertical and horizontal on the screen. The mouse movements here follow the two rotation axes. Click MiddleMouse again to return to a rotation axis perpendicular to the screen.
- ARROWKEYS: These keys move the mouse cursor exactly 1 pixel.
- Switching mode:
  RKEY: starts Rotate mode again.
  SKEY: switches to Size mode.
  GKEY: switches to Grab mode.
- Rotation mode can be terminated with: LeftMouse, SPACEBAR or ENTER: move to a new location.
- RightMouse or ESC: everything returns to the former state.

ALT + R

Clear Rotation. The X,Y,Z rotations of selected Objects are set to zero.

S

Size mode or scaling mode. Works on selected Objects and vertices. The degree of scaling is exactly linked to the mouse movement. Try to move from the (rotation) midpoint with the mouse. The midpoint is determined by the settings of the 3DHeader->Around buttons.

Alternatives for starting scaling mode:

- LeftMouse (click-hold-draw) draw a V-shaped line.

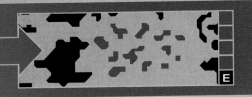

The following options are available in scaling mode:

- Limitors:
  CTRL: in steps of 0.1.
  SHIFT+CTRL: in steps of 0.01.
- MiddleMouse toggle: A short click restricts the scaling to the X, Y or Z axis. Blender calculates the appropriate axis based on the already initiated mouse movement. Click MiddleMouse again to return to free scaling.
- ARROWKEYS: These keys move the mouse cursor exactly 1 pixel.
- XKEY Make the horizontal scaling negative; this is also called an X-flip.
- YKEY Make the vertical scaling negative; this is also called a Y-flip.
- Switching mode:
  SKEY: starts Size mode again.
  RKEY: switches to Rotate mode.
  GKEY: switches to Grab mode.

Terminate Size mode with:

- LeftMouse, SPACEBAR or ENTER: move to a new location.
- RightMouse or ESC: everything returns to its previous state.

ALT + S

Clear Size. The X,Y,Z dimensions of selected Objects are set to 1.0.

SHIFT + S

Snap Menu. This menu offers a number of options for precisely specifying the position of Objects or vertices.

"Sel -> Grid": all selected Objects or vertices are moved to the closest grid position.
"Sel -> Curs": all selected Objects or vertices are moved to the 3DCursor position.
"Curs -> Grid": the 3DCursor is moved to the closest grid position.
"Curs -> Sel": the 3DCursor is moved to the selected Object. If there are multiple Objects or vertices, the 3DCursor is set to the midpoint. The 3DHeader->Around buttons determine what type of midpoint is meant here.

→ *Use the PopupMenu hotkeys 1KEY, 2KEY, etc. to select the options.*

T

Texture space mode. The position and dimensions of the texture space for the selected Objects can be changed in the same manner as described above for Grab and Size mode. To make this visible, the drawing flag EditButtons->TexSpace is set ON. A PopupMenu asks you to select: "Grabber" or "Size". Faster hotkeys: T-1 or T-2.

CTRL + T

Make Track. All selected Objects are given a rotation constraint directed at the active Object. The type of rotation and which axis is up and which one is directed at the Track Object are specified in the AnimButtons.

ALT + T

Clear Track. The tracking is turned off for all selected Objects. A PopupMenu allows you to maintain the current tracking as the rotation in the Objects.

U

Single User Menu. Use this menu to manage the (multi-) user structure. These operations only work on selected Objects and the DataBlocks that are linked to them.

"Object": if other Scenes also have a link to this Object, the link is deleted and the Object is copied. The Object now only exists in the current Scene. The links from the Object remain unchanged.
"Object & ObData": Similar to the previous command, but now the ObData blocks with multiple links are copied as well. All selected Objects are now present in the current Scene only, and each has a unique ObData (Mesh, Curve, etc.).
"Object & ObData & Materials+Tex": Similar to the previous command, but now Materials and Textures with multiple links are also copied. All selected Objects are now unique. They have unique ObData and each has a unique

Material and Texture block.
"Materials+Tex": Only the Materials and Textures with multiple links are copied.

V

Start or exit VertexPaint Mode.

ALT + V

Object-Image Aspect. This hotkey sets the X and Y dimensions of the selected Objects in relation to the dimensions of the Image Texture they have. Use this hotkey when making 2D Image compositions and multi-plane designs to quickly place the Objects in the appropriate relationship with one another.

ALT + W

Write Videoscape. The selected Mesh Object is saved as an ASCII file. Use the FileWindow to enter a file name. Blender adds the extension ".obj" to the Videoscape file.

X

Erase Selected. All selected Objects are deleted from the Scene and, if they are not linked to other Scenes, they are released. The ObData and other linked DataBlocks remain.

Z

DrawMode Solid ON/OFF. This is Zbuffered with the standard OpenGL lighting.

SHIFT + Z

DrawMode Shaded ON. This drawing mode, which is Zbuffered and Gouraud shaded, approaches the way in which Blender renders as closely as possible. It shows the situation from a single Camera frame.

CTRL + Z

Turn DrawMode Shaded ON and force a recalculation of DrawMode Shaded.

ALT + Z

Turn DrawMode Textured ON.

IpoHeader

WindowType (IconMenu)

As with every window header, the first button enables you to set the window type. Full Window (IconTog) Maximise the window or return it to the previous window display size; return to the old screen setting. HotKey: (ALT)CTRL+UPARROW

Home (IconBut)

All visible curves are displayed completely, centered in the window. HotKey: HOMEKEY.

IpoKeys (IconTog)

This is a drawing mode for the animation curves in the IpoWindow (the IpoCurves). Yellow vertical lines are drawn through all the vertices of the curves. Vertices of different curves at the same location in 'time' are joined together and can easily be selected, moved, copied or deleted. This method adds the ease of traditional key framing to the animation curve system. For Object Ipos, these IpoKeys can also be drawn and transformed in the 3DWindow. Changes in the 3D position are processed in the IpoCurves immediately.

Ipo Type

Depending on the active Object, the various Ipo systems can be specified with these buttons.

Object Ipo (IconRow)

Settings, such as the location and rotation, are animated for the active Object. All Objects in Blender can have this Ipo block.

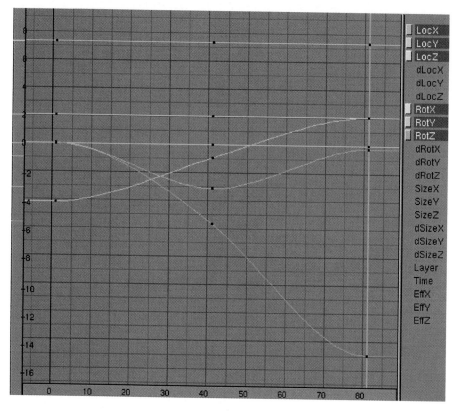

Material Ipo (IconRow)

Settings of the active Material are animated for the active Object. A NumBut is added as an extra feature. This button indicates the number of the active Texture channel. Eight Textures, each with its own mapping, can be assigned per Material. Thus, per Material Ipo, 8 curves in the row "OfsX, OfsY, ...Var" are available.

Speed Ipo (Icon Row)

If the active Object is a path Curve, this button can be used to display the Speed Ipo.

Lamp Ipo (IconRow)

If the active Object is a Lamp, this button can be used to animate light settings.

World Ipo (IconRow)

Used to animate a number of settings for the WorldButtons.

VertexKey Ipo (IconRow)

If the active Object has a VertexKey, the keys are drawn as horizontal lines. Only one IpoCurve is available to interpolate between the Keys.

Sequence Ipo (IconRow)

The active Sequence Effect can have an IpoCurve.

The DataButtons can be used to control the Ipo blocks themselves.

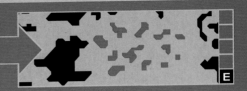

Ipo Browse (MenuBut)

Choose another Ipo from the list of available Ipos. The option "Add New" makes a complete copy of the current Ipo. This is not visible; only the name in the adjacent button will change. Only Ipos of the same type are displayed in the menu list.

IP: (TextBut)

Give the current Ipo a new and unique name. After the new name is entered, it appears in the list, sorted alphabetically.

Users (NumBut)

If this button is displayed, there is more than one user for the Ipo block. Use the button to make the Ipo "Single User".

Unlink Ipo (IconBut)

The current Ipo is unlinked.

Copy to Buffer (IconBut)

All selected IpoCurves are copied to a temporary buffer.

Paste from Buffer (IconBut)

All selected channels in the IpoWindow are assigned an IpoCurve from the temporary buffer. The rule is: the sequence in which they are copied to the buffer is the sequence in which they are pasted. A check is made to see if the number of IpoCurves is the same.

Extend mode Constant (IconBut)

The end of selected IpoCurves are horizontally extrapolated.

Extend mode Direction (IconBut)

The ends of selected IpoCurves continue extending in the direction in which they end.

Extend mode Cyclic (IconBut)

The full length of the IpoCurve is repeated cyclically.

Extend mode Cyclic Extrapolation(IconBut)

The full length of the IpoCurve is extrapolated cyclic.

View Zoom (IconBut, click - hold)

Move the mouse horizontally or vertically to zoom in or out on the IpoWindow. This is an alternative for CTRL+MiddleMouse.

View Border (IconBut)

Draw a rectangle to indicate what part of the IpoWindow should be displayed in the full window.

Lock (TogBut)

This buton locks the update of the 3DWindow while editing in the IpoWindow, so you can see changes maked to the Ipo in realtime in the 3DWindow. This option works extremely well with relative vertex keys.

©2000 Anthony C. D'agostino

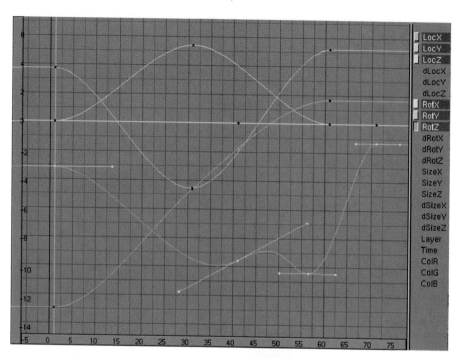

The Mouse

 (hold - draw)
These are the Gestures. Blender's gesture recognition works in two ways here:

Draw a straight line: start translation mode (Grabber).
Draw a V-shaped line: start scaling mode.

 CTRL + 🖱
Create a new vertex. These are the rules:

There is no IpoBlock (in this window) and one channel is selected: a new IpoBlock is created along with the first IpoCurve with one vertex. There is already an Ipo-Block, and a channel is selected without an IpoCurve: a new IpoCurve with one vertex is added, otherwise a new vertex is simply added to the selected IpoCurve. This is not possible if multiple IpoCurves are selected or if you are in EditMode.

🖱 (hold - move)
Depending on the position within the window:

- On the channels; if the window is not high enough to display them completely, the visible part can be shifted vertically.
- On the sliders; these can be moved. This only works if you are zoomed in.
- The rest of the window; the view is translated.

CTRL + 🖱 (hold - move)
Zoom in/out on the IpoWindow. You can zoom horizonaly or vertically using horional and vertical mouse movements.

🖱
Selection works the same here as in the 3DWindow: normally one item is selected. Use SHIFT to expand or reduce the selection (extend select).

If the IpoWindow is in IpoKey mode, the IpoKeys can be selected.
If at least 1 of the IpoCurves is in Edit-Mode, only its vertices can be selected. VertexKeys can be selected if they are drawn (horizontal lines), the IpoCurves can also be selected.

IpoWindow

The IpoWindow shows the contents of the Ipo block. Which one depends on the Ipo Type specified in the header. The standard IpoWindow has a grid with the time expressed horizontally in frames and vertical values that depend on the channel. There are 2 sliders at the edge of the IpoWindow. How far the Ipo-Window is zoomed in can be seen on the sliders, which can also be used to move the view. The right-hand part of the window shows the available channels.

To make it easier to work with rotation-IpoCurves, are displayed in degrees (instead of in radials). The vertical scale relation is: 1.0 'Blender unit' = 10 degrees.

In addition to the IpoCurves, the VertexKeys are also drawn here. These are horizontal blue lines; the yellow line visualises the reference Key.

Each channel can be operated with two buttons:

IpoCurve Select (TogBut)

This button is only displayed if the channel has an IpoCurve. The button is the same colour as the IpoCurve. Use the button to select IpoCurves. Multiple buttons can be deselected using SHIFT+LeftMouse.

Channel Select (TogBut)

A channel can be selected whether there is an IpoCurve or not. Only IpoCurves of selected channels are drawn. Multiple channels can be deselected using SHIFT+LeftMouse.

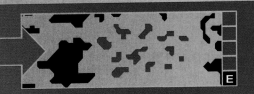

🖰 (click - hold - move)
Select and start translation mode, i.e. the Grabber. The selection can be made using any of the four selection methods discussed above.

SHIFT + 🖰

Extend the selection.

The HotKeys

PAD - − , PAD - +
Zoom in, zoom out.

PAGE UP
Select the next IpoKey. If more than one IpoKey is selected, the selection is shifted cyclically.

SHIFT + PAGE UP
Extend select the next IpoKey.

PAGE DOWN
Select the previous IpoKey. If more than one Object Key is selected, the selection is shifted cyclically.

SHIFT + PAGE DOWN
Extend select the previous IpoKey.

HOME
All visible curves are displayed completely, centered in the window.

TAB
All selected IpoCurves go into or out of EditMode. This mode allows you to transform individual vertices.

A
Select All / deselect All. If any item is selected, first everything is deselected. Placing the mouse cursor above the channels, (de)selects all channels where there is a curve.

B
Border select. Draw a rectangle with the LeftMouse; all items that fall within this rectangle are selected. Draw a rectangle with the RightMouse to deselect.

C
If one vertex or one IpoKey is selected, the current frame number is set to this position.

SHIFT + D
Duplicate Ipo. All selected vertices or IpoKeys are copied. Then translation mode is started automatically.

G
Translation mode (the Grabber). This works on selected curves, keys or vertices.

Alternatives for starting this mode:

RightMouse (click-hold-move)
LeftMouse (click-hold-draw) draw a straight line.

The following options are available in translation mode:

• Limitors:
  CTRL increments of 1 frame or vertical unit.
  SHIFT+CTRL increments of 0.1 frame or vertical unit.
  MiddleMouse toggle:
  A short click restricts the current translation to the X or Y axis. Blender calculates which axis to use, based on the already initiated mouse movement. Click MiddleMouse again to restore unlimited translation.
• ARROWKEYS:
  With these keys the mouse cursor can be moved exactly 1 pixel.
• Grabber can be terminated with:
  LeftMouse, SPACEBAR or ENTER: move to a new position.
  RightMouse of ESC: everything returns to the old position.

H
Toggle Handle align / free.

SHIFT + H
Set Handle auto. The selected Bezier handles are converted to auto type.

I
Insert Key. Vertices can be added to the visible curves in the IpoWindow. A PopupMenu asks you to make a choice:

"Current Frame"; all visible curves get a vertex on the current frame.
"Selected Keys"; (only in IpoKey mode) all selected IpoKeys get vertices for each visible curve, including IpoCurves that are not part of the IpoKey.

J
Join vertices. Selected vertices or IpoKeys can be joined. A PopupMenu asks you to make a choice:

"All Selected"; all selected vertices are replaced by a new one.
"Selected doubles": all selected vertices that are closer to each other than 0.9 frame are joined.

K
IpoKey mode ON/OFF. If the IpoBlock is Object IpoType, the Objects are redrawn with the option DrawKey ON (see the explanation under IpoHeader).

R
Recording mode. The X and Y movements of the mouse are linked to the height of the IpoCurve. Thus, this works with a maximum of two selected channels or IpoCurves. The old curve is completely deleted; the new one becomes a 'linear' type. You cannot change parts of curves with recording. The scale at which this happens is determined by the view of the IpoWindow.

A PopupMenu asks you to make a choice:

"Still"; the current frame is used as the starting point.
"Play anim"; the animation starts, allowing you to see the correlation with other animation systems.

During recording mode, the SPACEKEY or ENTER or LMB is used to stop recording. Use ESCKEY to undo changes.

S

Scaling mode. This works on selected IpoCurves and vertices. The degree of scaling is precisely linked to the mouse movement. Try to move from the (rotation) midpoint with the mouse. In IpoKey mode, you can only scale horizontally.

Alternatives for starting scaling mode:

- LeftMouse (click-hold-draw) draw a sharp angle; a V-shaped line. The following options are available in scaling mode:
- Limitors:
  TRL: in increments of 0.1.
  SHIFT+CTRL: in increments of 0.01.
  MiddleMouse toggle: A short click limits scaling to the X or Y axis. Blender calculates which axis to use based on the already initiated mouse movement. Click MiddleMouse again to return to free scaling.
- ARROWKEYS These keys allow you to move the mouse cursor exactly 1 pixel.
- XKEY Make the horizontal scaling negative, the X-flip.
- YKEY Make the vertical scaling negative, the Y-flip.
- Terminate size mode with: LeftMouse or SPACEBAR or ENTER: move to a new location. RightMouse or ESC: everything returns to its previous state.

SHIFT + S

Snap Menu.

"Horizontal": The selected Bezier handles are set to horizontal.
"To next": The selected handle or vertex is set to the same (Y) value as the next one.
"To frame": The selected handles or vertices are set to the exact frame values.
"To current frame": The selected handle or vertex is moved to the current frame.

T

If an IpoCurve is selected: "Ipo Type". The type of selected IpoCurves can be changed. A PopupMenu asks you to make a choice:

"Constant": after each vertex of the curve, this value remains constant, and is not interpolated.
"Linear": linear interpolation occurs between the vertices.
"Bezier": the vertices get a handle (i.e. two extra vertices) with which you can indicate the curvature of the interpolation curve.

If a Key is selected: "Key Type". The type of selected Keys can be changed.

"Linear": linear interpolation occurs between the Keys. The Key line is displayed as a broken line.
"Cardinal": fluent interpolation occurs between the Keys; this is the default.
"BSpline": extra fluent interpolation occurs between the Keys, four Keys are now involved in the interpolation calculation. Now the positions themselves cannot be displayed precisely, however. The Key line is shown as a broken line.

V

Vector Handle. The selected Bezier handles are converted to vector type.

X

Erase selected. The selected vertices, IpoKeys or IpoCurves are deleted. If there are selected VertexKeys, they are also deleted.

SequenceHeader

WindowType (IconMenu)

As with every window header, the first button allows you to set the type of window.

FullWindow (IconTog)

Maximise the window, or return to the previous window display size; return to the previous screen setting. Hotkey: CTRL+UPARROW

Home (IconBut)

All visible Sequences are completely displayed, centered in the window. Hotkey: HOMEKEY.

DisplayImage (IconTog)

The window shows the result of the Sequences, i.e. a picture.

ViewZoom (IconBut, click - hold)

Move the mouse to zoom into or out of the SequenceWindow. This is an alternative for CTRL+MiddleMouse. View Border (IconBut) Draw a rectangle to indicate what part of the SequenceWindow should be displayed in the full window.

Clear (Button)

Force a clear of all buffered images in memory.

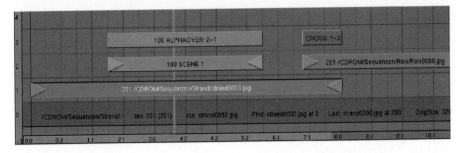

SequenceWindow

In the SequenceWindow you arrange your scenes, external pictures or movie files for the postproduction of your animation. The Strip in row 1 is a sequence of numbered jpeg-pictures. It will play for a few seconds and then "SCENE 1" in row 2 will be superimposed with the "ALPHAOVER" effect in row 3. The "ALPHAOVER" generates some shadows, which can be seen in the film-strip below. In "SCENE 1" (which is a normal Blender-scene) the titling is done with the usual animation features from Blender, which makes that system a very flexible titler.

In the end a transition of strip in row 1 and the following in row 2 is done with the CROSS effect. The numbers 1-2 are representing the row numbers the effect applies to. The result is a smooth fade between the two strips in row 1 and 2.

The mouse

The position of the mouse cursor becomes the current frame. If DisplayImage is ON, the Sequences at this position are read or calculated at this position.

 (hold - move)
Depending on the position within the window:

On the sliders; this can be moved. The rest of the window; the view is translated.

CTRL + (hold - move)
Zoom in/out on the IpoWindow. For ease of use, you can only zoom horizontally. Use the HeaderButton if you must zoom vertically as well.

Selection works the same way here as in the 3DWindow: normally a maximum of one Sequence strip is selected. Use SHIFT to extend or reduce the selection (extend select).

(click - hold - move)
Selects something and immediately starts translation mode, i.e. the Grabber.

SHIFT +
Extend selection.

The hotkeys

PAD -, PAD +
Zoom in, zoom out.

SHIFT + PAD +
Insert gap. One second is inserted at the current frame position. This only applies to strips that are totally to the right of the current frame.

ALT + PAD +
Insert gap. As above, but now 10 seconds are inserted.

SHIFT + PAD -
Remove gaps. All strips that are completely to the right of the current frame and do not start past the last frame are

repositioned so that there is no longer an empty space.

PAD .
The last selected strip is displayed completely.

HOME
All visible Sequences are displayed completely, centered in the window.

A
Select All / deselect All. If any strip is selected, everything is first deselected.

SHIFT + A
Add sequence. A PopupMenu asks you to make a choice. The first three are possible sources:

"Images"; Specify with FileSelect (with RightMouse select!), what pictures will form a strip. If only 1 picture is selected, the strip is lengthened to 50 frames. Directories can also be specified; each directory then becomes a separate strip in the SequenceWindow.
"Movie"; Specify with FileSelect (with LeftMouse or MiddleMouse!) what movie will comprise a strip
"Scene"; A PopupMenu asks you to specify the Scene that is to be inserted as a strip. The Scene is then rendered according to its own settings and processed in the Sequence system.

The following menu options are effects that work on pictures; two strips must be selected for this. The order of selection determines how the effects are applied.

"Cross"; a fluent transition from strip 1 to strip 2.
"GammaCross"; This is a gamma-corrected cross. It provides a more 'natural' transition in which lighter parts are inserted before darker parts.
"Add"; two strips are added together.
"Sub"; the second strip is subtracted from the first.
"Mul"; the strips are multiplied.
"AlphaOver"; the second strip, with its alpha, is placed over the first. Pictures with alpha are normally 32 bits.

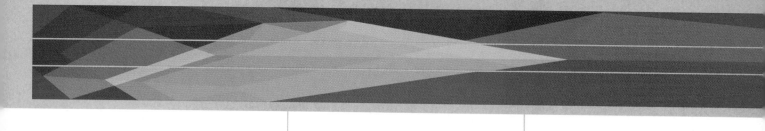

"AlphaUnder"; the first strip is placed behind the second, with the alpha of the second strip.
"AlphaOverDrop"; like "AlphaOver", but now with a drop shadow.

B

Border select. Draw a rectangle with the LeftMouse; all strips that fall within this rectangle are selected. Draw a rectangle with the RightMouse to deselect.

C

If one of the ends of a strip is selected (the triangles), the current frame is moved to this end. In all other cases, the Change menu is invoked. This menu allows you to change specific characteristics of the active strip.
If this is an Image strip:

"Change Images". The FileSelect appears and new pictures can be specified.

If this is an Effect strip:

"Switch a-b"; change the sequence of the effect.
"Recalculate"; force a recalculation of the effect.
"Cross, Gammacross, Add, ..."; change the type of effect.

If this is a Scene strip:

"Update Start and End"; the start and end frame of the Scene is processed in the strip again.

SHIFT + D

Add Duplicate. All selected strips are copied. Immediately thereafter, translation mode is started. The images in an Image strip are reused; they take up no extra memory.

F

"Set Filter". An extra Y filter can only be activated in Movie strips. This filter is for a stable video display with no flickering.

G

Translation mode (the Grabber). This works on selected strips or the (triangular) ends of selected strips. Alternative for starting this mode: Right-Mouse (click-hold-move). The following options are available in translation mode:

Limitors: SHIFT with finer translation.
MiddleMouse toggle: A short click limits the current translation to the X or Y axis. Blender calculates which axis to use based on the already initiated mouse movement. Click MiddleMouse again to return to unlimited translation.
ARROWKEYS: These keys can be used to move the mouse cursor exactly 1 pixel.
Grabber can be terminated with:
LeftMouse, SPACEBAR or ENTER: move to a new position.
RightMouse or ESC: everything returns to the old position.

M

Make Meta. The selected strips are combined into a Meta strip. This only occurs if no unselected strips are linked to the selection by effects. Use TABKEY to view the contents of a Meta or to leave the Meta. Metas can be inside other Metas, and behave exactly like a normal Sequence strip. When Metas are duplicated, their contents are not linked!

ALT + M

Un-Meta. The selected Meta is 'unpacked' again.

SHIFT + S

Snap menu. The PopupMenu offers you a choice:
"Sequence to frame"; the selected strips are placed with their starting point on the current frame.

X

Delete Sequence. The selected strips are deleted.

 OBCamera

OopsHeader

WindowType (IconMenu)

As with every window header, the first button allows you to set the window type.

Full Window (IconTog)

Maximise the window, or return to the previous window display size; return to the previous screen setting. HotKey: (ALT-)CTRL+UPARROW

Home (IconBut)

All visible blocks are displayed completely, centered in the window. HotKey: HOMEKEY.

View Zoom (IconBut, click - hold)

Move the mouse to zoom in or out of the OopsWindow. This is an alternative to CTRL+MiddleMouse.

View Border (IconBut)

Draw a frame to indicate what part of the OopsWindow should be displayed in the FullWindow.

Visible Select (IconTog)

This row of buttons determines what types of DataBlocks must be displayed. Relations between blocks are only shown if both blocks are visible.

These are:
"Lay": the layer setting of the Scene determines what Objects are drawn.
"Scene": all Scenes present are displayed.
"Object": all Objects of all visible Scenes are displayed, possibly limited by the "Lay" option.
Mesh
"Curve": this is also for Surface and Font blocks.

"MetaBall"
"Lattice"
"Lamp"
"Material"
"Texture"
"Ipo"
"Library"

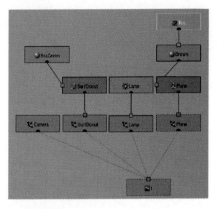

OopsWindow

The OopsWindow gives a schematic overview of the current structure. Blender is based on an Object-Oriented Programming System (OOPS!). The building blocks are universal DataBlocks that are assigned relationships using links. The different DataBlocks in the OopsWindow can be recognised by an icon and the colour. The DataBlocks have a clearly visible 'entrance' and 'exit' between which link lines are drawn.

The current Scene and the active Object have a frame with a broken line.

The functionality of the OopsWindow is limited to visualisation. Links are created using the available HotKeys (CTRL-L in the 3DWindow) and with the DataButtons in the Headers. Selected Objects are also selected in the OopsWindow, and vice versa.

In the accompanying example, we see the Scene at the bottom, with four linked Object blocks. The Object blocks have links to the specific ObData; such as

Mesh, Surface, Lamp. The Materials ("Brown" and "SeaGreen") are linked to the ObData and the Texture is linked to a Material.

The mouse

(hold - draw)
These are the Gestures. Blender's gesture recognition works in two ways here:

Draw a straight line: start translation mode.
Draw a V-shaped line: start scaling mode.

(hold - move)
The view is translated.

CTRL + (hold - move)
Zoom in or out of the OopsWindow.

Select works here in the normal fashion: normally a maximum of one DataBlock is selected. Use SHIFT to enlarge or reduce the selection (extend select).

(click - hold - move)
Select and start translation mode, the Grabber.

SHIFT +
Extend selection.

CTRL +
This selects and activates a DataBlock. This only works for Scenes and Objects.

The HotKeys

PAD-, PAD+
Zoom in, zoom out.

HOME
All visible blocks are displayed completely, centred in the window.

1, 2, ... =
The visible layers of the current Scene can be set. Use SHIFT for extend select.

A
Select All / deselect All. If one block is selected, everything is first deselected.

B

Border select. Draw a rectangle with the LeftMouse; all blocks that fall within this rectangle are selected. Draw a rectangle with the RightMouse to deselect the blocks.

G

Translation mode (the Grabber). This works on selected blocks. Alternatives for starting this mode:

RightMouse (click-hold-move)
LeftMouse (click-hold-draw)
draw a straight line.

The following options are available in translation mode:

• MiddleMouse toggle: A short click restricts the current translation to the X or Y axis. Blender calculates which axis to use based on the already initiated mouse movement. Click MiddleMouse again to restore unlimited translation.
• ARROWKEYS: The mouse cursor can be moved exactly 1 pixel with these keys.
• Grabber terminates with:
LeftMouse or SPACEBAR or ENTER: move to a new position.
RightMouse or ESC: everything returns to the old position.

L

Select Linked Forward. All DataBlocks that are linked by a selected DataBlock are also selected. In this way, the entire underlying structure can be selected, starting with a selected Scene block.

SHIFT + L

Select Linked Backward. All users of selected DataBlocks are selected. This allows you to visualise what Objects the Material uses, starting with a selected Material block.

S

Scaling mode. This works on selected blocks. Only the length of the links, i.e. the distance between the DataBalocks, can be transformed. The degree of scaling corresponds exactly to the mouse movement. Try to move the (rotation)

midpoint with the mouse. Alternatives for starting scaling mode: - LeftMouse (click-hold-draw), draw a sharp angle; a V-shaped line. The following options are available in scaling mode:
MiddleMouse toggle: A short click restricts the scaling to the X or Y axis. Blender calculates which axis to use based on the already initiated mouse movement. Click MiddleMouse again to return to free scaling.
ARROWKEYS: These keys move the mouse cursor exactly 1 pixel.
Exit size mode with:
LeftMouse or SPACEBAR or ENTER: move to a new location.
RightMouse or ESC: everything returns to its previous state.

SHIFT + S

Shuffle Oops. An attempt is made to minimise the length of the link lines for selected DataBlocks using parsed toggling.

ALT + S

Shrink Oops. The length of the link lines for the selected DataBlocks is shortened without causing the blocks to overlap.

The Textwindow is a simple but useful Texteditor, fully integrated into Blender. The main purpose of it is to write Python scripts, but it is also very useful to write comments in the Blendfile or to instruct other users about the purpose of the scene.

The TextWindow can be displayed with SHIFT-F11 or with adjusting the Icon-Menu in the Windowheader. As usual there is an IconBut to make the Text-Window fullscreen, the next MenuButton can be used to switch between the text-files, open new ones or adding new text buffers. The x-shaped Button deletes a textbuffer after a confirmation.

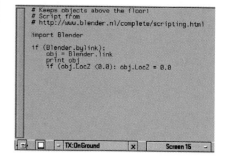

With the right MenuButton you can change the font for displaying the text.

With LeftMouse-Hold and dragging the mouse you can mark ranges of text for the usual cut, copy & paste functions. The keycommands are:

ALT - C

Copy the marked text into a buffer.

ALT - X

Cut out the marked text into a buffer.

ALT - V

Paste the text from buffer to the cursor in the textwindow.

ALT - S

Saves the text as a textfile, a FileWindow appears.

ALT - O

Loads a text, a FileWindow appears.

SHIFT - ALT - F

Pops up the Filemenu for the TextWindow.

ALT - J

Pops up a NumButton where you can specify a line number the cursor will jump to.

ALT - P

Executes the text as a Python script.

ALT - U

Unlimited Undo for the TextWindow.

ALT - R

Redo function, recovers the last Undo.

ALT - A

Mark the whole text.

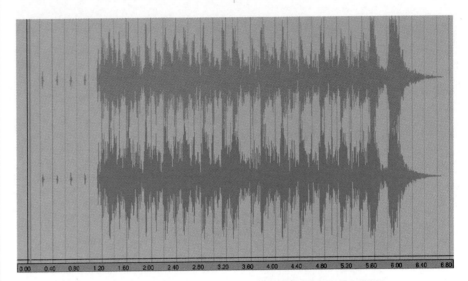

The SoundWindow is currently only useful for the realtime part of Blender, which is not covered by this manual.

It is used to load and visualise sounds. You can grab and zoom the window like every other window in Blender.

→ SO:Hey!.wav   Load
SoundBrowse (MenuButton)

WAV: 44100 kHz Stereo 16 bits
InfoText

◄‖ □⌂ → SO:Hey!.wav   Load WAV: 44100 kHz Stereo 16 bits

SoundHeader

◄‖ □⌂
WindowType (IconMenu)

As with every window header, the first button allows you to set the type of window.

FullWindow (IconTog)

Maximise the window, or return to the previous window display size; return to the previous screen setting. Hotkey: CTRL+UPARROW

Home (IconBut)

All visible Sequences are completely displayed, centered in the window. Hotkey: HOMEKEY.

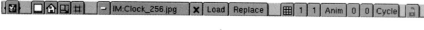

ImageHeader

WindowType (IconMenu)

As with every window header, the first button allows you to set the type of window.

FullWindow (IconTog)

Maximise the window, or return to the previous window display size; return to the previous screen setting. HotKey: (ALT-)CTRL+UPARROW

Home (IconBut)

The picture is displayed completely, centred in the window. HotKey: HOMEKEY.

Square UV - polygons (IconTog)

This option keeps the UV polygons square while UV-texturing

Clip UV with imagesize (IconTog)

Limits the UV-polygons to the imagesize

The Image blocks can be specified using the DataButtons.

Image Browse (MenuBut)

Select an Image from the list provided.

IM: (TextBut)

Give the current Image a new and unique name. After the new name is entered, it is displayed in the list alphabetically.

Load (But)

Load a new Image. A FileSelect asks you to specify what file.

Replace (But)

Replace the picture in the current Image block with a new one.

Tile (IconTog)

Sets the image to tile mode. This way you can make a repeating pattern with a small part of an image. With SHIFT-LeftMouse you indicate which part of the image should be used.

PartsX and PartsY (NumBut)

Defines the dimension of the tile mode. Currently only 4x4 is implemented.

Anim (IconTog)

Enables the texture-animation.

Animation start and end (NumBut)

Controls the start and end of the texture-animation.

Cycle (IconTog)

Switches between one-time and cyclic play.

Lock (IconTog)

When activated, changes made in the ImageWindow are shown in realtime in the 3DWindow.

ImageWindow
(see Fig.1)

Images in Blender are also DataBlocks. The ImageWindow is used for visualisation and UV-texturing of realtime-models.

The use of the mouse and HotKeys is:

(hold - move)
Translate the view.

PAD −, PAD +
Zoom in, zoom out.

HOME
The picture is displayed completely, centred in the window.

CTRL + N
Replace Image Names. A menu asks you to enter an old and a new file name. All file names for Images with the old name or a name which starts with corresponding characters are replaced by the new name. This utility is especially useful for changing directories.

Example:
"old" = /data/, "new" = /pics/textures/.
The file name "/data/marble.tga" is replaced by "/pics/textures/marble.tga".

Fig. 1

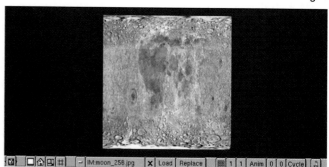

ImageSelectHeader

WindowType (IconMenu)

As with every window header, the first button allows you to set the type of window.

FullWindow (IconTog)

Maximise the window, or return to the previous window display size; return to the old screen setting. HotKey: CTRL+UPARROW

Remove (IconBut)

Delete the ".Bpib" help file in the current directory. A new ".Bpib" is only created once the directory is read again.

Dirview (IconTog)

Indicates whether the left part, where the directories are displayed, is shown.

Info (IconTog)

Indicates whether the lower part, where information about the active picture is displayed, is shown.

Images (IconTog)

Obsolete.

Magnify (IconTog)

The active picture is displayed twice as large.

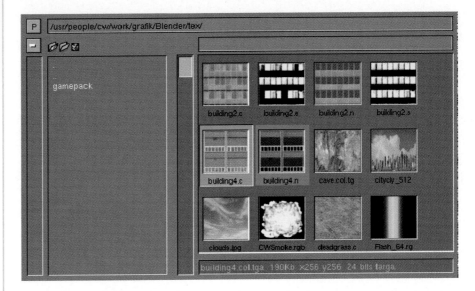

ImageSelectWindow

In parts of the Blender interface where pictures can be loaded, you generally have the option of using a FileSelect window or the ImageSelect window. For the most part, the functionality is the same. The ImageSelect window reads the directory and examines each file to see if it is a recognisable image. After the entire directory is scanned, the images are loaded and displayed as a thumbnail and saved in the ".Bpib" file. If a ".Bpib" file already exists, it is first read in and compared to the contents of the directory.

P (But)

Displays the parent directory. Also with: PKEY.

DirName: (TextBut)

This button displays the current directory.

Preset Directories (MenuBut)

The file $HOME/.Bfs contains a number of pre-sets that are shown in this menu. While a file is being read or written, the directory involved is temporarily added to the menu.

FileName: (TextBut)

The file name can be entered here.

Status Icons.

The different phases of ImageSelect: - Was a ".Bpib" file found? - Was the directory scanned completely? - Have all the pictures been read in?

The mouse and HotKeys

Activate a file. The file name is placed in the FileName button.

Activate a file and return to the previous window type.

Select a file.

ENTER / PAD ENTER
Close the ImageSelectWindow; return with a OK message. ESC Close the ImageSelectWindow; no action is performed.

PAGE DOWN

Scroll down one page.

PAGE UP

Scroll up one page.

P

Go to the parent directory.

To allow you to view sequential sequences of rendered frames or AVIs, Blender has a simple, but efficient animation playback option.

This playback is invoked with the "PLAY" button in the DisplayButtons. This button plays all of the numbered frames specified in the DisplayButtons->pics TextBut.

An alternative for starting the animation window is to type -a in the command line: blender -a . Blender first reads all the files in memory and then displays them as a flip book. Check in advance to make sure sufficient memory is available; you can see this with the FileWindow. Use ESCKEY to stop the reading process.

The commands available in the playback window are:

ESC

Close the window.

ENTER, **PAD ENTER**

Start playback.

←, **↓**

Stops the playback; if playback is already stopped, moves 1 frame back.

→, **↑**

Stops the playback; if playback is already stopped, moves 1 frame forward.

NUMPAD 0

Sets the playback at the first frame and switches 'cyclical' playback off. Pressing this key again turns cyclical playback on again and starts the playback at the beginning.

PAD 1 to **PAD 9**

The playback speed. 60, 50, 30, 25, 20, 15, 12, 10 and 6 frames per second, respectively.

(hold - move)
Move the mouse horizontally through the playback window to scroll through the frames.

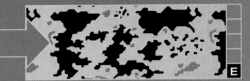

Chapter 13
The buttons

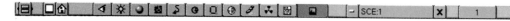

WindowType (IconMenu)

As with every window header, the first button enables you to set the window type.

FullWindow (IconTog)

Maximise the window, or return to the previous window display size; return to the old screen setting. HotKey: (ALT-)CTRL+UPARROW

Home (IconBut)

The optimal view settings for the current window are restored. HotKey: HOMEKEY. The following series of buttons determine the type of ButtonsWindow. In order, they are:

ViewButtons. (IconRow)

The 3DWindow settings for the window.

LampButtons (IconRow)

The settings of the active Lamp Object. HotKey: F4.

MaterialButtons (IconRow)

The settings of the active Material linked by the active Object. HotKey F5.

TextureButtons (IconRow)

The settings of the active Texture. This can be the Texture for a Material, Lamp or World. HotKey: F6.

AnimButtons (IconRow)

The (animation) settings of the active Object, including Particle Effects. HotKey: F7.

RealTimeButtons (IconRow)

Settings for real time 3D content. HotKey: F8

WorldButtons (IconRow)

The settings of the World linked by the current Scene.

EditButtons (IconRow)

The settings and EditMode options of the ObData linked by the active Object. HotKey: F9.

Face/PaintButtons (IconRow)

The VertexPaint and FaceSelect options. Only for an active Mesh Object.

RadiosityButtons (IconRow)

The Radiosity options.

ScriptButtons (IconRow)

Buttons to assign scripts.

DisplayButtons (IconRow)

The settings of the Scene. HotKey: F10.

Later sections deal with each button in detail.

This group of DataButtons is drawn based on the type of ButtonsWindow and the availability of the data to be visualised. The header for the Display-Buttons is shown here as an example.

Scene Browse (MenuBut)

Choose a different scene from the list of available scenes.

SCE: (TextBut)

Give the current Scene a new and unique name.

Delete Scene (But)

"OK? Delete Current Scene"

Current Frame. (NumBut)

The current frame number is displayed as a fixed part of the ButtonsHeader.

ButtonsWindow

A ButtonsWindow offers a number of extra facilities:

(hold-move)
If space is available, this can be used to horizontally or vertically move the view.

CTRL+ (hold-move)
Within certain limits, a ButtonsWindow can be enlarged or reduced.

PAD+
Zoom in.

PAD-
Zoom out.

HOME
The optimal view settings for the current window are restored.

If there is only one 3DWindow in the current Screen, the NumPad commands for the 3DWindow also work in the ButtonsWindow.

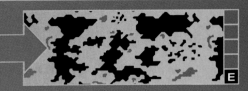

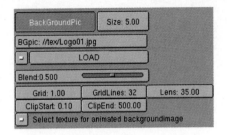

These buttons are not global; independent variables can be set for each 3DWindow independently, for the grid or the lens, for example. Use the HotKey SHIFT+F7 in the 3DWindow or the WindowType button in the 3DHeader.

Use SHIFT+F5 to restore the 3DWindow.

BackGroundPic (TogBut)

This option displays a picture in the background of the 3DWindow. Standard Image blocks are used; re-using an Image does not consume any additional memory.
The BackGroundPic is only drawn in ortho and Camera view. It is always centered around the global nulpoint.
In camera View, it is completely displayed in the viewport.

Size: (NumBut)

The size in Blender units for the width of the BackGroundPic. Only of interest in ortho.

ImageBrowse (MenuBut)

Select an existing Image from the list provided.

LOAD (But)

The window changes into an Image-SelectWindow. Use this to specify the picture to be used as the BackGroundPic. The picture is added to the Blender structure as an Image block.

Blend (NumSli)

The factor with which the grey of the 3DWindow is blended with the background picture.

TextureBrowse (MenuBut)

Specify a Texture to be used as the BackGroundPic. This only works for Image Textures. The TextureButtons have extensive options for an animated Image Texture, which allows you to achieve an animated BackGroundPic. Use this option for rotoscoping, for example. This is a technique in which video images are used as examples or as a basis for 3D animation.

Grid: (NumBut)

The distance between two grid lines. This value is also used to define minimum and maximum values for several buttons in Blender.

GridLines: (NumBut)

The number of lines that comprise the grid in perspective or Camera view. A value of zero means no grid at all.

Lens: (NumBut)

The 'lens' used for the perspective view. This is independent of the Camera.

ClipStart: (NumBut)

The start clipping value in perspective view mode.

ClipEnd: (NumBut)

The distance beyond which items are no longer displayed in perspective view mode. The ClipStart and ClipEnd limits also determine the resolution (actually the density) of the OpenGL zbuffer. Try to keep these values as close together as possible, so that the zbuffer can distinguish small differences.

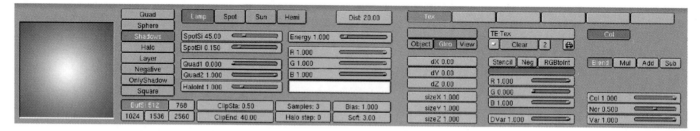

The settings in these ButtonsWindow visualise the Lamp DataBlock. The Lamp-Buttons are only displayed if the active Object is a Lamp. HotKey for LampButtons: F4.

The DataButtons in the Header indicate what Lamp block is visualised.

Lamp Browse (MenuBut)

Choose another Lamp block from the list provided.

LA: (TextBut)

Give the current Lamp a new and unique name.

Users (But)

If the Lamp Block is used by more than one Object, this button shows the total number of Objects. Press the button to make the Lamp "Single User". Then an exact copy is made.

Lamp options

Quad (TogBut)

The distance from the lamp is in inverse quadratic proportion to the intensity of the light. An inverse linear progression is standard (see also the buttons "Dist", "Quad1" and "Quad2").

Sphere (TogBut)

The lamp only sheds light within a spherical area around the lamp. The radius of the sphere is determined by the "Dist" button.

Shadows (TogBut)

The lamp can produce shadows. Shadow calculations are only possible with the Spot lamps. The render option "Shadows" must also be turned ON in the DisplayButtons. See also the shadow buffer buttons later in this section.

Halo (TogBut)

The lamp has a halo. This only works with Spot lamps. The intensity of the halo is calculated using a conic section. With the option "Halo step:" it also uses the shadow buffer (volumetric rendering).

The scope of the spot halo is determined by the value of "Dist".

Layer (TogBut)

Only Objects in the same layer(s) as the Lamp Object are illuminated. This enables you to use selective lighting, to give objects an extra accent or to restrict the effects of the lamp to a particular space. It also allows you to keep rendering times under control.

Negative (TogBut)

A lamp casts 'negative' light.

OnlyShadow (TogBut)

For spot lamps (with "Shadow" ON), only the shadow is rendered. Light calculations are not performed and where there are shadows, the value of "Energy" is reduced.

Square

Spotlamps can have square Spotbundles with this option. For a better control over shadows and for slide projector effects.

Lamp types

Lamp Spot Sun Hemi

Lamp (RowBut)

The standard lamp, a point light source.

Spot (RowBut)

The lamp is restricted to a conical space. The 3DWindow shows the form of the spotlight with a broken line. Use the sliders "SpotSi" and "SpotBl"

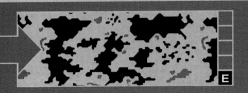

to set the angle and the intensity of the beam.

Sun (RowBut)

The light shines from a constant direction; the distance has no effect. The position of the Lamp Object is thus unimportant, except for the rotation.

Hemi (RowBut)

Like "Sun", but now light is shed in the form of half a sphere, a hemisphere. This method is also called directional ambient. It can be used to suggest cloudy daylight.

Dist: 20.00

Dist (NumBut)

For the lamp types "Lamp" and "Spot", the distance affects the intensity of the light. The standard formula is used for this: D = "Dist" button, a = distance to the lamp.

Light intensity = $D/(D + a)$.

This is an inverse linear progression. With the option "Quad", this becomes:

Light intensity = $D/(D + a*a)$.

Energy 1.000
R 1.000
G 1.000
B 1.000

Energy (NumSli)

The intensity of the light. The standard settings in Blender assume that a minimum of two lamps are used.

R, G, B (NumSli)

The red, green and blue components of the light.

SpotSi 45.00
SpotBl 0.150
Quad1 0.000
Quad2 1.000
HaloInt 1.000

SpotSi (NumSli)

The angle of the beam measured in degrees. Use for shadow lamp beams of less than 160 degrees.

SpotBl (NumSli)

The softness of the spot edge.

Quad1, Quad2 (NumSli)

The light intensity formula of a Quad Lamp is actually: Light intensity = $D / (D + (quad1 * a) + (quad2 * a * a))$ D = "Dist" button. a = distance to the lamp. The values of "quad1" and "quad2" at 1.0 produces the strongest quadratic progression. The values of "quad1" and "quad2" at 0.0 creates a special Quad lamp that is insensitive to distance.

HaloInt (NumSli)

The intensity of the spot halo. The scope of the spot halo is determined by "Dist".

Shadow Buffer

| BufSi 512 | 768 | ClipSta: 0.50 | Samples: 3 | Bias: 1.000 |
| 1024 | 1536 | 2560 | ClipEnd: 40.00 | Halo step: 0 | Soft: 3.00 |

Blender uses a shadow buffer algorithm. From the spotlight, a picture is rendered for which the distance from the spotlight is saved for each pixel. The shadow buffers are compressed, a buffer of 1024x1024 pixels requires, on average, only 1.5 Mb of memory.

This method works quite quickly, but must be adjusted carefully. There are two possible side effects:

Aliasing. The shadow edge has a block-like progression. Make the spot beam smaller, enlarge the buffer or increase the number of samples in the buffer.

Biasing. Faces that are in full light show banding with a block-like pattern. Set the "Bias" as high as possible and reduce the distance between "ClipSta" and "ClipEnd".

Bufsi 512, 768, 1024, 1536, 2560 (RowBut)

The size of the buffer in pixels. The value of DisplayButtons->Percentage (100%, 75%, ...) is multiplied by this.

ClipSta, ClipEnd (NumBut)

Seen from the spot lamp: everything closer than ClipSta always has light; everything farther away than ClipEnd always has shadow. Within these limits, shadows are calculated. The smaller the shadow area, the clearer the distinction the lamp buffer can make between small distances, and the fewer side effects you will have. It is particularly important to set the value of ClipSta as high as possible.

Samples (NumBut)

The shadow buffer is 'sampled'; within a square area a test is made for shadow 3*3, 4*4 or 5*5 times. This reduces aliasing.

Halo step (NumBut)

A value other than zero in the button "Halo step" causes the use of the shadow detection (volumetric rendering) for Halos. Low values cause better results and longer rendering times. A value of "8" works fine in most cases.

Soft (NumBut)

The size of the sample area. A large "Soft" value produces broader shadow edges.

Texture Channels

Texture Name (RowBut)

A Lamp has six channels with which Textures can be linked. Each channel has its own mapping, i.e. the manner in which the texture works on the lamp. The settings are in the buttons described below.

Mapping: coordinates input.

Each Texture has a 3D coordinate (the texture coordinate) as input. The starting point is always the global coordinate of the 3D point that is seen in the pixel to be rendered. A lamp has three options for this.

Object Name (TextBut)

The name of the Object that is used for the texture coordinates. If the Object does not exist, the button remains empty.

Object (RowBut)

Each Object in Blender can be used as a source for texture coordinates. To do this, an inverse transformation is applied to the global coordinate, which gives the local Object coordinate. In this way, the texture is linked with the position, size and rotation of the Object.

Glob (RowBut)

The global coordinate is passed on to the texture.

View (RowBut)

The view vector of the lamp; the vector of the global coordinate to the lamp, is passed on to the texture. If the lamp is a Spot, the view vector is normalised to the dimension of the spot beam, allowing use of a Spot to project a 'slide'.

Mapping: transform coordinates.

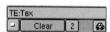

Use these buttons to adjust the texture coordinate more finely.

dX, dY, dZ (NumBut)

The extra translation of the Texture coordinate.

sizeX, sizeY, sizeZ (NumBut)

The extra scaling of the Texture coordinate.

Texture Block

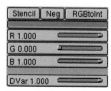

TE: (TextBut)

The name of the Texture block. The name can be changed with this button.

Texture Browse (MenuBut)

Select an existing Texture from the list provided, or create a new Texture Block.

Clear (But)

The link to the Texture is erased.

Users (But)

If the Texture Block has multiple users, this button shows the total number of users. Press the button to make the Texture "Single User". Then an exact copy is made.

Auto Name (But)

Blender assigns a name to the Texture.

Mapping: Texture input settings.

These buttons pass extra information to the Texture.

Stencil (TogBut)

Normally, textures are executed one after the other and placed over each other. A second Texture channel can completely replace the first. This option sets the mapping to stencil mode. No subsequent Texture can have an effect on the area the current Texture affects.

Neg (TogBut)

The inverse of the Texture is applied.

RGBtoInt (TogBut)

With this option, an RGB texture (affects colour) is used as an Intensity Texture (affects a value).

R, G, B (NumSli)

The colour with which an Intensity Texture blends with the current colour.

DVar (NumSli)

The value with which the Intensity Texture blends with the current value.

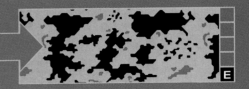

Mapping: output to.

Col (TogBut)

The Texture affects the colour of
the lamp.

Mapping: output settings.

These buttons adjust the output of
the Texture.

Blend (RowBut)

The Texture mixes the values.

Mul (Rowbut)

The Texture multiplies the values.

Add (RowBut)

The Texture adds the values.

Sub (RowBut)

The Texture subtracts the values.

Col (NumSli)

The extent to which the Texture affects
the colour.

Nor (NumSli)

The extent to which the Texture affects
the normal (not important here).

Var (NumSli)

The extent to which the Texture affects
the value (a variable, not important here).

©2000 Angel Quiijada Alvares

The settings in this ButtonsWindow visualise the Material DataBlock. The MaterialButtons are only displayed if the active Object has a Material. Hotkey: F5.

The DataButtons in the Header indicate what Material block is visualised.

Material Browse (MenuBut)

Select another Material from the list provided, or create a new block.

MA: (TextBut)

Give the current Material a new and unique name.

Users (But)

If the Material block is used by more than one Object, this button indicates the total number of users. Press the button to make the Material "Single User". An exact copy is created.

Remove Link (But)

Delete the link to the Material.

Auto Name (But)

Blender assigns a name to the Material.

Copy to buffer (IconBut)

The complete contents of the Material and all the mapping is copied to a temporary buffer.

Copy from buffer (IconBut)

The temporary buffer is copied to the Material.

Preview settings.

Plane (IconRow)

The preview plane only shows the X-Y coordinates.

Sphere (IconRow)

In the sphere-preview the Z axis is the vertical axis for the preview sphere; the X and Y axes revolve around this axis.

Cube (IconRow)

The cubic preview shows the Material preview mapped on three sides of a cube, allowing to see the three possible mappings.

Background (IconTog)

Use this button to select a light or a dark background.

Refresh (Icon)

Use this button to refresh the Material preview. This is mostly needed after changing frames while having a material-Ipo.

ME:Plane   OB ME

These buttons specify what the Material block is linked to, or must be linked to. By linking Materials directly to Objects, each Object is rendered in its own Material.

ME: (TextBut)

This Button indicates the block to which the Material is linked. This button can only be used to give the block another name. Possible blocks are:

ME: Material is linked to a Mesh (ObData) block.
CU: Material is linked to a Curve, Surface or Font (ObData) block.
MB: Material is linked to a MetaBall (ObData) block.
OB: Material is linked to the Object itself.

OB (RowBut)

Use this button to link the current Material to the Object. Any link to the ObData block remains in effect. Links can be removed with the Header button:

"Remove Link" ME or CU or MB (RowBut)

Use this button to link the current Material to the ObData of the Object. Any link to the Object block remains in effect. Links can be removed with the Header button: "Remove Link"

1 Mat 1 (NumBut)

An Object or ObData block may have more than one Material. This button can be used to specify which of the Materials must be displayed, i.e. which Material is active. The first digit indicates how many Materials there are; the second digit indicates the number of the active Material. Each face in a Mesh has a corresponding number: the 'Material index'. The number of indices can be specified with the EditButtons.

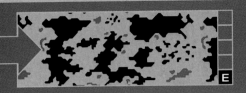
Curves and Surfaces also have
Material indices.

RGB (RowBut)

Most colour sliders in Blender have two
pre-set options: in this case, the colour is
created by mixing Red, Green, Blue.

HSV (RowBut)

The colour sliders mix colour with the
Hue, Saturation, Value system. 'Hue'
determines the colour, 'Saturation'
determines the amount of colour in
relation to grey and 'Value' determines
the light intensity of the colour.

DYN (RowBut)

Adjust parameters for the dynamics
optons.

The following buttons specify what type
of color is visualised in the sliders:

Mir (RowBut)

The mirror colour of the Material. This
affects a environment or reflection map.

Spec (RowBut)

Specularity, the colour of the sheen.

Color (RowBut)

The basic colour of the Material.

R, G, B (NumSli) or H, S, V (NumSli)

These mix the colour specified.

Ref (NumSli)

Reflectivity. The degree to which the
Material reflects the basic colour when
light falls on it.

Alpha (NumSli)

The degree of coverage, which can be
used to make Materials transparent. Use
the option "ZTransp" to specify that multiple transparent layers can exist. Without
this option, only the Material itself is
rendered, no matter what faces lie behind
it. The transparent information is saved in
an alpha layer, which can be saved as
part of a picture (see DisplayButtons).

Emit (NumSli)

The Material 'emits light', without
shedding light on other faces of course.

Ambient (NumSli)

The degree to which the global Ambient
colour is applied, a simple form of
environmental light. The global Ambient
can be specified in the World block,
using the WorldButtons. Ambient is
useful for giving the total rendering a
softer, more coloured atmosphere.

Zoffset (NumBut)

This button allows you to give the face
to be rendered an artificial forward offset
in Blender's Zbuffer system. This only
applies to Materials with the option
"ZTransp". This option is used to place
cartoon figures on a 3D floor as images
with alpha. To prevent the figures from
'floating', the feet and the shadows drawn
must be placed partially beneath the floor.
The Zoffset option then ensures that the
entire figure is displayed. This system
offers numerous other applications for
giving (flat) images of spatial objects the
appropriate 3D placement.

Spec (NumBut)

The degree of sheen (specularity) the
Material has.

Hard (NumBut)

The hardness of the specularity. A large
value gives a hard, concentrated sheen,
like that of a billiard ball. A low value
gives a metallic sheen.

SpTr (NumBut)

This button makes areas of the Material
with a sheen opaque. It can be used to
give transparent Materials a 'glass' effect.

Add (NumBut)

This option adds some kind of glow to
transparent objects, but only works with
the unified renderer.

TexFace (TogBut)

A texture assigned with the UV-Editor
gives the color information for the faces.

NoMist (TogBut)

The Material is insensitive to "Mist"
(see WorldButtons).

Traceable (TogBut)

This term stems from Blender's ray-trace
past. It specifies whether or not shadow
lamps can 'see' the current Material.

Turn the "Traceble" option OFF to prevent undesired shadows.

Shadow (TogBut)

This button determines whether the Material can receive a shadow, i.e. whether a shadow calculation is needed.

Shadeless (TogBut)

This button makes the Material insensitive to light or shadow.

Wire (TogBut)

Only the edges of faces are rendered (normal rendering!). This results in an exterior that resembles a wire frame. This option can only be used for Meshes.

VCol Light (TogBut)

If the Mesh vertex has colours (see Edit-Buttons), they are added to the Material as extra light. The colours also remain visible without lamps. Use this option to render radiosity-like models.

VCol Paint (TogBut)

If the Mesh vertex has colours, this button replaces the basic colour of the Material with these colours. Now light must shine on the Material before you can see it.

Halo (TogBut)

Instead of rendering the faces, each vertex is rendered as a halo. The lens flare effect is a part of the halo. This option can change certain MaterialButtons (see the following section).

ZTransp (TogBut)

Transitional Zbuffers can only render opaque faces. Blender uses a modified method to Zbuffer transparent faces. This method requires more memory and calculation time than the normal Zbuffer, which is why the two systems are used alongside each other.

Zinvert (TogBut)

The Material is rendered with an inverse Zbuffer method; front and back are switched.

Env (TogBut)

Environment option. The Material is not rendered and the Zbuffer and render buffers are 'erased' so that the pixel is delivered with Alpha = 0.0.

OnlyShadow (TogBut)

This option determines the alpha for transparent Materials based on the degree of shadow. Without a shadow the Material is not visible.

Texture name (RowBut)

A Material has eight channels to which Textures can be linked. Each channel has its own mapping, which is the effect the texture has on the material.

Copy to buffer (IconBut)

The complete mapping settings are copied to a temporary buffer.

Copy from buffer (IconBut)

The contents of the temporary buffer are copied to the mapping settings.

SepT (TogBut)

Separate Textures. This option forces only the current channel to be rendered with its corresponding Texture.

Mapping: coordinates as input.

Each Texture has a 3D coordinate (the texture coordinate) as input. The starting point is generally the global coordinate of the 3D point

that can be seen in the pixel to be rendered.

A Material has the following Mapping options:

UV (RowBut)

The U-V coordinates of a face or Nurbs surface from an Object make up the texture coordinates. U-V is a commonly used term for specifying the mathematical space of a flat or curved surface.

Object (RowBut)

Every Object in Blender can be used as a source for texture coordinates. For this, the Object's inverse transformation is applied to the global coordinate, which gives the local Object coordinate. This links the texture to the position, dimension and rotation of the Object. Generally, an Empty Object is used to specify the exact location of a Texture, e.g. to place a logo on the body of an airplane. Another commonly used approach is to have the 'Texture Object' move to achieve an animated texture.

Object Name (TextBut)

The name of the Object used for the texture coordinates. If the Object does not exist, the button remains empty.

Glob (RowBut)

The global coordinate is passed on to the Texture.

Orco (RowBut)

The standard setting. This is the original coordinate of the Mesh or another ObData block.

Stick (RowBut)

Sticky Texture. Blender allows you to assign a texture coordinate to Meshes, which is derived from the manner in which the Camera view sees the Mesh. The screen coordinate (only X,Y) for each

vertex is calculated and saved in the Mesh. This makes it appear as if the texture is projected from the Camera; the texture becomes "sticky" (see also "Make Sticky" in the EditButtons). Use "Sticky" to precisely match a 3D object with an Image Texture. Special morphing effects can also be achieved.

Win (RowBut)

The screen coordinate (X,Y) is used as a texture coordinate. Use this method to achieve 2D layering of different Images.

Nor (RowBut)

The normal vector of the rendered face is used as a texture coordinate. Use this method to achieve reflection mapping, which is the suggestion of mirroring using a specially pre-calculated Image.

Refl (RowBut)

The reflection vector of the rendered face is used as a texture coordinate. This vector points in a direction that makes the face appear to be mirrored. Use this option to suggest a reflected surface with procedural textures such as "Marble" or "Clouds" and of course for the use with the EnvMap texture.

Mapping: transform coordinates.

Use these buttons to more finely adjust the texture coordinate.

dX, dY, dZ (NumBut)

The extra translation of the texture coordinate. sizeX, sizeY, sizeZ (NumBut) The extra scaling of the texture coordinate.

Mapping: 3D to 2D

For Image Textures only; this determines the manner is which the 3D coordinate is converted to 2D.

Flat (RowBut)

The X and Y coordinates are used directly.

Cube (RowBut)

Depending on the normal vector of the face, the X-Y or the X-Z or the Y-Z coordinates are selected. This option works well for stones, marbles and other regular textures,

Tube (RowBut)

This creates a tube-shaped mapping. The Z axis becomes the central axis, X and Y revolve around it.

Sphere (RowBut)

This causes a sphere-shaped mapping. The Z axis becomes the central axis, X and Y revolve around it.

Mapping: switch coordinates.

The three rows of buttons indicate the new X, Y and Z coordinates. Normally, the X is mapped to X, the Y to Y and Z to Z. The first button switches a coordinate completely off.

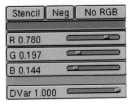

Texture Block

TE: (TextBut)

The name of the Texture block. The name can be changed with this button. Texture Browse (MenuBut) Select an existing Texture from the list provided, or create a new Texture Block.

Clear (But)

The link to the Texture is erased.

Users (But)

If the Texture Block has multiple users, this button displays the total number of users. Press the button to make the Texture "Single User". An exact copy is made.

Auto Name (But)

Blender assigns a name to the Texture.

Mapping: Texture input settings.

These buttons pass extra information to the Texture.

Stencil (TogBut)

Normally, textures are executed one after the other and laid over one another. A second Texture channel can completely replace the first. With this option, the mapping goes into stencil mode. No subsequent Texture can have an effect on the area the current Texture affects.

Neg (TogBut)

The effect of the Texture is reversed.

RGBtoInt (TogBut)

With this option, an RGB Texture (affects colour) is used as an Intensity texture (affects a value).

R, G, B (NumSli)

The colour with which an Intensity Texture blends with the current colour.

DVar (NumSli)

The value with which the Intensity Texture blends with the current value.

Mapping: output to.

Col (TogBut)

The texture affects the basic colour of the material.

Nor (TogBut)

The texture affects the rendered normal. Only important for Image Textures. The "Stucci" Texture does this itself.

Csp (TogBut)

The texture affects the specularity colour of the material.

Cmir (TogBut)

The texture affects the mirror colour of the material, filtered with Mir-RGB sliders.

Ref (Tog3But)

The texture affects the value of the material's reflectivity. There are three settings; the third setting reverses the effect

Spec (Tog3But)

The texture affects the value of specularity of the material. There are three settings.

Hard (Tog3But)

The texture affects the hardness value of the material. There are three settings.

Alpha (Tog3But)

The texture affects the alpha value of the material. There are three settings.

Emit (Tog3But)

The texture affects the "Emit" value of the material. There are settings.

Mapping: output settings.

These buttons change the output of the Texture.

]Mix (RowBut)

The Texture blends the values or colour.

Mul (Rowbut)

The Texture multiplies values or colour.

Add (RowBut)

The Texture adds the values or colour.

Sub (RowBut)

The Texture subtracts values or colour.

Col (NumSli)

The extent to which the texture affects colour.

Nor (NumSli)

The extent to which the texture affects the normal (not important here).

Var (NumSli)

The extent to which the texture affects a value (a variable).

The MaterialButtons, Halos

If a Material has the option "Halo" ON, a number of buttons change to specific halo settings. Lens flares can also be created here. Halos are rendered on the 3D location of the vertices. These are small, transparent round spots or pictures over which circles and lines can be drawn. They take Blender's Zbuffer into account; like any 3D element, they can simply disappear behind a face in the forefront.

Halos are placed over the currently rendered background as a separate layer, or they give information to the alpha layer, allowing halos to be processed as a post-process.

Only Meshes and Particle Effects can have halos. A Mesh with a halo is displayed differently in the 3DWindow; with small dots at the position of the vertices. Halos cannot be combined with 'ordinary' faces within one Mesh. Only one Material can be used per 'halo' Mesh.

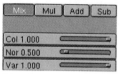

Flare (TogBut)

Each halo is now also rendered as a lens flare. This effect suggests the reflections that occur in a camera lens if a strong light source shines on it.

A Flare consists of three layers:

The ordinary halo, which has a 3D location, and can thus disappear behind a face.
The basic Flare, which is the same halo, but possibly with other dimensions.

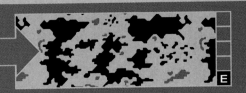

This is placed over the entire rendering as a post-process.
The sub Flares, multi-coloured dots and circles, that are also placed over the entire rendering as a post-process.

The "HaloSize" value not only determines the dimensions, but is also used to determine the visibility - and thus the strength - of the Flare rendered in the post-process. This way, a Flare that disappears slowly behind a face will decrease in size at a corresponding speed and gradually go out.

Rings (TogBut)

Determines whether rings are rendered over the basic halo.

Lines (TogBut)

Determines whether star-shaped lines are rendered over the basic halo.

Star (TogBut)

Instead of being rendered as a circle, the basic halo is rendered in the shape of a star. The NumBut "Star" determines the number of points the star has.

Halo (TogBut)

Turn this option OFF to return to a normal Material.

HaloTex (TogBut)

Halos can be given textures in two ways:

"HaloTex" OFF: the basic colour of each halo is determined by the texture coordinate of the halo-vertex.

"HaloTex" ON: each halo gets a complete texture area, in which, for example, an Image Texture is displayed completely in each basic halo rendered.

HaloPuno (TogBut)

The vertex normal ("Puno" in Blender's turbo language) is used to help specify the dimension of the halo. Normals that point directly at the Camera are the largest; halos with a normal that point to the rear are not rendered. If there are no vertex normals in the Mesh (the Mesh only consists of vertices) the normalised local coordinate of the vertex is used as the normal.

XAlpha

Extreme Alpha. Halos can 'emit light'; they can add colour. This cannot be expressed with a normal alpha. Use this option to force a stronger progression in the alpha.

ME:Plane.001	OB	ME	1 Mat 1
RGB			R 1.000
HSV			G 0.539
DYN	Ring	Line	Halo	B 0.000

Ring (RowBut)

With this option ON, the colour of the rings can be mixed with the RGB sliders.

Line (RowBut)

With this option ON, the colour of the lines can be mixed with the RGB sliders.

Halo (RowBut)

With this option ON, the colour of the basic halo can be mixed with the RGB sliders.

R, G, B (NumSli)

Use these sliders to mix the indicated colour.

HaloSize: 0.50
Alpha 1.000
Hard 34
Add 0.000

HaloSize (NumBut)

The dimension of the halo.

Alpha (NumSli)

The degree of coverage of the halo.

Hard (NumSli)

The hardness of the halo, a large value gives a strong, concentrated progression.

Add (NumSli)

Normally, the colour of halos is calculated during rendering, giving a light emitting effect. Set the "Add" value to 0.0 to switch this off and make black or 'solid' halos possible as well.

Rings: 4 | Lines: 8
Star: 4 | Seed: 2
lareSize: 1.00 | Sub Size: 1.00
FlareBoost: 0.100
Fl.seed: 0 | Flares: 1

Rings (NumBut)

The number of rings rendered over the basic halo.

Lines (NumBut)

The number of star-shaped lines rendered over the basic halo.

Star (NumBut)

The number of points on the star-shaped basic halo.

Seed (NumBut)

'Random' values are selected for the dimension of the rings and the location of the lines based on a fixed table. "Seed" determines an offset in the table.

FlareSize (NumBut)

The factor by which the post-process basic Flare is larger than the halo.

SubSize (NumBut)

The dimension of post-process sub Flares, multicoloured dots and circles.

FlareBoost (NumBut)

This gives the Flare extra strength.

Fl.seed (NumBut)

The dimension and shape of the sub Flares is determined by a fixed table with 'random' values. "Fl.seed" specifes an offset in the table.

Flares (NumBut)

The number of sub Flares.

The settings in this ButtonsWindow visualise the Texture DataBlock. These buttons are only displayed if:

the active Material has a Texure (see MaterialButtons).
the active Lamp has a Texture (see LampButtons).
the World block has a Texture (see WorldButtons)

Blender automatically selects the correct setting if the TextureButtons are called up from the MaterialButtons, LampButtons or WorldButtons. Hotkey: F6. Each Texture has a 3D coordinate (the texture coordinate) as input. What happens here is determined by the type of texture:

Intensity textures: return one value. The preview render in this window shows this as grey values.
RGB textures: returns three values; they always work on colour.
Bump textures: returns three values; they always work on the normal vector. Only the "Stucci" and "Image" texture can give normals.

TE:Clouds | 2 | X |

The DataButtons in the Header indicate what Texture block is visualised.

Texture Browse (MenuBut)

Select another Texture from the list provided, or create a new block.

TE: (TextBut)

Give the current Texture block a new and unique name.

Users (But)

If the Texture block has more than one user, this button shows the total. Press the button to make the Texture "Single User". An exact copy is then created.

Remove Link (But)

Delete the link to the Texture.

Auto Name (But)

Blender assigns a name to the Texture.

The standard TextureButtons

MA:Material
Mat | World | Lamp

This group of buttons determines the type of user from which the Texture must be displayed. Blender automatically selects the correct settings if the TextureButtons are invoked from the MaterialButtons, LampButtons or WorldButtons.

MA: (or LA: or WO:) (TextBut)

The name of the DataBlock that has a (possible) link to the Texture.

Mat (RowBut)

The Texture of the active Material is displayed.

World (RowBut)

The Texture of the World block is displayed.

Lamp (RowBut)

The Texture of the Lamp is displayed.

Blend

This group of buttons shows the channels. In this example, we see that of the eight available channels for the Material, only the first is linked to a Texture.

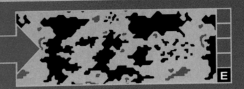

| None | Image | EnvMap | Plugin | Clouds | Wood | Marble | Magic | Blend | Stucci | Noise |

The program includes nine types of textures. These are described in detail later in this guide.

Default Vars (But)

Changes the values set for the type of texture to the standard values.

| Bright1.000 | Contr1.000 |

Bright (NumSli)

The 'brightness' of the colour or intensity of a texture. In fact, a fixed number is added or subtracted.

Contr (NumSli)

The 'contrast' of the colour or intensity of a texture. This is actually a multiplication.

Colorband

Use this option to create a smooth colour progression. Intensity textures are thus changed into an RGB texture. The use of Colorband with a sharp transition can cause aliasing.

Colorband (TogBut)

Switches the use of Colorband on or off.

Add (TogBut)

Adds a new colour to the Colorband.

Cur: (NumBut)

The active colour from the Colorband.

Del (TogBut)

Delete the active colour.

Pos: (NumBut)

The position of the active colour. Values range from 0.0 to 1.0. This can also be entered using LeftMouse (hold-move) in the Colorband.

E, L, S (RowBut)

The interpolation type with which colours are mixed, i.e. 'Ease', 'Linear' and 'Spline'. The last gives the most fluid progression.

A, R, G, B (NumSli)

The Alpha and RGB value of the active colour.

Image Texture

The Image Texture is the most frequently used and most advanced of Blender's textures. The standard bump-mapping and perspective-corrected MipMapping, filtering and anti-aliasing built into the program guarantee outstanding image quality (set the DisplayButtons->OSA ON for this). Because pictures are two-dimensionaal, you must specify in the mapping buttons how the 3D texture coordinate is converted to 2D; mapping is a part of the MaterialButtons.

InterPol (TogBut)

This option interpolates the pixels of an Image. This becomes visible when you enlarge the picture. Turn this option OFF to keep the pixels visible - they are correctly anti-aliased. This last feature is useful for regular patterns, such as lines and tiles; they remain 'sharp' even when enlarged considerably.

UseAlpha (TogBut)

Use the alpha layer of the Image.

CalcAlpha (TogBut)

Calcualte an alpha based on the RGB values of the Image.

NegAlpha (TogBut)

Reverses the alpha value.

MipMap (TogBut)

Generates a series of pictures, each half the size of the former one. This optimises the filtering process. When this option is OFF, you generally get a sharper image, but this can significantly increase calculation time if the filter dimension becomes large.

Fields (TogBut)

Video frames consist of two different images (fields) that are merged by horizontal line. This option makes it possible to work with field images. It ensures that when 'Fields' are rendered (DisplayButtons->Field) the correct field of the Image is used in the correct field of the rendering. MipMapping cannot be combined with "Fields".

| InterPol | UseAlpha | CalcAlpha | NegAlpha | MipMap | Fields | Rot90 | Movie | Anti | StField |

Rot90 (TogBut)

Rotates the Image 90 degrees when rendered.

Movie (TogBut)

Movie files (AVIs supported by Blender, SGI-movies) and 'anim5' files can also be used for an Image. To do this, set the "Frames" NumBut to the total number of frames.

Anti (TogBut)

Graphic images such as cartoons and pictures that consist of only a few colours with a large surface filling can be anti-aliased as a built in pre-process.

St Field (TogBut)

Normally, the first field in a video frame begins on the first line. Some frame grabbers do this differently!

Filter (NumBut)

The filter size used by the options "MipMap" and "Interpol".

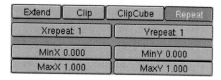

Load Image (But)

The (largest) adjacent window becomes an ImageSelectWindow. Specify here what file must be read to become an Image.

...(But)

This small button does the same thing, but now simply gives a FileSelect.

ImageBrowse (MenuBut)

You can select a previously created Image from the list provided. Image blocks can be reused without taking up extra memory.

File Name (TextBut)

Enter a file name here, after which a new Image block is created.

Users (But)

Indicates the number of users for the Image. The "Single User" option cannot be activated here. It has no significance for Images.

Pack (TogBut)

Indicates the packing of the image. Pressed (grey) means the image is packed into the Blend-file. Klicking on the Button packs or unpacks the image. If a unpack option is triggered the unpack-menu pops up.

UnPack file
Create //textures/WOOD_27.tga
Use /usr/people/cw/work/grafik/Blender/tex/WOOD_27.tga (identical)

Reload (But)

Force the Image file to be read again.

The following options determine what happens if the texture coordinate falls outside the Image.

Extend (RowBut)

Outside the Image the colour of the edge is extended.

Clip (RowBut)

Outside the Image, an alpha value of 0.0 is returned. This allows you to 'paste' a small logo on a large object.

ClipCube (RowBut)

The same as "Clip", but now the 'Z' coordinate is calculated as well. Outside a cube-shaped area around the Image, an alpha value of 0.0 is returned.

Repeat (RowBut)

The Image is repeated horizontally and vertically.

Xrepeat (NumBut)

The (extra) degree of repetition in the X direction.

Yrepeat (NumBut)

The (extra) degree of repetition in the Y direction.

MinX, MinY, MaxX, MaxY (NumBut)

Use these to specify a cropping, it appears that the Image actually becomes larger or smaller.

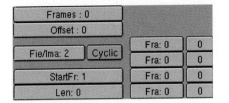

Frames (NumBut)

This activates the animation option; another image file (in the same Image block) will be read per rendered frame. Blender tries to find the other files by changing a number in the file name. Only the rightmost digit is interpreted for this. For example: 01.ima.099.tga + 1 becomes 01.ima.100.tga. The value of "Frames" indicates the total number of files to be used. If the option "Movie" is ON, this value must also be set. Now, however, a frame is continually taken from the same file.

Offset (NumBut)

The number of the first picture of the animation.

Fie/Ima (NumBut)

The number of fields per rendered frame. If no fields are rendered, even numbers must be entered here. (2 fields = 1 frame).

Cyclic (TogBut)

The animation Image is repeated cyclically.

StartFr: (NumBut)

The moment - in Blender frames - at which the animation Image must start.

Len (NumBut)

This button determines the length of the animation. By assigning "Len" a higher value than "Frames", you can create a still at the end of the animation. The "Fra:"-buttons allow you to create a simple montage within an animation Image. The left button, "Fra" indicates

the frame number, the right-hand button indicates how long the frame must be displayed.

Environment Maps

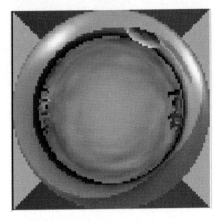

Blender allows three types of environment maps:

Static (RowBut)

The map is only calculated once during an animation or after loading a file.

Dynamic (RowBut)

The map is calculated each time a rendering takes place. This means moving Objects are displayed correctly in mirroring surfaces.

Load (RowBut)

When saved as an image file, environment maps can be loaded from disk. This option allows the fastest rendering with environment maps.

Free Data (But)

This action releases all images associated with the environment map. This is how you force a recalculation when using a Static map.

Save EnvMap (But)

You can save an environment map as an image file, in the format indicated in the DisplayButtons (F10).

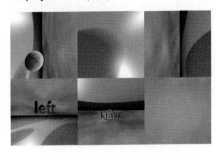

These buttons are drawn when the environment map type is "Load". The environment map image then is a regular Image block in the Blender structure.

Load Image (But)

The (largest) adjacent window becomes an ImageSelectWindow. Specify here what file to read in as environment map.

...(But)

This small button does the same thing, but now gives a FileSelect.

ImageBrowse (MenuBut)

You can select a previously loaded map from the list provided. EnvMap Images can be reused without taking up extra memory.

File Name (TextBut)

Enter an image file name here, to load as an environment map. Users (But) Indicates the number of users for the Image. Reload (But) Force the Image file to be read again.

| Ob:Sphere | | Filter : 1.00 |
| ClipSta 0.10 | ClipEnd 100.00 | CubeRes 224 |

Ob: (TextBut)

Fill in the name of an Object that defines the center and rotation of the environment map. This can be any Object in the current Scene.

Filter: (NumBut)

With this value you can adjust the sharpness or blurriness of the reflection.

Clipsta, ClipEnd (NumBut)

These values define the clipping boundaries when rendering the environment map images.

CubeRes (NumBut)

The resolution in pixels of the environment map image.

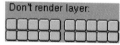

Don't render layer

Indicate with this option the faces that exist in a specific layer that are NOT rendered in the environment map.

Plugin texture

Plugins are pieces of compiled C-code which can be loaded by runtime, to extend a programs features.

After choosing "Load Plugin" you get a FileWindow which lets you choose a plugin. The plugins are platform specific, so be sure to load a plugin for your operating system.

Clouds texture

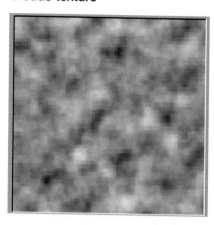

"Clouds" is a procedural texture. This means that each 3D coordinate can be translated directly to a colour or a value. In this case, a three-dimensional table with pseudo random values is used, from which a fluent interpolation value can be calculated with each 3D coordinate (thanks to Ken Perlin for his masterful article "An Image Synthesizer", from the SIGGRAPH proceedings 1985). This calculation method is also called ~(Perlin) Noise.

| Default | Color |

Default (RowBut)

The standard Noise, gives an Intensity.

Color (RowBut)

The Noise gives an RGB value.

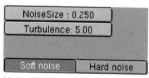

| NoiseSize : 0.250 |
| Turbulence: 5.00 |
| Soft noise | Hard noise |

NoiseSize (NumBut)

The dimension of the Noise table.

NoiseDepth (NumBut)

The depth of the Cloud calculation. A higher number results in a long calculation time, but also in finer details.

Soft Noise, Hard Noise (RowBut)

There are two methods available for the Noise function.

Wood texture

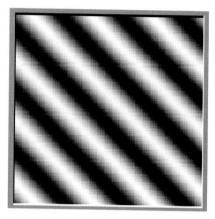

"Wood" is also a procedural texture. In this case, bands are generated based on a sine formula. You can also add a degree of turbulence with the Noise formula. It returns an Intensity value only.

| Bands | Rings | BandNoise | RingNoise |

Bands (RowBut)

The standard Wood texture.

Rings (RowBut)

This suggests 'wood' rings.

BandNoise (RowBut)

Applying Noise gives the standard Wood texture a certain degree of turbulence.

RingNoise (RowBut)

Applying Noise gives the rings a certain degree of turbulence.

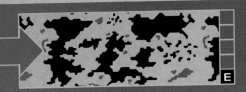

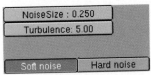

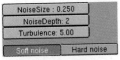

NoiseSize (NumBut)

The dimension of the Noise table.

Turbulence (NumBut)

The turbulence of the "BandNoise" and "RingNoise" types.

Soft Noise, Hard Noise (RowBut)

There are two methods available for the Noise function.

Marble texture

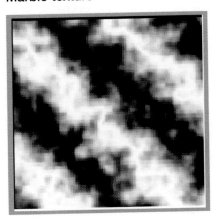

"Marble" is also a procedural texture. In this case, bands are generated based on a sine formula and Noise turbulence. It returns an Intensity value only.

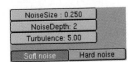

Soft, Sharp, Sharper (RowBut)

Three pre-sets for soft to more clearly defined Marble.

NoiseSize (NumBut)

The dimensions of the Noise table.

NoiseDepth (NumBut)

The depth of the Marble calculation. A higher value results in greater calculation time, but also in finer details.

Turbulence (NumBut)

The turbulence of the sine bands.

Soft Noise, Hard Noise (RowBut)

The Noise function works with two methods.

Magic texture

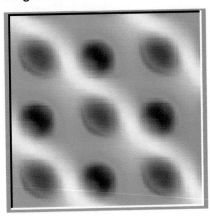

"Magic" is a procedural texture. The RGB components are generated independently with a sine formula.

Size (NumBut)

The dimensions of the pattern.

Turbulence (NumBut)

The strength of the pattern.

Blend texture

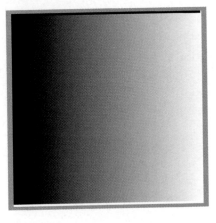

This is also a procedural texture. It generates a progression in Intensity.

Lin (RowBut)

A linear progression.

Quad (RowBut)

A quadratic progression. Ease (RowBut) A flowing, non-linear progression.

Diag (RowBut)

A diagonal progression.

Sphere (RowBut)

A progression with the shape of a three-dimensional ball.

Halo (RowBut)

A quadratic progression with the shape of a three-dimensional ball.

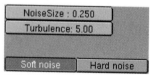

Flip XY

The direction of the progression is flipped a quarter turn.

Stucci texture

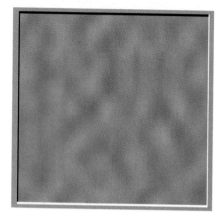

This procedural texture generates Noise-based normals.

Plastic (RowBut)

The standard Stucci. Wall In, Wall out (RowBut) This is where Stucci gets it name. This is a typical wall structure with holes or bumps.

NoiseSize (NumBut) The dimensions of the Noise table.

Turbulence (NumBut)

The depth of the Stucci.

Soft Noise, Hard Noise (RowBut)

There are two methods available for working with Noise.

Noise texture

Although this looks great, it is not Perlin Noise! This is a true, randomly generated Noise. This gives a different result every time, for every frame, for every pixel.

This ButtonsWindow visualises settings associated with animations, most of which are part of the Object DataBlock. It is the 'Build'- and the 'Particles'-Effect. Hotkey: F7.

The typical 'browse' MenuBut is missing here. Link Objects to other Scenes with the LinkMenu (CTRL+L).

OB: (TextBut)

Give the Object block a new and unique name. The Object is inserted again, sorted alphabetically.

Users (But)

If the Object block has multiple users, this button shows the total number of users. Press the button to make the Object "Single User". An exact copy is then created (exlusive the Object block).

Tracking buttons

In Blender, Objects can be assigned a rotation constraint:

Objects that always point in the direction of other Objects: CTRL+T, or "Make Track".
Objects as Children of a Curve path, where the curve determines the rotation ("Follow" button).
Particles can give rotations to Objects (see AnimButtons, Effects). Because Objects have a rotation of their own, it is advisable to first erase this using ALT+R. If the Object is a Child, then erase the "Parent Inverse" as well using ALT+P.

Use these buttons to indicate how tracking must work:

TrackX, Y, Z, -X, -Y, -Z (RowBut)

Specifies the direction axis; the axis that, for example, must point to the other Object.

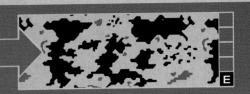
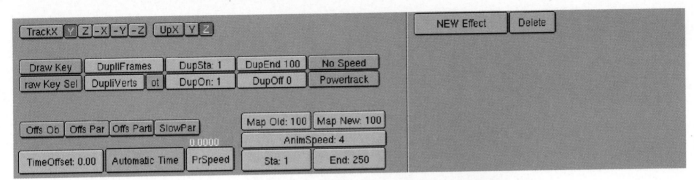

UpX, UpY, UpZ (RowBut)

Specify what axis must point 'up', in the direction of the (global) positive Z axis. If the "Track" axis is the same as the "Up" axis, this is turned off.

PowerTrack (TogBut)

This option completely switches off the Object's own rotation and that of its Parents. Only for Objects that 'track' to another Object.

DrawKey (TogBut)

Draw Key
Draw Key Sel

If Objects have an Object Ipo, they can be drawn in the 3Dwindow as key positions. Key positions are drawn with this option ON and the IpoKeys ON (in the IpoHeader). Hotkey: KKEY.

DrawKeySel (TogBut)

Limits the drawing of Object keys to those selected.

Duplicators

Blender can automatically generate Objects without actually creating them. To do this, an animation system must be created first. A 'virtual' copy of the Object will then be placed on every frame specified. It is also possible to have a virtual copy placed on each vertex (or particle). This can be used as a modelling tool as well. To do this, select the duplicated Objects and press CTRL-SHIFT+A ("Make Dupli's Real").

DupliFrames (TogBut)

No matter how the Object moves, with its own Object Ipos or on a Curve path, a copy of the Object is made for every frame from "DupSta" to "DupEnd". The "DupliFrames" system is built for the specified frame interval.

DupliVerts (TogBut)

Child Objects are duplicated on all vertices of this Object (only with Mesh).

DupSta, DupEnd (NumBut)

The start and end frame of the duplication.

DupOn, DupOff (NumBut)

Empty positions can be specified with the option "DupliFrames". For example: "DupOn" on '2', "DupOff" on '8' sets two copies on every 10 frames. The duplicated Objects

move over the animation system like a sort of train.

No Speed (TogBut)

The "DupliFrames" are set to 'still', regardless of the current frame.

Slurph (NumBut)

Slurph: 0   Relative Keys

This option is only available if there are VertexKeys. The "Slurph" value specifies a fixed delay for the interpolation of Keys per vertex. The first vertex comes first, the last vertex has a delay of "Slurph" frames. This effect makes quite special and realistic Key framing possible.

Watch the sequence of vertices carefully with Meshes. The sequence can be sorted with the commands EditButtons->Xsort and EditButons->Hash. Naturally, it is important that this occurs before the VertexKeys are created, because otherwise quite unpredictable things can occur (however, it can be nice for Halos).

Relative Keys (TogBut)

This button toggles between using standard vertex keyframing and the use of relative vertex keys. Relative vertex keys allowing mix, add or subtract multiple vertex key positions independently. Best suited for facial expression animations.

OffsOb (TogBut)

The "TimeOffset" value works on its own Object Ipo.

OffsPar (TogBut)

The "TimeOffset" value works on the Parent relationship of the Object.

OffsPart (TogBut)

The "TimeOffset" value works on the Particle Effect.

SlowPar (TogBut)

The value of "TimeOffset" is used to create a 'delay' in the Parent relationship. This delay is cumulative and depends on the previous frame. When rendering animations, the complete sequence must always be rendered, starting with the first frame.

TimeOffset (NumBut)

Depending on the previously mentioned pre-sets, the animation is shifted a number of frames. This does not work for VertexKeys.

Automatic Time (But)

This generates automatic "TimeOffset" values for all selected Objects. The start value is the value of the "TimeOffset" button. A requestor pops up and asks for the size of the interval. Blender looks at the Object's screen coordinates in the nearest 3DWindow and calculates the offset values from left to right.

PrSpeed (But)

The speed of the Object is printed.

Map Old, Map New (NumBut)

This button can be used to modify the internal time calculation. "Map Old" gives the previous value in frames; "Map New" specifies the number of frames that must be rendered. Only the mutual relations between these values are important. Use this only to speed up or slow down the entire animation system. The absolute value 'frame' now becomes relative, which can be quite confusing if the animation must still be modified.

AnimSpeed (NumBut)

The maximum speed of the real-time animation playback, expressed in hundredths of a second.

Sta, End (NumBut)

The start and end frame of an animation to be rendered or played real-time.

These buttons are only displayed if the active Object is a Curve.

PathLen (NumBut)

The length of the Curve path in frames, if there is no Speed Ipo.

CurvePath (TogBut)

Specifies that the Curve becomes a path. Children of this Curve now move over the curve. All Curves can become a path, but a 5th order Nurbs curve works best. It has no problems with movement and rotation discontinuity.

CurveFollow (TogBut)

The Curve path passes a rotation to the Child Objects. The 'Tracking' buttons determine which axis the path follows. In EditMode, horizontal lines are also drawn for a 3D curve. This determines the tilt, which is an extra axis rotation of the Child

Objects. The tilt can be changed using the TKEY. Curve paths cannot give uniform perpendicular (aligned with the local Z axis) rotations. In that case, the 'up' axis cannot be determined.

PrintLen (But)

The length of the path is printed in Blender units.

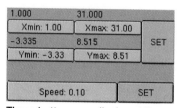

These buttons are displayed if an IpoWindow is present in the same Screen.

Xmin, Xmax, Ymin, Ymax (NumBut)

The numbers above these buttons specify the boundbox of all the visible curves in the IpoWindow. Use the buttons to enter a new value.

Set (But)

The new values of the boundbox are assigned to the visible curves in the IpoWindow.

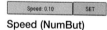

Speed (NumBut)

In certain cases, the exact speed of a translation caused by Object Ipos must be determined. Proceed as follows to do this:

In the IpoWindow, make only the LocX, LoxY, LocZ curves visible.
Set the IpoKey option ON (KKEY in the IpoWindow).
Select the keys that must be assigned a particular speed.
Only keys that already have a speed and direction can be changed.
If the speed is 0.0, nothing happens.
Press the "Set" Button.

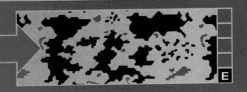

Anim Effects: Build

Three effects are currently built in: "Build", "Particles" and "Wave". Effects are a fixed part of the Object; they cannot have any links or multiple users.

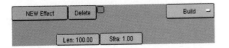

New Effect (But)

Create a new Effect.

Delete (But)

Delete the Effect.

Build (MenuBut)

Select an effect. The Build Effect works on Meshes, which are built up face by face over time. It also works on the vertices in Halo Meshes. The sequence in which this happens can be specified in the 3DWindow with CTRL+F: "Sort Faces" (not in EditMode). The faces of the active Mesh Object are sorted. The current face in the 3DWindow is taken as the starting point. The leftmost face first, the rightmost face last.

Len (NumBut)

The total time the building requires.

SFra (NumBut)

The frame number on which the Effect starts.

Anim Effects: Particles

Particles are halos (or Objects if the option "DupliVerts" is ON) that are generated more or less according to laws of physics. Use Particles for smoke, fire, explosions, a fountain, fireworks or a school of fish! With the Static option it is also possible to make fur or even plants.

A Particle system is pre-calculated as a pre-process (this can take some time). They can then be viewed in the 3DWindow in real time. Particles are a full-fledged part of Blender's animation system. They can also be controlled by Lattices. Only Meshes can have Particles.

Recalc All (But)

Recalc the particle-system after changing the animation of the emitter mesh. This updates the particle-system.

Static (TogBut)

Making static particles. Particles now don't animate or move anymore, they follow the Object's transformation. Static particles are generated one at each 'frame' for the entire 'Life' value. Use the "step" option to control this; step=2 means a particle at every two frames.

Tot (NumBut)

The total number of Particles. Particles require quite a bit of memory (not in the file!) and rendering time, so specify this value carefully.

Sta, End (NumBut)

The start and end frame between which Particles are generated.

Life (NumBut)

The life span of each Particle.

Keys (NumBut)

Not all Particle locations are calculated and remembered for each frame for the entire particle system. This is only done for a fixed number of key positions between which interpolations are performed. A larger number of "Keys" gives a more fluid, detailed movement. This makes significant demands on the memory and time required to calculate the system.

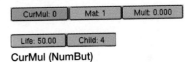

CurMul (NumBut)

Particles can 'multiply themselves' at the end of their lives. For each generation, certain particle settings are unique. This button determines which generation is displayed.

Mat (NumBut)

The Material used for the current generation of Particles.

Mult (NumBut)

This determiness whether the particles multiply themselves. A value of 0.0 switches this off. A value of 1.0 means that each Particle multiplies itself. The particle system itself ensures that the total number of Particles is limited to the "Tot" value.

Life (NumBut)

The age of the Particles in the following generation.

Child (NumBut)

The number of children of a Particle that has multiplied itself.

RandLife (NumBut)

A factor that ascribes the age of Particles a (pseudo) random variation.

Seed (NumBut)

The offset in the random table.

Face (TogBut)

With this option particles are not only emited from vertices, but also from the faces of the mesh.

Bspline (TogBut)

The Particles are interpolated from the keys using a B-spline formula. This gives a much more fluid progression, but the particles no longer pass exactly through the key positions.

Vect (TogBut)

This gives particles a rotation direction. This can be seen in the Halo rendering. Particles that duplicate Objects now also give a rotation to these Objects. VectSize (TogBut) The extent to which the speed of the "Vect" Particle works on the dimensions of the Halo.

Norm (NumBut)

The extent to which the vertex normal of the Mesh gives the Particle a starting speed. If the Mesh has no faces (and thus no vertex normals) the normalised local vertex coordinate is used as the starting speed.

Ob (NumBut)

The Extent to which the speed of the Object gives the Particle a starting speed. This makes a rotating cube become a sort of 'sprinkler'.

Rand (NumBut)

The extent to which a (pseudo) random value gives the Particle a starting speed.

Tex (NumBut)

The extent to which the Texture gives the Particle a starting speed. For this, only the last Texture of the Material is used, in channel number 8.

Damp (NumBut)

Use of damping reduces the speed, like a sort of friction.

Force X, Y, Z (NumBut)

A standard, continually present force. This can simulate the effect of gravity or wind.

Texture X, Y, Z (NumBut)

A standard force that works on a Particle, determined by the texture. Textures can have an effect on the movement of Particles. The 3D coordinate of the Particle is passed to the texture per Particle key.

Int (RowBut)

The Intensity that is passed back from the texture is used as a factor for the standard texture force (previous three buttons).

RGB (RowBut)

The colour of the texture has a direct effect on the speed of the Particle: Red on the X, Green on the Y and Blue on the Z component of the speed.

Grad (RowBut)

The gradient of the texture is calculated. This is the mathematical derivitive. Four samples of the texture are combined to produce a speed vector. With procedural textures, such as Clouds, this method gives a very beautiful, turbulent effect. Set the number of "Keys" as high as possible to see the sometimes rather subtle twisting.

Nabla (NumBut)

The dimension of the area in which the gradient is calculated. This value must be carefully adjusted to the frequency of the texture.

Anim Effects: Wave

The Wave Effect adds a animated Wave to a Mesh. It is not limited to flat objects but can also be used to make a sphere 'wobble'.

The Wave Effect can be accessed from the AnimButtons F7 while the mesh is active. Choose 'NEW Effect' and change it with the MenuButton to 'Wave'.

Wave Type (But)

Per default you have then a XY Wave on your Object. With the Buttons X and Y you can enable or disable the wave generation for an axis, look at the image below for the three basic effects. The Button "Cycl" makes the generation cyclic in the animation.

Time Sta (NumBut)

When (in frames of the animation) the wave generation should start.

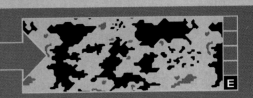
Lifetime (NumBut)

How long (in frames) a wave exists.

Damptime (NumBut)

How many frames the wave should extenuate.

| Sta x: 0.00 | Sta y: 0.00 |

Sta X, Sta Y (NumBut)

Starting Position of the Wave.

Speed:0.500	
Heigth:0.500	
Width:1.500	
Narrow:1.500	

Speed (NumSli)

Speed the Wave travels, can also be negative.

Height (NumSli)

Amplitude of the Wave.

Width (NumSli)

Width of the wave (wavelength).

Narrow (NumSli)

How narrow the next wave follows.

The RealtimeButtons are meant for making interactive 3D animations in Blender. Blender acts then as a complete developement tool for interactive worlds including a gameEngine to play the worlds. All is done without compiling the game or interactive world. Just press PKEY and it runs in realtime.

This guide does not cover the realtime part of Blender, because it is a complex process which needs the full attention of a seperate book. However we would like to give you an overview of what can be done with Blender. Visit our website www.blender.nl to see the latest developements of the gameEngine and find tutorials giving you a start in interactive 3D graphics.

Sector	Prop	Actor	Dynamic	MainActor
Do Fh	Rot Fh	Mass: 1.00		Size: 0.230
Damp: 0.092		RotDamp: 0.170		
ADD property				
Del	Int ⌐	Name:prop	0	D

The RealtimeButtons can be logical seperated in to parts. The left part contains global settings for elements of the game. If I talk about games here I use it for all kind of interactive 3D content, Blender is not limited to games.

This includes settings for general physics, like the damping or mass. Here you also define if an object should be calculated with the build in physic or should be handled static or forming a level.

Here you can also define properties of game objects, these properties can carry values which describe attributes of

the object like variables in a programming language.

The right part of the RealtimeButtons is the comand center to add game logic to your objects and worlds. It consists of the sensors, controlers and actuators.

Sensors are like the senses of a lifeform, they react on keypresses, collisions, contact with materials, timer events or values of properties.

The controlers are collecting events from the sensors and are able to calculate them to a result. Simple actuators are just doing a AND for example to test if a key is pressed and a certain time is over. There are also OR actuators and you also can use python-scripting to do more complex stuff.

The actuator can then actually do things to the objects. This can be applying forces to objects to move or rotate them, playing predefined animations (via IPOs) or adding new objects.

The logic is connected (wired) with the mouse amongst the sensors, controlers and actuators. After that you are immediately able to play the game! If you discover something in the game you don't like, just stop, edit and restart. This way you get fantastic turnaround times in your developement.

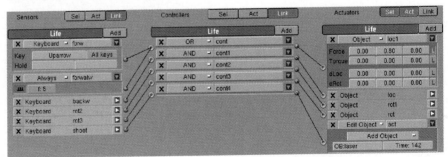

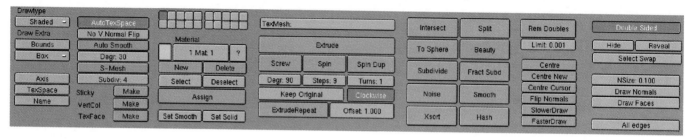

EditButtons, general, F9KEY

The settings in this ButtonsWindow visualise the ObData blocks and provide tools for the specific EditModes. Certain buttons are redrawn depending on the type of ObData. The types are: Mesh, Curve, Surface, Text, MetaBall, Lattice, Ika and Camera. This section describes the buttons that appear for nearly all ObData. Later in the text, the buttons are grouped per ObData type. A complete overview of all HotKeys for EditMode is provided in the 3DWindow section.

The DataButtons in the Header specify what block is visualised. Mesh is used as an example here, but the usage of the other types of ObData is identical.

Mesh Browse (MenuBut)

Select another Mesh from the list provided.

ME: (TextBut)

Give the current block a new and unique name. The new name is inserted in the list, sorted alphabetically.

Users (But)

If the block is used by more than one Object, this button shows the total number of Objects. Press the button to change this to "Single User". An exact copy is then created.

OB: (TextBut)

Give the current Object a new and unique name. The new name is inserted in the list, sorted alphabetically.

This group of buttons specifies Object characteristics. They are displayed here for ease.

DrawType (MenuBut)

Choose a preference for the standard display method in the 3DWindow from the list provided. The "DrawType" is compared with the "Draw-Mode" set in the 3D header; the least complex method is the one actually used.

The types, in increasing degree of complexity, are:

Bounds. A bounding object in the dimensions of the object is drawn.
Wire. The wire model is drawn.
Solid. Zbuffered with the standard OpenGL lighting.
Shaded. This display, which uses Gouraud shading, is the best possible approach to the manner in which Blender renders. It depicts the situation of a single frame from the Camera. Use CTRL+Z to force a recalculation.

The "Draw Extra" options are displayed above the selected DrawType.

BoundBox (TogBut)

A bounding object is displayed in the dimensions of the object.

Box (MenuBut)

With this MenuButton you can choose between different bound-objects.

Axis (TogBut)

The axes are drawn with X, Y and Z indicated.

TexSpace (TogBut)

The texture space. This can be different from the BoundBox. It is displayed with broken lines.

Name (TogBut)

The name of the Object is printed at the Object centre.

Do Centre (But)

Each ObData has its own local 3D space. The null point of this space is placed at the Object centre. This option calculates

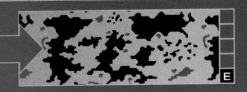

a new, centred null point in the ObData. This may change texture coordinates.

Centre New (But)

As above, but now the Object is placed in such a way that the ObData appears to remain in the same place.

Centre Cursor (But)

The new null point of the object is the 3DCursor location.

The layer setting of the Object. Use SHIFT+LeftMouse to activate multiple layers.

Material indices

Objects and ObData can be linked to more than one Material. This can be managed with these buttons.

1 Mat 1 (NumBut)

This button can be used to specify which Material should be shown, i.e. which Material is active. The first digit indicates the amount of Materials, the second digit indicates the index number of the active Material. Each face in a Mesh has a corresponding number: the 'Material index'. The same is true of Curves and Surfaces.

? (But)

In EditMode, this Button indicates what index number, and thus what Material, the selected items have.

New (But)

Make a new index. The current Material is assigned an extra link. If there was no Material, a new one is created.

Delete (But)

Delete the current index. The current Material gets one less link. The already used index numbers are modified in the ObData.

Select (But)

In EditMode, everything is selected with the current index number.

Deselect (But)

In EditMode, everything is deselected with the current index number.

Assign (But)

In EditMode, the current index number is assigned to the selected items.

EditButtons, Mesh

AutoTexSpace (TogBut)

This option calculates the texture area automatically, after leaving EditMode. You can also specify a texture area yourself (Outside EditMode, in the 3DWindow; TKEY), in which case this option is turned OFF.

No V.Normal Flip (TogBut)

Because Blender normally renders double-sided, the direction of the normal (towards the front or the back) is automatically corrected during rendering. This option turns this automatic correction off, allowing "smooth" rendering with faces that have sharp angles (smaller than 100 degrees). Be sure the face normals are set consistently in the same direction (CTRL+N in EditMode).

AutoSmooth (TogBut)

Automatic smooth rendering (not faceted) for meshes. Especially interesting for imported Meshes done in other 3D applications. The Button "Set smooth" also has to be activated to make "Auto Smooth" work. The smoothing isn't displayed in the 3DWindow.

Degr: (NumBut)

Determines the degree in which faces can meet and still get smoothed by "Auto Smooth".

S-Mesh (TogBut)

The S-Mesh option turns a Mesh Object into a S-Mesh. S-Mesh means procedural smooth subdivision of Mesh objects.

Subdiv: (NumBut)

Number of subdivisions for S-Meshes.

Make Sticky (But)

Blender allows you to assign a texture coordinate to Meshes that is derived from the way the Camera view sees the Mesh. The screen coordinates (only X,Y) are calculated from each vertex and these coordinates are stored in the Mesh. As if the texture is permanently projected and fixed on the Mesh as viewed from the Camera; it becomes "sticky". Use "Sticky" to match a 3D object exactly with the Image Texture of a 3D picture. This option also allows you to create special morphing effects. If the image is already "sticky", the button allows you to remove this effect.

Make VertCol (But)

A colour can be specified per vertex. This is required for the VertexPaint option. If the Object DrawType is "Shaded", these colours are copied to the vertex colours.

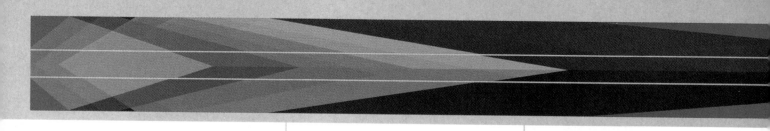

This allows you to achieve a radiosity-like effect (set MaterialButtons->VertCol ON). If the Mesh is "Double Sided", this is automatically turned off.

Make TexFace (But)

Assigns a texture per face. WIll be automaticly set when you use the UV-Editor to texture a realtime model.

TexMesh (TextBut)

Enter the name of another Mesh block here to be used as the source for the texture coordinates. Morphing-like effects can then be achieved by distorting the active Mesh. For example, a straight stream of water (as an animated texture) can be placed in a winding river.

Extrude (But)

The most important of the Mesh tools: Extrude Selected. "Extrude" in EditMode converts all selected edges to faces. If possible, the selected faces are also duplicated. Grab mode starts immediately after this command is executed. If there are multiple 3DWindows, the mouse cursor changes to a question mark. Click at the 3DWindow in which "Extrude" must be executed. HotKey: EKEY.

Screw (But)

This tool starts a repetitive "Spin" with a screw-shaped revolution on the selected vertices. You can use this to create screws, springs or shell-shaped structures.

Spin (But)

The "Spin" operation is a repetitively rotating "Extrude". This can be used in every view of the 3DWindow,

the rotation axis is always through the 3DCursor, perpendicular to the screen. Set the buttons "Degr" and "Steps" to the desired value.

If there are multiple 3DWindows, the mouse cursor changes to a question mark. Click at the 3DWindow in which the "Spin" must occur.

Spin Dup (But)

Like "Spin", but instead of an "Extrude", there is duplication.

Degr (NumBut)

The number of degrees the "Spin" revolves.

Steps (NumBut)

The total number of "Spin" revolutions, or the number of steps of the "Screw" per revolution.

Turns (NumBut)

The number of revolutions the "Screw" turns.

Keep Original (TogBut)

This option saves the selected original for a "Spin" or "Screw" operation. This releases the new vertices and faces from the original piece.

Clockwise (TogBut)

The direction of the "Screw" or "Spin", clockwise, or counterclockwise.

Extrude Repeat (But)

This creates a repetitive "Extrude" along a straight line. This takes place perpendicular to the view of the 3DWindow.

Offset (NumBut)

The distance between each step of the "Extrude Repeat". HotKey: WKEY.

Intersect (But)

Select the faces (vertices) that need an intersection and press this button. Blender now intersects all selected faces with each other.

Split (But)

In EditMode, this command 'splits' the selected part of a Mesh without removing faces. The split sections are no longer connected by edges. Use this to control smoothing. Since the split parts can have vertices at the same position, we recommend that you make selections with the LKEY. HotKey: YKEY.

To Sphere (But)

All selected vertices are blown up into a spherical shape, with the 3DCursor as a midpoint. A requester asks you to specify the factor for this action. HotKey: WKEY.

Beauty (TogBut)

This is an option for "Subdivide". It splits the faces into halves lengthwise, converting elongated faces to squares. If the face is smaller than the value of "Limit", it is no longer split in two. Subdivide (But) Selected faces are divided into quarters; all edges are split in half. HotKey: WKEY.

Fract Subd (But)

Fractal Subdivide. Like "Subdivide", but now the new vertices are set with a random vector up or down. A requestor asks you to specify the amount. Use this to generate landscapes or mountains.

Noise (But)

Here Textures can be used to move the selected vertices up a specific amount. The local vertex coordinate is used as the texture coordinate. Every Texture type works with this option. For example, the Stucci produce a landscape effect. Or use Images to express this in relief.

Smooth (But)

All edges with both vertices selected are shortened. This flattens sharp angles. HotKey: WKEY.

Xsort (But)

Sorts the vertices in the X direction. This creates interesting effects with Vertex-Keys or 'Build Effects' for Halos.

Hash (But)

This makes the sequence of vertices completely random.

Rem Doubles (But)

Remove Doubles. All selected vertices closer to one another than "Limit" are combined and redundant faces are removed.

Flip Normals (But)

Toggles the direction of the face normals. HotKey: WKEY.

SlowerDraw, FasterDraw. (But)

When leaving EditMode all edges are tested to determine whether they must be displayed as a wire frame. Edges that share two faces with the same normal are never displayed. This increases the recognisability of the Mesh and considerably speeds up drawing.

With "SlowerDraw" and "FasterDraw", you can specify that additional or fewer edges must be drawn when you are not in EditMode.

Double Sided (TogBut)

Only for display in the 3DWindow; can be used to control whether double-sided faces are drawn. Turn this option OFF if the Object has a negative 'size' value (for example an X-flip).

Hide (But)

All selected vertices are temporarily hidden. HotKey: HKEY.

Reveal (But)

This undoes the "Hide" option. HotKey: ALT+H.

Select Swap (But)

Toggle the selection status of all vertices.

NSize (NumBut)

The length of the face normals, if they have been drawn.

Draw Normals (NumBut)

Indicates that the face normals must be drawn in EditMode.

Draw Faces (NumBut)

Indicates that the face must be drawn (as Wire) in EditMode. Now it also indicates whether faces are selected.

AllEdges (NumBut)

After leaving EditMode, all edges are drawn normally, without optimisation.

EditButtons, Curve and Surface

These options convert selected curves.

Poly (But)

A polygon only gives a linear interpolation of vertices.

Bezier (But)

Vertices in a Bezier curve are grouped in threes; the handles. The most frequently used curve type for creating letters or logos.

Bspline (But)

(Obsolete.-cw-)

Cardinal (But)

(Obsolete.-cw-)

Nurb (But)

A Nurbs curve is mathematically quite 'pure'. For example: it can be used to create perfect circles.

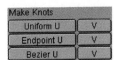

Nurbs curves have knots, a row of numbers that specify the exact curve. Blender offers three pre-sets for this:

Uniform U, V (But)

Sets the knots to create a uniform distribution. Use this for closed curves or surfaces.

Endpoint U, V (But)

Sets the knots so that the first and last vertices are always included.

Bezier U, V (But)

Sets the knots table in such a way that the Nurbs behave like a Bezier.

Order U, V (NumBut)

The order is the 'depth' of the curve calculation. Order '1' is a point, order '2' is linear, order '3' is quadratic, etc. Always use order '5' for Curve paths. Order '5' behaves fluently under all circumstances, without annoying discontinuity in the movement.

ResloIU, V (NumBut)

The resolution in which the interpolation occurs; the number of points that must be generated between two vertices in the curve.

Set Weight (But)

Nurbs curves have a 'weight' per vertex; the extent to which a vertex participates in the interpolation. This button assigns the "Weight" value to all selected vertices.

Weight (But)

The weight that is assigned with "Set Weight".

1.0, sqrt(2)/4, sqrt(3)/9 (But)

A number of pre-sets that can be used to create pure circles and spheres.

DefResolU (NumBut)

The standard resolution in the U direction for curves.

Set (But)

Assigns the value of "DefResolU" to all selected curves.

Back (TogBut)

Specifies that the back side of (extruded) 2D curves should be filled.

Front (TogBut)

Specifes that the front side of (extruded) 2D curves should be filled.

3D (TogBut)

The curve may now have vertices on each 3D coordinate; the front and back side are never rendered.

Width: 1.000
Ext1: 0.000
Ext2: 0.000
BevResol: 0
BevOb:

These buttons are only drawn for Curve and Font Objects.

Width (NumBut)

The interpolated points of a curve can be moved farther apart or brought closer together.

Ext1 (NumBut)

The depth of the extrude.

Ext2 (NumBut)

The depth of the standard bevel.

BevResol (NumBut)

The resolution of the standard bevel; the bevel eventually becomes a quarter circle.

BevOb (TextBut)

The 'bevel' Object. Fill in the name of another Curve Object; this now forms the bevel. For each interpolated point on the curve, the 'bevel Object' is, as it were, extruded and rotated. With this method, for example, you can create the rails of a roller coaster with a 3D curve as the base and two small squares as bevels. Set the values "ResolU" of both Curves carefully, given that this beveling can generate many faces.

Hide	Reveal
Select Swap	
Subdivide	
NSize: 0.100	

Hide (But)

All selected vertices are hidden temporarily.

Reveal (But)

This undoes the "Hide" operation.

Select Swap (But)

Toggle the selection status of all vertices.

Subdivide (But)

Create new vertices or handles in curves.

NSize (NumBut)

This determines the length of the 'tilt' lines in 3DCurves.

Spin (But)

This button is only available for Surface Objects. It makes selected Nurb curves a surface of revolution. The rotation axis runs perpendicular to the screen through the 3DCursor.

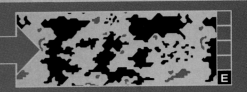

EditButtons, Font

Font type (MenuBut)

Select a font from the list.

Load Font (But)

In the FileSelect Window, this specifies an "Adobe type 1" file that must be read.

Pack Font (IconTog)

To pack the font into the *.blend.

ToUpper (But)

In EditMode, changes all letters into capitals or, if there are no small letters, changes all capitals to small letters.

Left (RowBut)

All text is left-aligned.

Right (RowBut)

All text is right-aligned.

Middle (RowBut)

The text is centered.

Flush (RowBut)

The text is spread out to full length; the length of the longest sentence.

TextOnCurve (TextBut)

Enter the name of a Curve Object here; this now forms the line along which the text is placed.

Size: 1.000	Linedist: 1.000
Spacing: 1.000	Y offset: 0.00
Shear: 0.000	X offset: 0.00

Size (NumBut)

The letter size.

Linedist (NumBut)

The distance between two lines of text.

Spacing (NumBut)

The size of the space between two letters.

Yoffset (NumBut)

This shifts the text up or down. For adjusting "TextOnCurve".

Shear (NumBut)

Changes the letters to italics.

Xoffset (NumBut)

This moves the text left or right. For adjusting "TextOnCurve".

Ob Family (TextBut)

You can create fonts yourself within a Blender file. Each letter from this Font Object is then replaced by any Object you chose, and is automatically duplicated. This means that you can type with Objects! Objects to be considered as letters must belong to the same 'family'; they must have a name that corresponds to the other letter Objects and with the name that must be entered in this button. Important: set the option AnimButtons >DupliVerts ON!

For example:

"Ob Family" = Weird.
The Objects that are to replace the letters a and b are called 'Weirda' and 'Weirdb', respectively.

Width: 1.000
Ext1: 0.000
Ext2: 0.000
BevResol: 0
BevOb:

Width (NumBut)

The interpolated points of a text can be moved farther apart or brought closer together.

Ext1 (NumBut)

The depth of the extrude.

Ext2 (NumBut)

The depth of the standard bevel.

BevResol (NumBut)

The resolution of the standard bevel; the bevel eventually becomes a quarter circle.

BevOb (TextBut)

The 'bevel' Object. Fill in the name of a Curve Object; this now forms the bevel. For each interpolated point on the curve, the 'bevel Object' is, as it were, extruded and rotated.

Set the values "ResolU" of both Text and Curve carefully, given that this beveling can generate many faces.

EditButtons, MetaBall

Wiresize:0.400	
Rendersize:0.200	
Threshold:0.600	

WireSize (NumSli)

Determines the resolution of the MetaBall displayed in the 3DWindow. Be careful with small values, as they use a lot of memory.

RenderSize (NumSli)

The resolution of the rendered MetaBall.

Threshold (NumSli)

This value determines the global 'stiffness' of the MetaBall.

Always (RowBut)

In EditMode, the MetaBall is completely recalculated during transformations.

HalfRes (RowBut)

The MetaBall is calculated in half resolution.

Fast (RowBut)

The MetaBall is only recalculated after the transformation.

In EditMode these Buttons apply to the active Ball:

Stiffness (NumSli)

The stiffness can be specified separately per 'ball', only for the active ball.

Len (NumSli)

MetaBall elements can also be tube-shaped. This button specifies the length of the active ball.

Negative (Tog)

The active 'ball' has a negative effect on the other balls.

Ball (RowBut)

The standard type.

TubeX, TubeY, TubeZ (RowBut)

The active 'ball' becomes a tube; in the X, Y of Z direction.

EditButtons, Lattice

Meshes and Surfaces can be deformed with Lattices, provided the Lattice is the Parent of the Mesh or Surface.

U, V, W (NumBut)

The three dimensions of the Lattice. If a new value is entered here, the Lattice is placed in a regular, standard position.

Lin, Card, B (NumBut)

The manner in which the deformation is calculated can be specified per dimension of the Lattice. The options are: Linear, Cardinal spline and B spline. The last option gives the most fluid deformation.

Make Regular (But)

This option sets the Lattice in a regular, standard position.

Outside (TogBut)

This type Lattice only displays vertices on the outside. The inner vertices are interpolated linearly. This makes working with large Lattices simpler.

EditButtons, Ika

Set Reference (But)

The reference position of an Ika determines the position from which the Ika

is calculated towards the user-specified position. This results in a sort of 'memory', a rest mode to which the Ika can always return. A slightly bent form works best as a reference. This position is also evaluated if the IKA has a Skeleton deformation; this is the state in which no deformation occurs.

Lock XY Plane (But)

With this option you are limiting the effector to the XY-plane, to avoid annoying Y-axis flips. This type is default now and much stabler to work with. Known problem: rotating an Ika (with RKEY) is not well defined, so it is better to disable inverse kinematics first with TABKEY and then rotate it.

XY Constraint (NumBut)

Amount of constrain to the XY Plane.

Mem (NumSli)

This is the extent to which the reference position has an effect on the Ika setting. Set this value to 0.0 to create a completely slack chain.

Iter (Num)

The number of iterations of the Ika calculation. To achieve a natural expression, this value can be kept low. During animation or transformation, the Ika then moves to the desired position slowly.

Limb Weight (NumBut)

These numbers give a relationship factor per limb for how stiff or heavy the limb is in relation to other limbs.

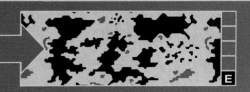

	Deform Max Dist	Deform Weight
Ika.002 (0):	0.00	1.000
Ika.002 (1):	0.00	1.000
Ika.002 (2):	0.00	1.000
Ika.002 (3):	0.00	1.000

Skeleton Weight (NumBut)

A Skeleton deformation can consist of multiple Ika Objects. These numbers determine the extent to which each Ika contributes to deformation.(Deform Weight) and how far this influence reaches (Deform Max Dist). A "Deform Max Dist" of zero works with a global fall-off, like in older Blender versions.

EditButtons, Camera

```
Lens: 35.00
ClipSta: 0.10
ClipEnd: 100.00
```

Lens (NumBut)

This number is derived from the lens values of a photo camera: '120' is telelens, '50' is normal, '28' is wide angle.

ClipSta, ClipEnd (NumBut)

Everything that is visible from the Camera's point of view between these values is rendered. Try to keep these values close to one another, so that the Zbuffer functions optimally.

```
DrawSize: 0.500
Ortho   ShowLimits
        Show Mist
```

DrawSize (NumBut)

The size in which the Camera is drawn in the 3DWindow.

Ortho (TogBut)

A Camera can also render orthogonally. The distance from the Camera then has no effect on the size of the rendered objects.

ShowLimits (TogBut)

A line that indicates the values of "ClipSta" and "ClipEnd" is drawn in the 3DWindow near the Camera.

ShowMist (TogBut)

A line that indicates the area of the 'mist' (see WorldButtons) is drawn near the Camera in the 3DWindow.

©2000 Willem Zwarthoed

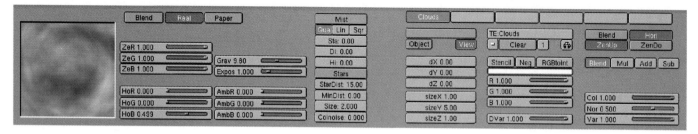

The settings in this ButtonsWindow visualise the World DataBlock. It is linked to a Scene, and can therefore be reused by other Scenes. This block contains the settings for standard backgrounds ('sky'), mist effects and the built-in star generator. The ambient colour and exposure time can be set here as well.

The DataButtons in the Header indicate which World block is active.

World Browse (MenuBut)

Select another World from the list provided, or create a new block.

WO: (TextBut)

Give the current World block a new and unique name.

Users (But)

If the World block has more than one user, this button shows the total number of users. Press the button to make the World "Single User". An exact copy is then created.

Remove Link (But)

Delete the link to the World.

Sky options.

Where the alpha in the rendering is less than 1.0, a sky colour is filled in. The alpha is then no longer usable for post-processing (unless the sky is black).

Blend (TogBut)

This option renders the background, e.g. a sky, with a natural progression. At the bottom of the image is the horizon colour, at the top, the colour of the zenith. The progression is not linear, but bent in the shape of a ball, depending on the lens value of the Camera.

Real (TogBut)

The option "Real" makes the position of the horizon real; the direction in which the camera is pointed determines whether the horizon or the zenith can be seen. This also influences the generated texture coordinates.

Paper (TogBut)

This option makes the "Blend" (if this is selected) or the texture coordinates completely flat, at 'viewport' level.

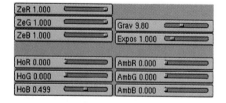

ZeR, ZeG, ZeB (NumSli)

The colour of the zenith. This is the point directly above or directly below an observer (on the earth!).

HoR, HoG, HoB (NumSli)

The colour of the horizon.

AmbR, AmbG, AmbB (NumSli)

The colour of the environmental light, the ambient. This is a rather primitive way to make the entire rendering lighter, or to change the colour temperature.

Grav (NumSli)

This slider defines the gravity for the realtime part of Blender.

Expos (NumSli)

The lighting time, exposure. In fact, this causes a global strengthening or reduction in all the lamps. Use this to give the rendering more contrast.

Mist (TogBut)

Activates the rendering of mist. All rendered faces and halos are given an extra alpha value, based on their distance from the camera. If a 'sky' colour is specified, this is filled in behind the alpha.

Qua, Lin, Sqr (RowBut)

Determines the progression of the mist. Quadratic, linear or inverse quadratic (square root), respectively. "Sqr" gives a thick 'soupy' mist, as if the picture is rendered underwater.

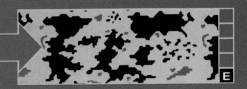

Sta (NumBut)

The start distance of the mist, measured from the Camera.

Di (NumBut)

The depth of the mist, with the distance measured from "Sta".

Hi (NumBut)

With this option, the mist becomes thinner the higher it goes. This is measured from Z = 0.0. If the value of "Hi" is set to zero, this effect is turned off.

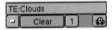

Stars (TogBut)

Blender has an automatic star generator. These are standard halos that are only generated in the sky. With this option ON, stars are also drawn in the 3DWindow (as small points).

StarDist (NumBut)

The average distance between two stars. Do not allow this value to become too small, as this will generate an overflow.

MinDist (NumBut)

In reality, stars are light years apart. In the Blender universe, this distance is much smaller. To prevent stars from appearing too close to the Camera, you can set a "MinDist" value. Stars will never appear within this distance.

Size (NumBut)

The average screen dimensions of a star.

ColNoise (NumBut)

This value randomly selects star colour.

Texture Channels

Texture name (RowBut)

A World has six channels with which Textures can be linked. This is only used for the sky. Each channel has its own mapping; i.e. the effect the texture has on the sky. The settings are in the buttons described below.

Mapping: coordinates input.

Each Texture has a 3D coordinate (the texture coordinate) as input. A sky has three options for this.

Object Name (TextBut)

The name of the Object that is used as a source for the texture coordinates. If the Object does not exist, the button remains empty.

Object (RowBut)

Each Object in Blender can be used as a source for texture coordinates. To accomplish this, an inverse transformation is used to obtain the local Object coordinate. This links the texture to the position, dimensions and rotation of the Object.

View (RowBut)

The view vector of the camera is passed on to the texture.

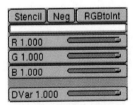

Mapping: transform coordinates.

Use these buttons to more finely adjust the buttons texture coordinate.

dX, dY, dZ (NumBut)

The extra translation of the texture coordinate.

sizeX, sizeY, sizeZ (NumBut)

The extra scaling of the texture coordinate.

Texture Block

TE: (TextBut)

The name of the Texture block. Use this button to change the name.

Texture Browse (MenuBut)

Choose an existing Texture from the list provided, or create a new Texture Block.

Clear (But)

The link to the Texture is erased.

Users (But)

If the Texture Block has more than one user, this button shows the total number of users. Press the button to make the Texture "Single User". An exact copy is then created.

Auto Name (But)

Blender assigns a name to the Texture.

Mapping: Texture input settings.

These buttons pass extra information on to the Texture.

Stencil (TogBut)

Textures are normally executed one after the other and layed over one another. A second Texture channel can completely replace the first one. This option sets the mapping to stencil mode. No subsequent Texture can operate where this Texture is operating.

Neg (TogBut) The Texture operation is reversed.

RGBtoInt (TogBut)

This option causes an RGB texture (works on colour) to be used as an Intensity texture (works on a value).

R, G, B (NumSli)

The colour that an Intensity texture blends with the current colour.

DVar (NumSli)

The value that an Intensity texture blends with the current value.

Mapping: output to.

Blend (TogBut)

The texture works on the colour progression in the sky.

Hori (TogBut)

The texture works on the colour of the horizon.

ZenUp (TogBut)

The texture works on the colour of the zenith above.

ZenDown (TogBut)

The texture works on the colour of the zenith below.

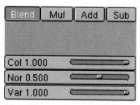

Mapping: output settings.

These buttons adjust the output of the Texture.

Blend (RowBut)

The Texture blends the values.

Mul (Rowbut)

The Texture multiplies the values.

Add (RowBut)

The Texture adds the values.

Sub (RowBut)

The Texture subtracts the values.

Col (NumSli)

The extent to which the texture works on colour.

Nor (NumSli)

The extent to which the texture works on the normal (not applicable here).

Var (NumSli)

The extent to which the texture works on a value (a single variable).

In Blender, the vertices of a Mesh can be assigned a colour, using EditButtons->"Make VertCol". Then, you can change the colour manually, as if you are painting the Mesh (start vertexPaint mode with VKEY in the 3DWindow). This Buttons-Menu has no HotKey, and can only be invoked in the ButtonsHeader with the 'brush' IconBut.

The second part of these Buttons is to set drawmodes needed for the UV-Editor.

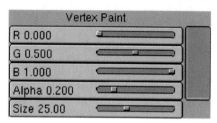

R, G, B (NumSli)

The active colour used for painting.

Alpha (NumSli)

The extent to which the vertex colour changes while you are painting.

Size (NumSli)

The size of the brush, which is drawn as a circle during painting.

Mix (RowBut)

The manner in which the new colour replaces the old when painting: the colours are mixed.

Add (RowBut)

The colours are added.

Sub (RowBut)

The paint colour is subtracted from the vertex colour.

Mul (RowBut)

The paint colour is multiplied by the vertex colour.

Filter (RowBut)

The colours of the vertices of the painted face are mixed together, with an "alpha" factor.

Area	Soft	Normals
Set	Mul: 1.00	Gamma: 1.000

Area (TogBut)

In the back buffer, Blender creates an image of the painted Mesh, assigning each face a colour number. This allows the software to quickly see what faces are being painted. Then, the software calculates how much of the face the brush covers, for the degree to which paint is being applied. You can set this calculation with the option "Area".

Soft (TogBut)

This specifies that the extent to which the vertices lie within the brush also determine the brush's effect.

Normals (TogBut)

The vertex normal (helps) determine the extent of painting. This causes an effect as if painting with light.

Set (But)

The "Mul" and "Gamma" factors are applied to the vertex colours of the Mesh.

Mul (NumBut)

The number by which the vertex colours can be multiplied.

Gamma (NumBut)

The number by which the clarity of the vertex colours can be changed.

The "Face Select"-Buttons are meant for use with the UV-Editor, especially usefull with the realtime engine but also to use UV-Textures for rendering. They become active if you enter the FaceSelectMode with FKEY or with the FaceSelectIcon in the 3DWindow header. These buttons display the settings for the active face when in FaceSelect mode (FKEY or the FaceSelect icon in the 3DWindow header).

When multiple faces are selected you have to use the button "Copy Drawmode" to assign the settings to all selected faces. More about the FaceSelect mode and using UV texture coordinates you can read in the UV-texturing chapter.

Tex (TogBut)

Faces with this attribute are rendered textured in the textured view and the realtime engine. If no texture is assigned to the face it will be rendered in a bright purple.

Tiles (TogBut)

Images can have a tile-mode assigned. In the ImageWindow header you can indicate how many tiles an Image will be subdivided in. This button tells Blender to use this tilemode for the active face.

Light (TogBut)

The faces with this attribute are calculated with light in the realtime engine and the shaded views.

Invisible (TogBut)

This attribute makes faces invisible.

Collision (TogBut)

Faces with this attribute are taken into account for the realtime collision detection.

Shared (TogBut)

In Blender vertex colours are stored in each Face, thus allowing a different colour for individual faces without having to add vertices. With this option, you can make sure that vertex colours are blended across faces if they share vertices.

Twoside (TogBut)

Faces with that attribute are rendered two sided.

ObColor (TogBut)

Each Object in Blender has an RGB colour that can be animated with Ipo-curves. With this option the realtime engine uses this "ObColor" instead of the vertex colours.

Halo (TogBut)

The faces are rendered as halos, which means the normals always pointing to the camera.

Shadow (TogBut)

Faces with this option set acting as shadow in the realtime engine. In fact the face 'drops' on the floor. So you have to make sure that the normal of the face points to the Z-axis. The face has to be located in the center of the Object (or slightly above). Best effect gives a texture with an alpha channel.

Opaque (RowBut)

The colour of the textured face is normally rendered as colour.

Add (RowBut)

This option makes the face being rendered transparent. The colour of the face is added to what has already being drawn, thus achieving a bright 'lightbeam'-like effect.
Black areas in the texture are transparent, white is full bright.

Alpha (RowBut)

Depending on the alpha channel of the image texture, the polygon is rendered transparant.

Copy DrawMode	Copy UV+tex	Copy VertCol

To copy the drawmodes from the active to the selected faces use these Buttons.

Copy DrawMode (But)

Copy the drawmode.

Copy UV+tex (But)

Copys UV information and textures.

Copy VertCol (But)

Copys the vertex colours.

Most rendering models, including ray-tracing, assume a simplified spatial model, highly optimised for the light that enters our 'eye' in order to draw the image. You can add reflection and shadows to this model to achieve a more realistic result. Still, there's an important aspect missing!

When a surface has a reflective light component, it not only shows up in our image, it also shines light at surfaces in its neighbourhood. And vice-versa. In fact, light bounces around in an environment until all light energy is absorbed (or has escaped!).

In closed environments, light energy is generated by 'emittors' and is accounted for by reflection or absorption of the surfaces in the environment. The rate at which energy leaves a surface is called the 'radiosity' of a surface.

Unlike conventional rendering methods, radiosity methods first calculate all light interactions in an environment in a view-independent way. Then, different views can be rendered in realtime.

In Blender, Radiosity is more of a modelling tool than a rendering tool. It is the integration of an external tool and still has all the properties (and limits) external tools.

The output of Radiosity is a Mesh Object with vertex colours. These can be re-touched with the VertexPaint option or rendered using the Material properties "VertexCol" (light colour) or "VColPaint"

(material colour). Even new Textures can be applied, and extra lamps and shadows added.

Currently the Radiosity system doesn't account for animated Radiosity solutions. It is meant basically for static environments, realtime (architectural) walk-throughs or just for fun to experiment with a simulation driven lighting system.

Go! A quickstart

1 Load the file called "radio.blend" from the CDROM. You can see the new RadioButtons menu displayed already.
2 Press the button "Collect Meshes". Now the selected Meshes are converted into the primitives needed for the Radiosity calculation. Blender now has entered the Radiosity mode, and other editing functions are blocked until the button "Free Data" has been pressed.
3 Press the button "GO". First you will see a series of initialisation steps (at a P200, it takes a few seconds), and then the actual radiosity solution is calcu-lated. The cursor counter displays the current step number. Theoretically, this process can continue for hours. Fortunately we are not very interested in the precise correctness of the solution, instead most environments display a satisfying result within a few minutes. To stop the solving process: press ESC.
4 Now the Gouraud shaded faces display the energy as vertex colours. You can clearly see the 'colour bleeding' in the walls, the influence of a coloured object near a neutral light-grey surface. In this phase you can do some postprocess editing to reduce the number of faces or filter the colours. These are described in detail in the next section.
5 To leave the Radiosity mode and save the results press "Replace Meshes" and "Free Radio Data". Now we have a new Mesh Object with vertex colours. There's also a new Material added with the right proprties to render it (Press F5 or F12).

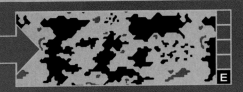

The same steps can be done with the examples "room.blend" and "radio2.blend".

The Blender Radiosity method

During the later eighties and early nineties radiosity was a hot topic in 3D computer graphics. Many different methods were developed. The most successful solutions were based at the "progressive refinement" method with an "adaptive subdivision" scheme.

(Recomended further reading: the web is stuffed with articles about radiosity, and almost every recent book about 3D graphics covers this area. The best still is "Computer Graphics" by Foley & van Dam et al.).

To be able to get the most out of the Blender Radiosity method, it is important to understand the following principles:

Finite Element Method

Many computer graphics or simulation methods assume a simplification of reality with 'finite elements'. For a visual attractive (and even scientifically proven) solution, it is not always necessary to dive into a molecular level of detail. Instead, you can reduce your problem to a finite number of representative and well-described elements. It is a common fact that such systems quickly converge into a stable and reliable solution. The Radiosity method is a typical example of a finite element method.

Patches and Elements

In the radiosity universe, we distinguish between two types of 3D faces:

1 Patches. These are triangles or squares which are able to send energy. For a fast solution it is important to have as few of these patches as possible. But, because the energy is only distributed from the Patch's center, the size should be small enough to make a realistic energy distribution. (For example, when a small object is located above the Patch center, all energy the Patch sends then is obscured by this object).
2 Elements. These are the triangles or squares used to receive energy. Each Element is associated to a Patch. In fact, Patches are subdivided into many small Elements. When an element receives energy it absorbs part of it (depending on the Patch colour) and passes the remainder to the Patch. Since the Elements are also the faces that we display, it is important to have them as small as possible, to express subtle shadow boundaries.

Progressive Refinement

This method starts with examining all available Patches. The Patch with the most 'unshot' energy is selected to shoot all its energy to the environment. The Elements in the environment recieve this energy, and add this to the 'unshot' energy of their associated Patches.

Then the process starts again for the Patch NOW having the most unshot energy.

This continues for all the Patches until no energy is received anymore, or until the 'unshot' energy has converged below a certain value.

The hemicube method

The calculation of how much energy each Patch gives to an Element is done through the use of 'hemicubes'. Exactly located at the Patch's center, a hemicube consist of 5 small images of the environment. For each pixel in these images, a certain visible Element is colour-coded, and the transmitted amount of energy can be calculated. Especially by the use of specialised hardware the hemicube method can be accellerated significantly.

In Blender, however, hemicube calculations are done "in software".

This method is in fact a simplification and optimisation of the 'real' radiosity fomula (form factor differentiation). For that reason the resolution of the hemicube (the number of pixels of its images) is important to prevent aliasing artefacts.

Adaptive subdivision

Since the subdivision of a Mesh defines the quality of the Radiosity solution, automatic subdivision schemes have been developed to define the optimal size of Patches and Elements.

Blender has two automatic subdivision methods:

1 Subdivide-shoot Patches. By shooting energy to the environment, and comparing the hemicube values with the actual mathematical 'form factor' value, errors can be detected that indicate a need for further subdivision of the Patch. The results are smaller Patches and a longer solving time, but a higher realism of the solution.
2 Subdivide-shoot Elements. By shooting energy to the environment, and detecting high energy changes (frequencies) inside a Patch, the Elements of this Patch are subdivided one extra level. The results are smaller Elements and a longer solving time and probably more aliasing, but a higher level of detail.

Display and Post Processing

Subdividing Elements in Blender is 'balanced', that means each Element differs a maximum of '1' subdivide level with its neighbours.

This is important for a pleasant and correct display of the Radiosity solution with Gouraud shaded faces.

Usually after solving, the solution consists of thousands of small Elements. By filtering these and removing 'doubles', the number of Elements can be reduced significantly without destroying the quality of the Radiosity solution.

Blender stores the energy values in 'floating point' values. This makes settings for dramatic lighting situations possible, by changing the standard multiplying and gamma values.

Rendering and integration in the Blender environment

The final step can be replacing the input Meshes with the Radiosity solution (button "Replace Meshes"). At that moment the vertex colours are converted from a 'floating point' value to a 24 bits RGB value. The old Mesh Objects are deleted and replaced with one or more new Mesh Objects. You can then delete the Radiosity data with "Free Data".

The new Objects get a default Material that allows immediate rendering. Two settings in a Material are important for working with vertex colours:

VColPaint. This option treats vertex colours as a replacement for the normal RGB value in the Material. You have to add Lamps in order to see the radiosity colours. In fact, you can use Blender lighting and shadowing as usual, and still have a neat radiosity 'look' in the rendering.
VertexCol. This option better should have been called "VertexLight". The vertex-colours are added to the light when rendering. Even without Lamps, you can see the result. With this option, the vertex colours are pre-multiplied by the Material RGB colour. This allows fine-tuning of the amount of 'radiosity light' in the final rendering.

The RadiosityButtons

See Figure 1

As with everything in Blender, Radiosity settings are stored in a datablock. It is attached to a Scene, and each Scene in Blender can have a different Radiosity 'block'. Use this facility to divide complex environments into Scenes with independent Radiosity solvers.

Phase 1: preparing the models

Only Meshes in Blender are allowed as input for Radiosity. It is important to realise that each face in a Mesh becomes a Patch, and thus a potential energy emittor and reflector.

Typically, large Patches send and receive more energy than small ones. It is therefore important to have a well-balanced input model with Patches large enough to make a difference!

When you add extremely small faces, these will (almost) never receive enough energy to be noticed by the "progressive refinement" method, which only selects, Patches with large amounts of unshot energy.

You assign Materials as usual to the input models. The RGB value of the Material defines the Patch colour. The 'Emit' value of a Material defines if a Patch is loaded with energy at the start of the Radiosity simulation. The "Emit" value is multiplied with the area of a Patch to calculate the initial amount of unshot energy.

Textures in a Material are not taken account for.

Collect Meshes

Collect Meshes (But)

All selected and visible Meshes in the current Scene are converted to Patches. As a result some Buttons in the interface change colour. Blender now has entered the Radiosity mode, and other editing

functions are blocked until the button "Free Data" has been pressed.

The "Phase" text prints the number of input patches. Important: check the number of "emit:" patches, if this is zero nothing interesting can happen!

Default, after the Meshes are collected, they are drawn in a pseudo lighting mode that clearly differs from the normal drawing. The 'collected' Meshes are not visible until "Free Radio Data" has been invoked.

Phase 2: subdivision limits

Blender offers a few settings to define the minimum and maximum sizes of Patches and Elements.

Collect Meshes (But)

You can always restart the entire Radiostiy process with this button.

Limit Subdivide (But)

With respect to the values "PaMax" and "PaMin", the Patches are subdivided. This subdivision is also automatically performed when a "GO" action has started.

PaMax, PaMin, ElMax, ElMin (NumBut)

The maximum and minimum size of a Patch or Element. These limits are used during all Radiosity phases. The unit is expressed in 0,0001 of the boundbox size of the entire environment.

ShowLim, Z (TogBut)

This option visualises the Patch and Element limits. By pressing the 'Z' option, the limits are drawn rotated differently. The white lines show the Patch limits, cyan lines show the Element limits.

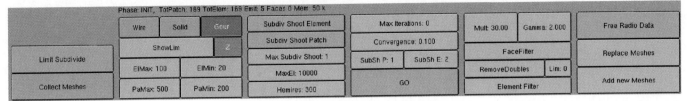

Figure 1

Wire, Solid, Gour (RowBut)

Three drawmode options are included which draw independent of the indicated drawmode of a 3DWindow. Gouraud display is only performed after the Radiosity process has started.

Phase 3: adaptive subdividing, GO!

Subdiv Shoot Element	Max Iterations: 0
Subdiv Shoot Patch	Convergence: 0.100
Max Subdiv Shoot 1	SubSh P: 1 SubSh E: 2
MaxEl: 10000	GO
Hemires: 300	

Hemires (NumBut)

The size of a hemicube; the colour-coded images used to find the Elements that are visible from a 'shoot Patch', and thus receive energy. Hemicubes are not stored, but are recalculated each time for every Patch that shoots energy. The "Hemires" value determines the Radiosity quality and adds significantly to the solving time.

MaxEl (NumBut)

The maximum allowed number of Elements. Since Elements are subdivided automatically in Blender, the amount of used memory and the duration of the solving time can be controlled with this button. As a rule of thumb 20,000 elements take up 10 Mb memory.

Max Subdiv Shoot (NumBut)

The maximum number of shoot Patches that are evaluated for the "adaptive subdivision" (described below). If zero, all Patches with 'Emit' value are evaluated.

Subdiv Shoot Patch (But)

By shooting energy to the environment, errors can be detected that indicate a need for further subdivision of Patches. The subdivision is performed only once each time you call this function. The results are smaller Patches and a longer solving time, but a higher realism of the solution. This option can also be automatically performed when the "GO" action has started. Subdiv Shoot Element (But) By shooting energy to the environment, and detecting high energy changes (frequencies) inside a Patch, the Elements of this Patch are selected to be subdivided one exta level. The subdivision is performed only once each time you call this function. The results are smaller Elements and a longer solving time and probably more aliasing, but a higher level of detail. This option can also be automatically performed when the "GO" action has started.

GO (But)

With this button you start the Radiosity simulation. The phases are:

1. Limit Subdivide. When Patches are too large, they are subdivided.
2. Subdiv Shoot Patch. The value of "SubSh P" defines the number of times the "Subdiv Shoot Patch" function is called. As a result, Patches are subdivided.
3. Subdiv Shoot Elem. The value of "SubSh E" defines the number of times the "Subdiv Shoot Element" function is called. As a result, Elements are subdivided.
4. Subdivide Elements. When Elements are still larger than the minimum size, they are subdivided. Now, the maximum

amount of memory is usually allocated.
5. Solve. This is the actual 'progressive refinement' method. The mouse cursor displays the iteration step, the current total of Patches that shot their energy in the environment. This process continues until the unshot energy in the environment is lower than the "Convergence" or when the maximum number of iterations has been reached.
6. Convert to faces. The elements are converted to triangles or squares with 'anchored' edges, to make sure a pleasant not-discontinue Gouraud display is possible.

This process can be terminated with ESC during any phase.

SubSh P (NumBut)

The number of times the environment is tested to detect Patches that need subdivision. (See option: "Subdiv Shoot Patch").

SubSh E (NumBut)

The number of times the environment is tested to detect Elements that need subdivision. (See option: "Subdiv Shoot Element").

Convergence (NumBut)

When the amount of unshot energy in an environment is lower than this value, the Radiosity solving stops.

The initial unshot energy in an environment is multiplied by the area of the Patches. During each iteration, some of the energy is absorbed, or disappears when the environment is not a closed volume. In Blender's standard coordinate system a typical emittor (as in the example files) has a relative small area. The convergence value is divided by a factor of 1000 before testing for that reason.

Max iterations (NumBut)

When this button has a non-zero value, Radiosity solving stops after the indicated iteration step.

Phase 4: editing the solution

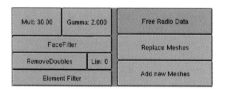

Element Filter (But)

This option filters Elements to remove aliasing artefacts, to smooth shadow boundaries, or to force equalized colours for the "RemoveDoubles" option.

RemoveDoubles (But)

When two neighbouring Elements have a displayed colour that differs less than "Lim", the Elements are joined.

Lim (NumBut)

This value is used by the previous button. The unit is expressed in a standard 8 bits resolution; a colour range from 0 - 255.

FaceFilter (But)

Elements are converted to faces for display. A "FaceFilter" forces an extra smoothing in the displayed result, without changing the Element values themselves.

Mult, Gamma (NumBut)

The colourspace of the Radiosity solution is far more detailed than can be expressed with simple 24 bit RGB values. When Elements are converted to faces, their energy values are converted to

an RGB colour using the "Mult" and "Gamma" values. With the "Mult" value you can multiply the energy value, with "Gamma" you can change the contrast of the energy values.

Add New Meshes (But)

The faces of the current displayed Radiosity solution are converted to Mesh Objects with vertex colours. A new Material is added that allows immediate rendering. The input-Meshes remain unchanged.

Replace Meshes (But)

As previous, but the input-Meshes are removed.

Free Radio Data (But)

All Patches, Elements and Faces are freed in Memory. You always must perform this action after using Radiosity to be able to return to normal editing.

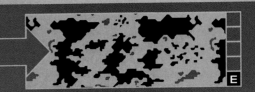
ScriptLinks -
Linking scripts to Blender

Python scripts can be attached to DataBlocks with the ScriptButtons window, and assigned events that define when they should be called.

The ScriptButtons are accessed via the icon in the the ButtonsWindow header.

ScriptLinks can be added for the following DataBlocks

Objects - Available when an Object is active
Cameras - Available when the active Object is a Camera
Lamps - Available when the active Object is a Lamp
Materials - Available when the active Object has a Material
Worlds - Available when the current scene contains a World

When you are able to add a script link an icon appears in the header, similar to the ones that are used in the IPO Window. Selecting one of the icons brings up the ScriptLink buttons group in the left of the ScriptButtons window.

| FrameChanged ⌄ | FrameScript.py | 1 Scr: 1 | New | Del |

DataBlocks can have an arbitrary number of ScriptLinks attached to them - additional links can be added and deleted with the "New" and "Del" buttons, similar to Material Indices. Scripts are executed in order, beginning with the script linked at index one.

When you have at least one scriptlink the Event type and link buttons are displayed. The link button should be filled in with the name of the Text object to be executed. The Event type indicates at what point the script will be executed,

FrameChanged - This event is executed every time the user changes frame, and during rendering and animation playback.

To provide more user interaction this script is also executed continuously during editing for Objects.
Redraw - This event is executed every time Blender redraws its Windows.

Scripts that are executed because of events being triggered receive additional input by objects in the Blender module.

The Blender.bylink object is set to True to indicate that the script has been called by a ScriptLink (as opposed to the user pressing Alt-P in the Textwindow).
The Blender.link object is set to contain the DataBlock which referenced the script, this may be a Material, Lamp, Object, etc.

The Blender.event object is set to the name of the event which triggered the ScriptLink execution. This allows one script to be used to process different event types.

Scene ScriptLinks

The ScriptLink buttons for Scenes are always available in the ScriptButtons, and function exactly in the manner described above. Events available for SceneScriptLinks are:

FrameChanged - This event is executed every time the user changes frame, and during rendering and animation playback.
OnLoad - This event is executed whenever the Scene is loaded, ie. when the file is initially loaded, or when the user switches to the current scene.
Redraw - This event is executed every time Blender redraws its Windows.

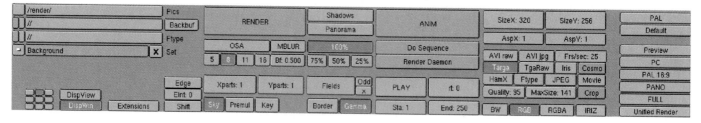

This button field contains all the settings and commands that involve displaying and rendering. All of these data are part of the Scene block. They must thus be set separately for each Scene within a Blender file. Hotkey: F10.

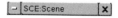

In the header of the ButtonsWindow you get a SceneBrowse for that reason.

Pics (TextBut)

Enter the name of the directory to which the rendered image must be written if the "ANIM" command is given and, when required, the first few letters of the file name. Blender automatically assigns files a number, frame 1 becoming 0001. In this example, pictures are written as the files /render/0001, /render/0002 etc. If you enter "/render/rt" in the button, the files will be called /render/rt0001, /render/rt0002... Blender creates the specified directories itself if they do not already exist. The small square button to the left of the TextBut is used to invoke a FileSelect. Use it to select the output directory, and possibly a file name, and press ENTER to assign this to the TextBut.

Backbuf (TextBut)

Enter a name of a image file to be used as a background. Blender uses the rendered alpha to determine the extent to which this background is visible. A code can be processed into the file name, which allows an already rendered

animation to be used as a background. Be sure that a '#' is placed at the end. This is replaced by the current (four-digit) frame number. For example: /render/work/rt.# becomes /render/work/rt.0101 at frame 101. The two small buttons to the left of the TextBut invoke an ImageSelect or a FileSelect Window. Specify the file and press ENTER to assign it to the TextBut.

BackBuf (TogBut)

Activate the use of a background picture.

Ftype (TextBut)

Use an "Ftype" file, to indicate that this file serves as an example for the type of graphics format in which Blender must save images. This method allows you to process 'colour map' formats. The colourmap data are read from the file and used to convert the available 24 or 32 bit graphics. If the option "RGBA" is specified, standard colour number '0' is used as the transparent colour. Blender reads and writes (Amiga) IFF, Targa, (SGI) Iris and CDi RLE colourmap formats. Here, as well, the two small button to the left of the TextBut can be used to invoke an ImageSelect or a FileSelect window.

Extensions (TogBut)

Filename extensions (*.xxx) will be added to the filename, needed mostly for Windows systems.

Each Scene can use another Scene as a "Set". This specifies that the two Scenes must be integrated when rendered. The current Lamps then have an effect on both Scenes. The render settings of

the Set, such as the Camera, the layers and the World used, are replaced by those of the current Scene. Objects that are linked to both Scenes are only rendered once. A Set is displayed with light gray lines in the 3DWindow. Objects from a Set cannot be selected here.

Window Location (TogBut)

These nine buttons visualise the standard position in which the Render Window appears on the screen. The setting in the example specifies that the Window must be at the top in the middle.

DispView (TogBut)

The rendering can also be displayed in the 3DWindow instead of in a separate window. This occurs, independent of the resolution, precisely within the render borders of Camera view. Use F11 to remove or recall this image.

DispWin (TogBut)

The rendering occurs in a separate window. Use F11 to move this window to the foreground or background.

Edge (TogBut)

In a post-render process an outline will be added to the objects in the rendering. Together with special prepared materials, this causes a cartoon-like picture.

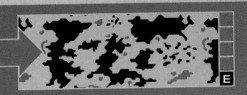

Eint: (NumBut)

Sets the intensity for the edge-rendering. Too high values causes outlining of single polygones.

Shift (TogBut)

With the unified renderer the outlines are shifted a bit.

All (TogBut)

Also consider transparent faces for edge-rendering with the unified renderer.

RENDER (But)

Start the rendering. This is a 'blocking' process. A square mouse cursor indicates that Blender is busy. Hotkey: F12.

Rendering can also take place in the 'background'. Use the command line for this:

```
blender -b file.blend -f 100
```

This will render frame 100 and save the images to disk.

OSA (TogBut)

OverSampling. This option turns anti-aliasing on, to achieve 'soft' edges and perfectly displayed Image textures. OSA rendering generally takes 1.5 to 2 times longer than normal rendering.

5, 8, 11, 16 (RowBut)

Blender uses a Delta Accumulation rendering system with jittered sampling. These numbers are pre-sets that specify the number of samples; a higher value produces better edges, but slows down the rendering.

MBLUR (TogBut)

This option mimics a natural (or long) shutter time by accumulating multiple frames.

The number-button "Bf:" defines the length of the shutter time.
The value of "Osa" (5,8,11,16) defines the number of accumulated images. Setting the "OSA" option makes each acumuled image having antialising.

Xparts, Yparts (NumBut)

OSA rendering of large images, in particular, can take up a lot of memory. In addition to all the shadow buffers and texture maps and the faces themselves, this takes up 10 to 16 bytes per pixel. For a 2048x1024 picture, this requires a minimum of 32 Mb free memory. Use this option to subdivide the rendering into 'parts'. Each part is rendered independently and then the parts are combined. The "Xparts" are particularly important when rendering "Ztransp" faces.

Sky (RowBut)

If a World has 'sky', this is filled in in the background. The alpha is not altered, but the transparent colours 'contaminate' the background colours, which makes the image less suitable for post-processing.

Premul (RowBut)

'Sky' is never filled in. The alpha in the picture is delivered as "Premul": a white pixel with alpha value 0.5 becomes: (RGBA bytes) 128, 128, 128, 128. The colour values are thus multiplied by the alpha value in advance. Use "Premul" alpha for post-processing such as filtering or scaling. Remember to select the "RGBA" option before saving. When Blender reads RGBA files, "Premul" is considered the standard.

Key (RowBut)

'Sky' is never filled in. The alpha and colour values remain unchanged. A white pixel with an alpha value of 0.5 becomes: (RGBA bytes) 255, 255, 255, 128. What this means is especially clear when rendering Halos: the complete transparency information is in the (hidden) alpha layer. Many drawing programs work better with "Key" alpha.

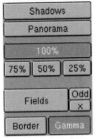

Shadows (TogBut)

This turns shadow rendering on. Shadow can only be created by Spot Lamps.

Panorama (TogBut)

Blender can render panoramas. To do this, a number of pictures are rendered, where the number in question corresponds with the value of "Xparts". For each 'part', the Camera is rotated in such a way that a continuous panorama is created. For the width of the panorama of the Camera Lens, adjust the "Xparts" and the "SizeX" for the picture. The total width of the picture, in pixels becomes: Xparts * SizeX. These are the settings for a 360 degree panorama: Xparts = 8, SizeX = 720, lens =38.6.

100%, 75%, 50%, 25% (RowBut)

These pre-sets allow you to render smaller pictures. It also affects the size of 'shadow buffers'.

Fields (TogBut)

Specifies that two separate fields are rendered. Each field is a complete picture.

The two fields are merged together in such a way that a 'video frame' is created.

Odd (TogBut)

This option indicates that the first field in a video frame begins on the first line. x (TogBut) With "Field" rendering, this switches the time difference between the two fields off (0.5 frame).

Border (TogBut)

This allows you to render a small cut-out of the image. Specify a render 'border' with SHIFT+B in the 3DWindow (in Camera view of course). A cut-out is always inserted in a complete picture, including any "BackBuf" that may be present. Set the option "Crop" ON to turn this off.

Gamma (TogBut)

Colours cannot be normally added together without consequences, for example when rendering anti-aliasing. This limitation is caused by the way light is displayed by the screen: the colour value 0.4 does not appear half as strong as 0.8 (in actuality it is nearly 0.56!). This can be solved by assigning the display-hardware an extremely high gamma correction: gamma 2.3 or even higher. This gives a really pale image with 'washed out' dark tints to which dithering must be applied. Blender renders everything internally already gamma-corrected. This produces a more stable anti-aliasing for the eye, i.e. anti-aliasing that does not 'swim'. To see this difference, render a "Shadeless" white plane with OSA - and with and without "Gamma". The only time this option should be set to OFF is when Blender is used for image composition.

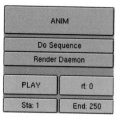

ANIM (But)

Start rendering a sequence. This is a 'blocking' process. A square mouse cursor indicates that Blender is busy. Animations can also be rendered in the 'background'. Use the command line for this: blender -b file.blend -a.

Do Sequence (TogBut)

Specifies that the current Sequence strips must be rendered. To prevent memory problems, the pictures of the complete Sequence system are released per rendering, except for the current frame.

RenderDeamon (TogBut)

Indicates to the external network render utility that the current Scene must be rendered.

Play (But)

This starts an animation playback window. All files from the "Pics" directory are read and played.

rt (NumBut)

For debugging purposes.

Sta, End (NumBut)

The start and end frame of an ANIM rendering.

SizeX, SizeY (NumBut)

The size of the rendering in pixels. The actual value is also determined by the percentage buttons (100%, 75%, etc.).

AspX, AspY (NumBut)

The pixel relationship. The pixels in monitors and video cards are not usually exactly square. These numbers can be used to specify the relative dimension of a pixel.

These buttons specify the graphics file format in which images are saved.

AVI raw (RowBut)

Uncompressed AVI files. AVI is a commonly used format on Windows plattforms.

AVI jpeg (RowBut)

JPEG compessed AVI files.

Frs/sec (NumBut)

Framerate for the AVI formats.

Targa (RowBut)

This is a commonly used, RLE-compressed standard.

TgaRaw (TogBut)

Raw Targa output as alternative for standard (RLE) Targa. Needed for some broken software.

Iris (RowBut)

The standard for SGI software.

JPEG (RowBut)

This lossy format can produce strong compression. Use "Quality" to indicate how much compression you want.

 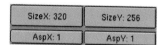

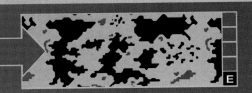

Cosmo (RowBut)

Only for SGI: specifies that Cosmo hardware must be used to compress SGI Movies.

HamX (RowBut)

A self-developed 8 bits RLE format. Creates extremely compact files that can be displayed quickly. To be used only for the "Play" option.

Ftype (RowBut)

This switches the Ftype option ON. See the description of the "Ftype" TextBut.

Movie (RowBut)

Only for SGI: Blender writes SGI movies.

Quality (NumBut)

Specifies the quality of the JPEG compression. Also for Movies.

MaxSize (NumBut)

For Movies: the average maximum size of each Movie frame in Kbytes. The compression factor can then vary per frame.

Crop (NumBut)

Specifies that the "Border" rendering must not be inserted in the total image. For Sequences, this switches the automatic picture scaling off. If the pictures are enlarged, the outside edges are cut off.

BW (RowBut)

After rendering, the picture is converted to black & white. If possible, the results are saved in an 8 bit file.

RGB (RowBut)

The standard. This provides 24 bit graphics.

RGBA (RowBut)

If possible (not for JPEG), the alpha layer is also saved. This provides 32 bit graphics.

IRIZ (RowBut)

Only for Iris format graphics: the Zbuffer is added to the graphics as a 32 bit extra layer.

A number of presets: (In the future, this will be replaced by a user-defined script).

PAL (But)

The European video standard: 720 x 576 pixels, 54 x 51 aspect.

Default (But)

Like "PAL", but here the render settings are also set.

Preview (But)

For preview rendering: 320 x 256 pixels.

PC (But)

For standard PC graphics: 640 x 480 pixels.

PAL 16:9 (But)

Wide-screen PAL.

PANO (But)

A standard Panorama setting.

FULL (But)

For large screens: 1280 x 1024 pixels.

The buttons

237

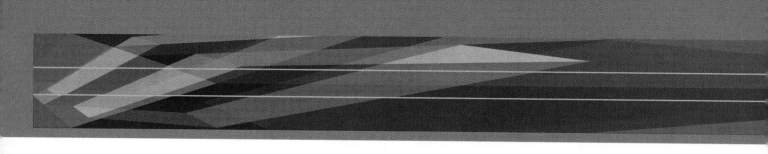

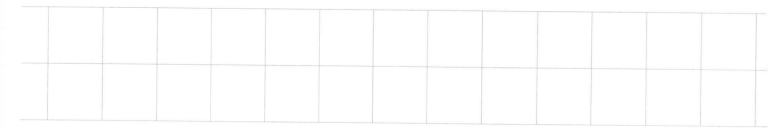

Chapter 14
Appendix

At the time this guide was written there were six supported platforms for Blender, namely: Windows, Linux, SGI Irix, Sun Solaris, BeOS and FreeBSD.

We plan to have an Apple Macintosh version soon. Some of these versions also have sub-versions to support different CPUs or graphic subsystems. Blender is one of the few real multi-platform applications and we've aimed to provide a simple and reliable installation to minimize hardware and platform conflicts.

Therefore we've made the installation process as easy as possible. Generally the installation consists of three simple steps:

1 Get Blender from the CDROM or by downloading it (only ca. 1.3MB for Windows!)
2 Uncompress the archive
3 Start Blender

For Windows there is an installer that will take care of all procedures.

We also provide unpacked directories on the CDROM supplied with this book, so that you can just can copy the directory containing the suitable version to your harddisk.

The basic requirements for a system to be capable of running Blender are:

• working OpenGL drivers
• minimum 16bit colour (65536 colours) display a 3-Buttons mouse is highly recommended

Getting help

If you run into problems, you can consult the FAQs (frequently asked questions) on our website, or send an e-mail to our support team at "support@blender.nl". Please include a precise description of the problem, details of your system specification, and which Blender version you are using.
This information will greatly assist us to resolve your query as soon as possible.

You can also post a message on our "Questions and Answers" discussion forum:
"http://www.blender.nl/discussion/list.php?f=2".
Here you will find many experienced Blender users who are prepared to answer any question you might have concerning Blender.

In every Blender archive there is also a README file containing further information relevant to that specific version.

For problems regarding various 3D hardware, we also have a discussion area on our website. The address is: "http://www.blender.nl/discussion/list.php?f=5". Use of the search function here is highly recommended; it is highly possible that the query you have has already been solved!

Installation on Windows systems

The Windows version will work on 32bit versions of Windows (Windows 9x, Windows ME, Windows NT and Windows 2000). Get the installer archive from our website, or locate it on the CDROM.

Double click on the installer icon. The installer will load and presents you with a splash screen and some important information about Blender. Read this information and click "Next" to proceed to the next screen.

In the "Choose Setup Folder" screen, enter a valid path where you want to install Blender. Optionally you can browse to a directory using the "browse"-button next to the path. The path's default is "C:\Blender".

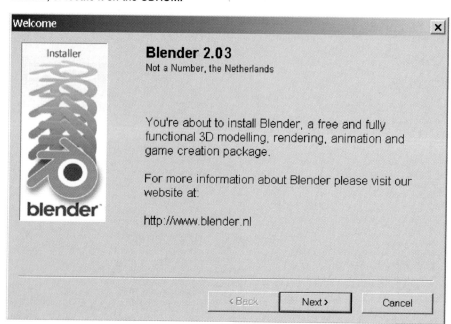

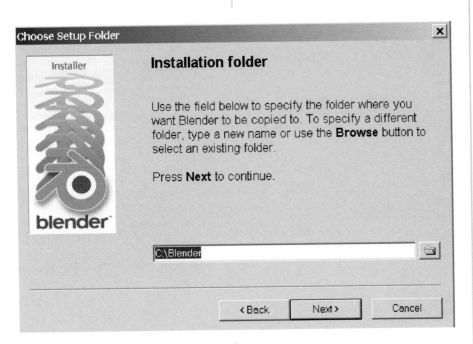

Installation folder

Use the field below to specify the folder where you want Blender to be copied to. To specify a different folder, type a new name or use the **Browse** button to select an existing folder.

Press **Next** to continue.

`C:\Blender`

The installer offers you the option to start Blender after the installation. To start Blender later, you can use the automatically created shortcut on your desktop, or use the entry in the start-menu.

At first start Blender will copy his preference files ".B.blend" and ".Bfs" to the Windows directory or to a directory named in the $HOME environment variable. Be sure that Blender has the permission to do that.

Blender for Windows comes with a small version of Python ("python.dll"). If you want to use the full power of Python, install a complete Python distribution (www.python.org) and delete the file "python.dll" in the Blender directory.

Installation on Unix platforms

Installation SGI Irix

For SGI Irix, there are currently two versions available, "blender2.04-irix-6.2-mips.tar.gz" for Irix 6.2 and "blender2.04-irix-6.5-mips.tar.gz" for Irix 6.5. Copy the archive-file to a directory where you would like to install.

Then use the following commands (bold, the rest is the output of the commands) in the shell to extract it:

o2cw 1%
gunzip blender2.04-irix-6.5-mips.tar.gz
o2cw 2%
tar xvf blender2.04-irix-6.5-mips.tar
x blender2.04-irix-6.5-mips/README, 1474 bytes, 3 blocks
x blender2.04-irix-6.5-mips/blender, 4174904 bytes, 8155 blocks
x blender2.04-irix-6.5-mips/copyright.txt, 1238 bytes, 3 blocks
x blender2.04-irix-6.5-mips/plugins/Makefile, 146 bytes, 1 block
x blender2.04-irix-6.5-mips/plugins/bmake, 1591 bytes, 4 blocks

x blender2.04-irix-6.5-mips/plugins/include/floatpatch.h, 2566 bytes, 6 blocks
x blender2.04-irix-6.5-mips/plugins/include/iff.h, 5822 bytes, 12 blocks
x blender2.04-irix-6.5-mips/plugins/include/plugin.h, 2841 bytes, 6 blocks
x blender2.04-irix-6.5-mips/plugins/include/util.h, 3007 bytes, 6 blocks
x blender2.04-irix-6.5-mips/plugins/sequence/Makefile, 100 bytes, 1 block
x blender2.04-irix-6.5-mips/plugins/sequence/blur.c, 4063 bytes, 8 blocks
x blender2.04-irix-6.5-mips/plugins/sequence/scatter.c, 4371 bytes, 9 blocks
x blender2.04-irix-6.5-mips/plugins/sequence/showzbuf.c, 1913 bytes, 4 blocks
x blender2.04-irix-6.5-mips/plugins/texture/Makefile, 100 bytes, 1 block
x blender2.04-irix-6.5-mips/plugins/texture/clouds2.c, 2909 bytes, 6 blocks
x blender2.04-irix-6.5-mips/plugins/texture/tiles.c, 3039 bytes, 6 blocks

Now enter the newly created directory and start Blender:

o2cw 3% **cd blender2.04-irix-6.5-mips**
o2cw 4%**./blender**

Linux and FreeBSD versions

For Linux Blender is available for Intel compatible CPUs (i386), Alpha and PowerPC.

There are static and dynamic versions. Static versions supply the needed libraries bound to the executable, so you will not need to install them. But we highly recommend you use the dynamic versions, since this will also allow you to use 3Dhardware acceleration. Revert to use the static versions should you encounter problems with the dynamic version.

Blender for FreeBSD comes in a static and dynamic linked version. Following you will find an example explaining how to unpack on Linux, the same commands apply for FreeBSD.

```
cw@mero /tmp >tar xzvf blender2.04-
linux-glibc2.1.2-i386.tar.gz
blender2.04-linux-glibc2.1.2-i386/
blender2.04-linux-glibc2.1.2-i386/
README
blender2.04-linux-glibc2.1.2-i386/
copyright.txt
blender2.04-linux-glibc2.1.2-i386/plugins/
blender2.04-linux-glibc2.1.2-i386/plugins/
Makefile
blender2.04-linux-glibc2.1.2-i386/plugins/
bmake
blender2.04-linux-glibc2.1.2-i386/plugins/
include/
blender2.04-linux-glibc2.1.2-i386/plugins/
include/floatpatch.h
blender2.04-linux-glibc2.1.2-i386/plugins/
include/iff.h
blender2.04-linux-glibc2.1.2-i386/plugins/
include/plugin.h
blender2.04-linux-glibc2.1.2-i386/plugins/
include/util.h
blender2.04-linux-glibc2.1.2-i386/plugins/
sequence/
blender2.04-linux-glibc2.1.2-i386/plugins/
sequence/Makefile
blender2.04-linux-glibc2.1.2-i386/plugins/
sequence/blur.c
blender2.04-linux-glibc2.1.2-i386/plugins/
sequence/scatter.c
blender2.04-linux-glibc2.1.2-i386/plugins/
sequence/showzbuf.c
blender2.04-linux-glibc2.1.2-i386/plugins/
sequence/blur.so
blender2.04-linux-glibc2.1.2-i386/plugins/
sequence/scatter.so
blender2.04-linux-glibc2.1.2-i386/plugins/
sequence/showzbuf.so
blender2.04-linux-glibc2.1.2-i386/plugins/
texture/
blender2.04-linux-glibc2.1.2-i386/plugins/
texture/Makefile
blender2.04-linux-glibc2.1.2-i386/plugins/
texture/clouds2.c
blender2.04-linux-glibc2.1.2-i386/plugins/
texture/tiles.c
blender2.04-linux-glibc2.1.2-i386/plugins/
texture/clouds2.so
blender2.04-linux-glibc2.1.2-i386/plugins/
texture/tiles.so
blender2.04-linux-glibc2.1.2-i386/blender
```

Now enter the newly created directory
and start Blender:

```
cw@mero /tmp >cd blender2.04-linux-
glibc2.1.2-i386
cw@mero /tmp/blender2.04-linux-
glibc2.1.2-i386 >./blender
```

This procedure is the same for all
versions, but of course the filenames
differ. On the first start Blender copies the
preference files ".B.blend" and ".Bfs" into
your home directory.

Sun Solaris

The procedure is pretty similar as that for
other Unix-like systems. The difference is
that you need to unpack the archive with
the command "uncompress".

BeOS

Blender works on BeOS x86 version 4.5
and later, also on the free version 5.0.

When downloading a version from the
internet, BeOS automatically recognizes
a ZIP-archive and starts the
"Expand-O-Matic" application.

When you want to use a version from
the CDROM, browse to the CDROM with
the "Tracker" (the BeOS filemanager) and
click the ZIP-file. This will also start the
"Expand-O-Matic".

Enter the desired destination directory for
Blender in the text field "Destination" and
click on "Expand". Blender will be
installed.

After unzipping, drag the
"libpython.1.5.so" on the symbolic link
"Drag libpython.1.5.so" to complete the
installation. Now you can either click on
Blender to start it, or create a shortcut for
it on your desktop.

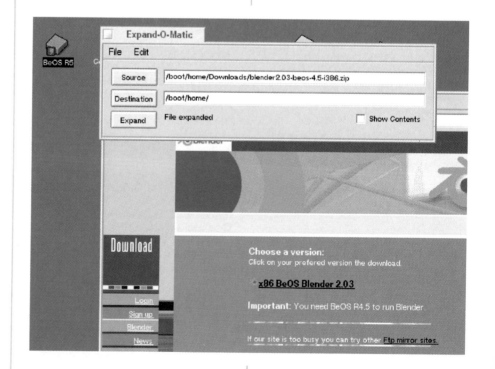

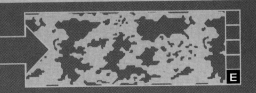
Active
Blender makes a distinction between selected and active. Only one Object or item can be active at any given time, for example to allow visualisation of data in buttons.

Alpha
The alpha value in an image denotes opacity, used for blending and anti-aliasing.

Ambient light
Light that exists everywhere without any particular source. Ambient light does not cast shadows, but fills in the shadowed areas of a scene.

Animate
To give motion to an object or a group of objects over time.

Animation
A series of images that create an illusion of movement when displayed rapidly in sequence.

Anti-aliasing
Algorithm designed to reduce the stair-stepping artifacts that result from drawing graphic primitives on a raster grid.

AVI
"Audio Video Interleaved". A container format for video with synchronized audio. An AVI-file can contain different compressed video and audio-streams.

Back-buffer
Blender uses two buffers to draw the interface in. This double-buffering system allows one buffer to be displayed, while drawing occurs on the back-buffer. For some applications in Blender the back-buffer is used to store colour-coded selection information.

Beveling
Beveling removes sharp edges from an extruded object by adding additional material around the surrounding faces. Bevels are particularly useful for flying logos, and animation in general, since they reflect additional light from the corners of an object as well as from the front and sides.

Bezier Curve
A curved line defined by its functional control points.

Bounding box
A six-sided box drawn on the screen that represents the maximum extents of an object.

Bump map
A grayscale image used to give a surface the illusion of ridges or bumps. In Blender bump maps are called Nor-maps.

Channel
1 Some DataBlocks can be linked to a series of other DataBlocks. For example, a Material has eight channels to link Textures to.
2 Each Ipo block has a fixed number of available channels. These have a name (LocX, SizeZ, enz.) which indicates how they can be applied. When you add an IpoCurve to a channel, animation starts up immediately.

Child
Objects can be linked to each other in hierarchical groups. The Parent Object in such groups passes its transformations through to the Child Objects.

Clipping
Removing, before drawing occurs, of vertices and faces which are outside the field of view.

Collision Detection
The ability of objects to register contact with other objects.

Compositing
The process of combining multiple images, or layers, into a single image.

Curve
Series of vertices between which interpolation occurs, allowing for fluid and detailed procedural shapes.

DataBlock (or 'block')
The general name for an element in Blender's Object Oriented System.

Double-buffer
Blender uses two buffers (images) to draw the interface in. The content of one buffer is displayed, while drawing occurs on the other buffer. When drawing is complete, the buffers are switched.

Environment Map
Texture mapping technique to mimic a mirroring surface.

Extend select
Add new selected items to the current selection.

Extrusion
The creation of a three-dimensional object by pushing out a two-dimensional outline to give it height, like a cookie-cutter. It is often used to create 3D text.

Face
The triangle and square polygons that form the basis for Meshes, or for rendering.

Field
Frames from videos in NTSC or PAL format are composed of two interlaced fields.

Flag
A programming term for a variable that indicates a certain status.

Flat shading
A fast rendering algorithm that simply gives each facet of an object a single colour. It yields a solid representation of objects without taking a long time to render. Pressing ZKEY switches to flat shading in Blender.

Fps
Frames per second. All animations, video, and movies are played at a certain rate. Above ca. 15fps the human eye cannot see the single frames and is tricked into seeing a fluid motion. NTSC uses 30fps, PAL 25fps, and movies 24fps.

Frame
A single picture taken from an animation or video.

Frame Rate
The speed at which frames are displayed. Normally denoted in fps (frames per second).

Game Engine
The code that Blender uses to run games, including the game physics.

Gouraud shading
A rendering algorithm that provides more detail. It averages colour information from adjacent faces to create colours. It is more realistic than flat shading, but less realistic than Phong shading or ray-tracing. Hotkey in Blender is CTRL-Z.

Hierarchy
Objects can be linked to each other in hierarchical groups. The Parent Object in such groups passes its transformations through to the Child Objects.

Inverse Kinematics (or IKA)
A character animation tool which allows the animator to move the endpoint of a hierarchically linked chain to determine a character's position.

Ipo
The main animation curve system. Ipo blocks can be used by Objects for movement, and also by Materials for animated colours.

IpoCurve
The Ipo animation curve.

Item
The general name for a selectable element, e.g. Objects, vertices or curves.

Keyframe
A frame in a sequence that specifies all of the attributes of an object. The object can then be changed in any way and a second keyframe defined. Blender automatically creates a series of transition frames between the two keyframes, a process called "tweening."

Lathe
A lathe object is created by rotating a two-dimensional shape around a central axis. It is convenient for creating 3D objects like glasses, vases, and bowls. In Blender this is called "spinning".

Lattice
Three dimensional grid of vertices, used to deform meshes, surfaces, and particles.

Layer
A visibility flag for Objects, Scenes and 3DWindows. This is a very efficient method for testing Object visibility.

Lens Flare
Artifact created by a light source shining directly into a (camera) lens.

Link
The reference from one DataBlock to another. It is a 'pointer' in programming terminology.

Local
1 Each Object in Blender defines a local 3D space, bounded by its location, rotation and size. Objects themselves reside in the global 3D space.
2 A DataBlock is local, when it is read from the current Blender file. Non-local blocks (library blocks) are linked parts from other Blender files.

Material
Contains all the information about the appearance of an object, such as colour, sheen, and the mapping of textures.

Mapping
The relationship between a Material and a Texture is called the 'mapping'. This relationship is two-sided. First, the information that is passed on to the Texture must be specified. Then the effect of the Texture on the Material is specified.

Mesh
This is the triangle and quad mesh data forming an object. It contains vertices, faces and normals.

MetaBalls
Spherical or tubical objects that can operate on each other's shape.

MPEG-I
Video compression standard by the "Motion Pictures Expert Group". Due to its small size and platform independence, it is ideal for distributing video files over the internet.

MPEG
"Motion Pictures Expert Group"

Normal
An imaginary ray pointing out from the surface of a polygon, and perpendicular to that surface.

Normap
Blender term for bumpmap.

NTSC
TV standard by the "National Television Standards Committee". Most common industry standard used in the USA and Japan.

NURBS
Non-Uniform Rational Bezier Curve. A mathematical description of a curved surface.

ObData block
The first and most important DataBlock linked by an Object. This block defines the Object type, e.g. Mesh or Curve or Lamp.

Object
The basic 3D information block. It contains a position, rotation, size and transformation matrices. It can be linked to other Objects for hierarchies or deformation. Objects can be 'empty' (just an axis) or have a link to ObData, the actual 3D information: Mesh, Curve, Lattice, Lamp, etc.

Orthographic View
A view in which an object's distance from the viewer has no effect on the size at which it is drawn.

PAL
"Phase Alternating Line", a TV standard common for Europe.

Parent
An object that is linked to another object, as the parent is linked to the child in a parent-child relationship. A parent object's coordinates become the center of the world for any of its child objects.

Parenting
The process of creating a hierarchical organization of objects in a scene.

Particles
Non-volume, non-surface 2D pixels in 3D space, to which forces can be applied.

Path
Special type of curve. Any curve can become a path, any objects parented to a path will use it as a trajectory.

Perspective View
In a perspective view, the further an object is from the viewer, the smaller it appears. See orthographic view.

Pivot
A point that normally lies at an object's geometric center. An object's position and rotation are calculated in relation to its pivot-point. However, an object can be moved off its center point, allowing it to rotate around a point that lies outside the object.

Pixel
A single dot of light on the computer screen; the smallest unit of a computer graphic. Short for "picture element."

Plug-In
A piece of (C-)code to load during run-time. This way it is possible to extend the functionality of Blender without a need for recompiling. In Blender we have Texture plug-ins and Sequencer plug-ins.

Point Light
A light source that emanates from a single point in space in all directions.

Polygon
A two-dimensional, closed non-intersecting geometric figure. Polygons can be triangles or squares. Also called 'faces' in Blender.

Primitives
Basic 3D geometric shapes like a cube, sphere, cylinder or cone. The building blocks for more complex objects.

Procedural Textures
Random patterns (such as marble, wood, and clouds) generated by mathematical algorithms. Each 3D coordinate can be translated directly into a colour or a value.

Proportional Editing Tool (PET)
Adds a magnet like function to Grab, Scale, and Rotate.

Python
The interpreted, interactive, object-oriented programming language that can be used with Blender to manipulate data.

Radiosity
A method to calculate softer, more natural shadows.

Render
To create a two-dimensional representation (i.e. a picture for print or to display on the monitor) of an object based on its shape and surface properties.

Rotation
Moving an object around a specific center and axis.

Scale
Changing the size of an object along one or all axis.

Scene
The basis of the 3D world. A virtual stage that determines what, and how much, will be rendered.

Selected
Blender makes a distinction between selected and active. Any number of Objects can be selected at once.

Almost all key commands have an effect on selected Objects.

Single User
DataBlocks with only one user.

Skinning
Stretching a surface over a series of 2-dimensional "ribs" or cross-sections.

S-Mesh
Subdivision mesh. Each face is calculated with a smooth subdivision on the fly.

Smoothing
A rendering procedure that performs vertex-normal interpolation across a face before lighting calculations begin. The individual facets are then no longer visible.

Surface
Special type of nurbs curve, with interpolation in two dimensions (U and V).

Text
Special type of curve. Only Postscript Type 1 is supported.

Title Safe
An area which is completely visible on all consumer TVs. In Blender, this area is denoted by the inner dotted line in the Camera view.

Toolbox
Menu containing almost all keyboard commands (hotkey: spacebar).

Transform
Change a location, rotation, or size. Usually applied to Objects or vertices.

Transparency
A surface property that determines how much light passes through an object without being altered.

User
When another DataBlock references a DataBlock, it has a user.

Vertex (vertices)
The general name for a 3D point. Besides an X,Y,Z coordinate, a vertex can have colour, a normal vector and a section flag.

Volumetric Light
Light with some type of volume perceived. This is done with HALO Spots.

Wireframe
A representation of a three-dimensional object that shows only the lines of its contours, hence the name "wireframe."

X, Y, Z axes
The three axes of the world's three-dimensional coordinate system. In the front view, the X axis is an imaginary horizontal line running left to right; the Z axis is a vertical line; and Y axis is a line that comes out of the screen toward you. In general, any movement parallel to one of these axes is said to be movement along that axis.

X, Y, and Z coordinates
The X coordinate of an object is measured by drawing, through its centerpoint, a line that is perpendicular to the X axis. The distance from where that line intersects the X axis to the 0 point of the X axis is the object's X coordinate. The Y and Z coordinates are measured in a similar manner.

Zbuffer
For a Zbuffer image, each pixel is associated a Z-value, derived from the distance in 'eye space' from the Camera. Before each pixel of a polygon is drawn, the existing Zbuffer value is compared to the Z-value of the polygon at that point. It is a common and fast visible-surface algorithm.

Zoom
Modification of the camera's focal length. This is done with a camera's 'lens' setting.

©2000 Petr Vlk

©2000 Luis Gervasio

INDEX

INDEX

INDEX